MW01071560

- Go to **awmi.net/sg420** to download PDFs of the following resources for each lesson in this study guide:
  - Outlines
  - Discipleship Questions
  - Scriptures
- Share as many copies as you'd like.
- These documents are not for resale.

You've Already Got It!

{ So Quit Trying to Get It. }

by
Andrew Wommack

STUDY GUIDE

Unless otherwise indicated, all Scripture quotations are taken from the *King James Version* of the Bible.

The author has emphasized some words in Scripture quotations with underline.

You've Already Got It! Study Guide
ISBN 978-1-59548-152-8

Copyright © 2014 by Andrew Wommack Ministries, Inc.
P.O. Box 3333
Colorado Springs, CO 80934-3333

www.awmi.net

Printed in the United States of America. All rights reserved under International Copyright Law. Contents and/or cover may not be reproduced in whole or in part in any form without the express written consent of the publisher.

CONTENTS

INTRODUCTION

Like the dog on the cover, most Christians spend their entire lives chasing something they already have. They're always asking the Lord to do something—to bless, heal, deliver, or prosper them—when in truth, they are seeking what they've already been given. They believe God *can* do anything, but not that He *has* (past tense) done very much.

However, the book of Ephesians was written from an entirely different perspective: Everything has already been accomplished in Christ and given to the born-again believer. It's both already done and already ours!

A victorious Christian isn't seeking victory but rather enforcing the victory already won through the death, burial, and resurrection of Jesus Christ. We aren't trying to win a battle; we're coming from a battle that has already been won. Jesus has conquered, and we're enforcing His conquest (Rom. 8:37).

As believers, we aren't trying to get something from God; we're fighting to receive the full manifestation of what is already ours in Christ. We aren't trying to get healed; we're fighting because we've already been healed, and the devil is trying to steal it. We aren't begging God to prosper us financially; we're fighting the good fight of faith to see the prosperity manifest that's already been given to us. We aren't asking God to bless us, because He has already commanded His blessing upon us. Through believing we've already got it, talking like we've already got it, and acting like we've already got it, we appropriate what the Lord has provided.

IT'S ALREADY DONE!

Understanding that God has already blessed, healed, and prospered you removes the legalistic performance mentality. You won't struggle under feelings of condemnation and unworthiness anymore, because you'll recognize that everything has already been given. In fact, it was supplied long before you ever came along. And since it's a gift (not based on your performance), your worthiness—or lack thereof—has nothing to do with it.

How can you doubt that God would give you something that you know He has already supplied? You can't! The knowledge that He's already done it eliminates all doubt. No more will you pray, "O God, I know You can, but will You please do it for me?" You'll know that it is already done. The question is: Will you receive?

If you understand and embrace these truths, you'll be ruined for much of what's being called Christianity today. The proclamation that "God *can* heal, bless, deliver, and prosper you" sounds good on the surface but is just a profession of what *can* happen. The Word declares, "God has already healed, blessed, delivered, and prospered you." Can you see the difference?

ENJOY GOD'S PROVISION

This study contains the truths you need to begin experiencing a much greater manifestation of God's power in your life. Your faith will be quickened, your heart encouraged, and your feet firmly set on His pathway of victory.

Stop chasing your tail, and start enjoying God's abundant provision!

HOW TO USE YOUR STUDY GUIDE

Whether you are teaching a class, leading a small group, discipling an individual, or studying on your own, this study guide is designed for you! Here's how it works:

Each lesson consists of the **Lesson** text, **Outline**, **Teacher's Guide**, **Discipleship Questions**, **Answer Key**, and **Scriptures**. Some studies also have additional information.

Outline for Group Study:
I. If possible, briefly review the previous lesson by going over the **Answer Key/Teacher's Guide** answers for the **Discipleship Questions/Teacher's Guide** questions.

II. Read the current **Lesson** text or **Teacher's Guide** aloud (or section—e.g., 1.1, 1.2, etc.).
   A. Be sure that each student has a copy of the **Outline**.
   B. While the **Lesson** text, **Teacher's Guide**, or section is being read, students should use their **Outlines** to follow along.

III. Once the **Lesson** text, **Teacher's Guide**, or section is read, facilitate discussion and study using the **Discipleship Questions** or **Teacher's Guide** questions.
   A. Read aloud one question at a time.
   B. The group should use their **Outlines** to assist them in answering the questions.
   C. Have them read aloud each specifically mentioned scripture before answering the question.
   D. Discuss the answer/point from the **Lesson** text, as desired.
   E. As much as possible, keep the discussion centered on the scriptures and the **Lesson** text, **Teacher's Guide**, or section points at hand.
   F. Remember, the goal is understanding (Matt. 13:19).
   G. One individual should not dominate the discussion; instead, try to draw out the quieter ones for the group conversation.
   H. Repeat the process until all of the questions are discussed/answered.

Materials Needed:
   Study guide, Bible, and enough copies of the **Outline, Discipleship Questions**, and **Scriptures** for each student. (PDFs of the **Outlines, Discipleship Questions**, and **Scriptures** can be downloaded via the URL located on the first page of this study guide.)

Outline for Personal Study:
I. Read the current **Lesson** text, **Teacher's Guide**, or section.
   A. Read additional information, if provided.
   B. Meditate on the given scriptures, as desired.
II. Answer the corresponding **Discipleship Questions** or **Teacher's Guide** questions.
III. Check your work with the **Answer Key/Teacher's Guide** answers.

Materials Needed:
   Study guide, Bible, and a writing utensil.

HOW DESPERATE ARE YOU?
LESSON 1

While ministering once in a church, I noticed how the pastor and his congregation wholeheartedly sang these songs about how "desperate" for God they were. Don't get me wrong: I like those tunes and their overall message. However, I prefer to sing "I'm in love with You" instead of "I'm desperate for You."

Desperate comes from the Latin word meaning "to despair" (*American Heritage Dictionary*). Check out these dictionary definitions:

1. Reckless or violent because of despair, driven to take any risk.
2. Undertaken as a last resort.
3. Nearly hopeless, critical, grave, i.e. a desperate illness.
4. Marked by, arising from, or showing despair; despairing, i.e. the desperate look of hunger.
5. In an unbearable situation because of need or anxiety, i.e. desperate for recognition.
6. Extreme because of fear, danger, or suffering greatly, i.e. in desperate need.

Synonyms for *despair* are hopelessness, desperation, despondency, depression, discouragement, and dejection. All of these nouns denote emotional states marked by a lowness of spirits or loss of hope. Despair and hopelessness stress the utter absence of hope and often imply a sense of powerlessness or resignation. Desperation implies absence of grounds for hope, but adds the idea of fighting back, often blindly or recklessly.

When you sing "Lord, I'm desperate for You," what do you mean? Are you saying, "Lord, I'm in love with You and want You more than anything else"? If so, that's fine. But according to the dictionary, you're really saying, "I'm in despair because of this extremely unbearable situation. There are no grounds for hope, but I'm anxiously, recklessly, and violently fighting back anyway." If that's what you mean by being "desperate for the Lord," it's absolutely wrong!

HUNGRY?

The only reason for a Christian to be desperate is if that person doesn't understand what God has already done. The Lord has already blessed us, healed us, delivered us, and prospered us. He loves us and nothing will ever change that. The only reason to be hopeless, helpless, and in despair is if we don't know who we are and what we have in Christ.

We need a full revelation of what Jesus has done for us! That doesn't mean we won't ever have problems. But in the midst of them, we can say, "Father, You've already supplied this before I ever had the need. I know it's there, so I'm drawing near to You. Thank You for revealing it to me." Christians should never be hopeless or full of despair.

When you sing "I'm hungry for God," what do you mean? If you're expressing desire, that's fine: "God, I love You and want You more than anything else!" However, a closer look at the dictionary definition of *hunger* reveals it can also refer to the hurt, pain, agony, depression, and despair that accompany not having your needs met.

Many people sing "God, I'm desperate and hungry for You" and mean "I'm so miserable. Life is terrible, but I'm looking for You. You're my answer, and I believe that out there—somewhere—You're *going* to do something to meet my needs." That's the complete opposite of the revelation of God's Word!

"WHAT'S WRONG WITH THIS PICTURE?"

This church had just sung those songs about how "desperate" and "hungry" they were. "O God, we need a move. Touch us. Please, Lord, do something new." I stood up to speak and asked, "How many of you are hungry for God? How desperate for Him are you?" They all clapped and cheered loudly.

Then I said, "John 6:35 declares, *'And Jesus said unto them, I am the bread of life: he that cometh to me shall never hunger; and he that believeth on me shall never thirst.'*"

I asked them, "What's wrong with this picture? All of you just stood and acknowledged that you're hungry and thirsty. Yet this says that you'll never hunger or thirst again. Jesus told the woman at the well the same thing: *'But whosoever drinketh of the water that I shall give him shall never thirst; but the water that I shall give him shall be in him a well of water springing up into everlasting life'*" (John 4:14). They immediately became so quiet, you could've heard a pin drop.

Now, don't misunderstand what I'm saying. I use the term "getting hungry for God" in the sense that you have a deep yearning for Him. My good friend Bob Nichols says, "As long as you can live without more of God, you will" and "As long as you can live without more healing, you will." You could plug a number of different things in there like peace, joy, prosperity, etc., but the point is, you must hunger for—strongly desire and focus on—the things of God in order to experience them.

The Lord doesn't come to those who just passively seek Him; you must pursue Him wholeheartedly.

> *For I know the thoughts that I think toward you, saith the Lord, thoughts of peace, and not of evil, to give you an expected end…[13] And ye shall seek me, and find me, when ye shall search for me with all your heart.*
>
> **JEREMIAH 29:11 & 13**

This type of hunger is godly.

But if by "hunger" you mean "O Lord, I'm just so empty. I have no joy, no peace, no hope. God, where are You? I'm desperate for You," that's not right and that's not faith. Yet this is what's being proclaimed and modeled in the body of Christ today as being a "normal" experience. It's like a person who's sitting in front of a twelve-course meal. Everything they could ever want is there, but they keep crying, "I'm so hungry!" They just want pity or somebody to stick the food in their mouth for them. Personally, I have no sympathy for someone sitting before such a feast and whining about how "desperate" they are. If you're hungry, eat!

DRAW FROM YOUR WELL

God has already given us everything. There's a well of living water on the inside of every born-again believer. It's not the Lord's fault if we're hungry and thirsty. It's not time to ask Him to come and touch us; it's time for us to start taking, eating, and drinking of what He's already given.

I'm not saying there's no place for a Christian to ever have problems or discouragement or that we should always be perfect and just deny reality. Believers do experience hunger in the sense that they feel empty, and God seems like a million miles away. But when you experience that, it's wrong to approach Him, saying, "O Lord, I just don't feel Your love. Please love me. Do something to show me You care!" You might as well have said "God, You haven't done anything" because you're blaming Him for your feelings of emptiness and hunger.

Through the revelation contained in this study, I've learned that God loves me infinitely more than I can ever comprehend or need. He can't love me more or give me any more love than what I already have. Knowing this has kept me out of depression and discouragement for over forty years.

There were times when such feelings tempted me. I've had issues and terrible things happen, just like anybody else. I've even had thoughts like, *Man, just get in your pickup and drive. Don't ever come back! I can't stand it anymore. Just walk away!* Although I've had these thoughts, I don't give in to them, because I also have this revelation that God loves me and has already provided everything I need.

So, instead of giving in to hunger, discouragement, and despair, I remind myself of God's Word. I don't ever say, "Lord, that's the way it is. Now You must do something brand-new to touch me. I'm looking for something else from You." That would be an insult against what He's already done. Instead, I pray, "Father, this is absolutely wrong. John 6:35 says that I should never hunger or thirst again. I know that on the inside of me, there is so much love, joy, and peace—all the fruit of the Spirit (Gal. 5:22-23). Everything I need is already there. So, Father, I know that You have done Your part. It's not Your fault if I'm tempted with depression, discouragement, giving up, and quitting. It's my fault. I'm not focused on You. I've let my eyes be taken off of You and put on the problems of this world." I'll just separate myself and spend a day or so fasting, praying, and seeking God. What I'm doing is mining what the Lord has already placed within me. Instead of asking Him to give me something new, I draw out the life that He's already given.

That's why I can truthfully tell you that I haven't been depressed in over forty years. I've been tempted with depression. I've had feelings of depression hit me. But within ten or fifteen minutes, I just decide that I don't like depression, and I refuse to have it. God has given me such joy inside that I can choose to rejoice at all times (Phil. 4:4).

NOT PASSIVE

The Word says, *"I will bless the LORD at all times: his praise shall continually be in my mouth"* (Ps. 34:1).

This isn't telling you to just "fake it till you make it." Rather, this is talking about drawing out what's inside of you.

As I've drawn on the joy that God has already placed within my born-again spirit, I've lived a consistently victorious life. In the midst of great adversity, I've experienced continual joy and peace. It's not because I'm never tempted with the other, but it's because I know in my heart that God has already done His part.

I haven't become passive and said, "God, I'm waiting on You." Many people do that and languish while waiting for an epiphany. They sing, "I'm so desperate and hungry! O God, where are You? I'm just a poor wayfaring pilgrim, and it's so miserable down here." Instead, I pray, "Father, I know this isn't right. This isn't what You've done. Your Word shows me that You've already blessed me. I praise You for what You've done!" I start focusing on the Lord and His Word and draw out His abundant life from within me.

That's why I haven't had discouragement or depression last for more than a very short time for over forty years now. I simply refuse to yield to it or let it have its effect in my life. That's awesome!

Many people desire these same results, but they think the way to achieve them is to passively ask God to do something and then sit back and wait. If things don't change and victory—healing, prosperity, blessings, deliverance—doesn't instantly come, they get upset with the Lord, asking, "God, why aren't You doing anything?" That's not it at all.

The Lord has already done everything. However, if you're not seeing it manifest, it's not God who hasn't given—but you who haven't received! Come with me as I take you on a journey that will teach you how to receive what God has already done for you.

HOW DESPERATE ARE YOU?
LESSON 1 – OUTLINE

I. The Lord has already blessed us, healed us, delivered us, and prospered us.

    A. The only reason to be hopeless, helpless, and in despair is if we don't know who we are and what we have in Christ.

    B. We need a full revelation of what Jesus has done for us!

    C. That doesn't mean we won't ever have problems, but in the midst of them, we can say, "Father, You've already supplied this before I ever had the need. I know it's there, so I'm drawing near to You. Thank You for revealing it to me."

    D. Christians should never be hopeless or full of despair.

And Jesus said unto them, I am the bread of life: he that cometh to me shall never hunger; and he that believeth on me shall never thirst.

JOHN 6:35

But whosoever drinketh of the water that I shall give him shall never thirst; but the water that I shall give him shall be in him a well of water springing up into everlasting life.

JOHN 4:14

    E. The Lord doesn't come to those who just passively seek Him—we must pursue Him wholeheartedly.

For I know the thoughts that I think toward you, saith the LORD, thoughts of peace, and not of evil, to give you an expected end…[13] And ye shall seek me, and find me, when ye shall search for me with all your heart.

JEREMIAH 29:11 AND 13

II. God has already given us everything.

    A. There's a well of living water on the inside of every born-again believer.

    B. It's not time to ask Him to come and touch us.

    C. It's time for us to start taking, eating, and drinking of what He's already given.

III. Through the revelation contained in this study, I've learned that God loves me infinitely more than I can ever comprehend or need.

A. There were times when depressing and discouraging feelings tempted me.

B. Although I've had these thoughts, I don't give in to them, because I also have this revelation that God loves me and has already provided everything I need.

C. So, instead of giving in to hunger, discouragement, and despair, I remind myself of God's Word.

D. I'll just separate myself and spend a day or so fasting, praying, and seeking God.

E. What I'm doing is mining what the Lord has already placed within me. Instead of asking Him to give me something new, I draw out the life that He's already given.

IV. God has given me such joy inside that I can choose to rejoice at all times (Phil. 4:4).

I will bless the LORD at all times: his praise shall continually be in my mouth.

PSALM 34:1

A. As I've drawn on the joy that God has already placed within my born-again spirit, I've lived a consistently victorious life.

B. In the midst of great adversity, I've experienced continual joy and peace.

C. It's not because I'm never tempted with the other, but because I know in my heart that God has already done His part.

D. I start focusing on the Lord and His Word and draw out His abundant life from within me.

V. The Lord has already done everything.

A. However, if you're not seeing it manifest, it's not God who hasn't given—but you who haven't received!

B. Come with me as I take you on a journey that will teach you how to receive what God has already done for you.

HOW DESPERATE ARE YOU?
LESSON 1 – TEACHER'S GUIDE

1.   The Lord has already blessed us, healed us, delivered us, and prospered us. The only reason to be hopeless, helpless, and in despair is if we don't know who we are and what we have in Christ. We need a full revelation of what Jesus has done for us! That doesn't mean we won't ever have problems. But in the midst of them, we can say, "Father, You've already supplied this before we ever had the need. We know it's there, so we're drawing near to You. Thank You for revealing it to us." Christians should never be hopeless or full of despair (John 6:35 and 4:14). The Lord doesn't come to those who just passively seek Him—we must pursue Him wholeheartedly (Jer. 29:11 and 13).

2.   God has already given us everything. There's a well of living water on the inside of every born-again believer. It's not time to ask Him to come and touch us; it's time for us to start taking, eating, and drinking of what He's already given.

3.   Through the revelation contained in this study, we'll learn that God loves us infinitely more than we can ever comprehend or need. There will be times when depressing and discouraging feelings tempt us. Although we'll have these thoughts, we won't give in to them, because we'll also have this revelation that God loves us and has already provided everything we need. So instead of giving in to hunger, discouragement, and despair, we'll remind ourselves of God's Word. We'll just separate ourselves and spend a day or so fasting, praying, and seeking God. What we're doing is mining what the Lord has already placed within us. Instead of asking Him to give us something new, we'll draw out the life that He's already given.

1. A. Read John 6:35, 4:14; Jeremiah 29:11, and 13. What is the only reason to be hopeless, helpless, and in despair? (We don't know who we are and what we have in Christ)
    B. Does the Lord come to those who just passively seek Him? (No, we must pursue Him wholeheartedly)
2. A. Who has already given us everything? (God)
    B. What's on the inside of every born-again believer? (A well of living water)
3. A. Instead of giving in to hunger, discouragement, and despair, what must we remind ourselves of? (God's Word)
    B. What are we doing when we separate ourselves and spend a day or so fasting, praying, and seeking God? (We're mining what the Lord has already placed within us)
    C. Instead of asking Him to give us something new, what must we draw out? (The life that He's already given)

4.   God has given us such joy inside that we can choose to rejoice at all times (Phil. 4:4 and Ps. 34:1). As we draw on the joy that God has already placed within our born-again spirits, we'll live a consistently victorious life. In the midst of great adversity, we'll experience continual joy and peace. It's not because we're never tempted with the other, but because we know in our hearts that God has already done His part. We start focusing on the Lord and His Word and draw out His abundant life from within us.

5.   The Lord has already done everything. However, if we're not seeing it manifest, it's not God who hasn't given—but us who haven't received! Come, let's go on a journey that will teach us how to receive what God has already done for us.

4.   A.   Read Philippians 4:4 and Psalm 34:1. As we draw on the joy that God has already placed within our born-again spirits, what will happen? (We'll live consistently victorious lives)
     B.   In order to experience continual joy and peace in the midst of great adversity, what must we know in our hearts? (That God has already done His part)
5.   A.   What has the Lord already done? (Everything)
     B.   If we're not seeing it manifest, is it God who hasn't given or us who haven't received? (Us who haven't received)

HOW DESPERATE ARE YOU?
LESSON 1 – DISCIPLESHIP QUESTIONS

1. Who was speaking in John 6:35?

2. What did He say He is?

3. Those who come to Him shall never what?

4. Who shall never thirst?

5. Who was speaking in John 4:14?

6. Whosoever drinks of the water He gives shall never what?

7. Who gives this water?

8. What shall this water be in them?

9. Springing up into what?

10. According to Jeremiah 29:11 and 13, who is thinking toward us?

11. What is He thinking?

12. To give us what?

13. When shall we seek Him and find Him?

14. According to Galatians 5:22-23, what is the fruit of the Spirit?

15. Against such fruit, there is no what?

16. Philippians 4:4 commands us to what?

17. When?

18. According to Psalm 34:1, whom shall we bless?

19. When?

20. Where shall His praise be continually?

HOW DESPERATE ARE YOU?
LESSON 1 – ANSWER KEY

1. Jesus

2. *"The bread of life"*

3. Hunger

4. Those who believe on Him

5. Jesus

6. Thirst

7. Jesus

8. A well of water

9. Everlasting life

10. The Lord

11. Thoughts of peace, and not of evil

12. An expected end

13. When we search for Him with all our hearts

14. Love, joy, peace, long-suffering, gentleness, goodness, faith, meekness, and temperance

15. Law

16. Rejoice in the Lord

17. Always

18. The Lord

19. At all times

20. In our mouths

HOW DESPERATE ARE YOU?
LESSON 1 – SCRIPTURES

JOHN 6:35
And Jesus said unto them, I am the bread of life: he that cometh to me shall never hunger; and he that believeth on me shall never thirst.

JOHN 4:14
But whosoever drinketh of the water that I shall give him shall never thirst; but the water that I shall give him shall be in him a well of water springing up into everlasting life.

JEREMIAH 29:11
For I know the thoughts that I think toward you, saith the Lord, thoughts of peace, and not of evil, to give you an expected end.

JEREMIAH 29:13
And ye shall seek me, and find me, when ye shall search for me with all your heart.

GALATIANS 5:22-23
But the fruit of the Spirit is love, joy, peace, longsuffering, gentleness, goodness, faith, [23] Meekness, temperance: against such there is no law.

PHILIPPIANS 4:4
Rejoice in the Lord alway: and again I say, Rejoice.

PSALM 34:1
I will bless the Lord at all times: his praise shall continually be in my mouth.

CHECK YOUR RECEIVER
LESSON 2

Ephesians was written from the perspective of what has already taken place. Paul's opening comments in this letter were—

Paul, an apostle of Jesus Christ by the will of God, to the saints which are at Ephesus, and to the faithful in Christ Jesus: [2] Grace be to you, and peace, from God our Father, and from the Lord Jesus Christ. [3] Blessed be the God and Father of our Lord Jesus Christ, who hath blessed us with all spiritual blessings in heavenly places in Christ.

EPHESIANS 1:1-3, EMPHASIS MINE

Notice the terminology here: "Blessed be God who *has*—past tense, it's already been done—blessed us with all spiritual blessings."

Some people argue, "Well, this means only in spiritual things, in an ethereal realm, not in practical, personal ways. It's just in heavenly places that we've been blessed." Really, *"all spiritual blessings in heavenly places in Christ"* is just an old English way of expressing the truth that God has already blessed us with everything—and it's in the spiritual realm.

Everything that God has done for you has already been deposited into your born-again spirit. Although it's already there, you must draw it out of the spirit and into the physical realm.

If God has already blessed you, which Ephesians 1:3 clearly reveals, then why do you keep asking Him to bless you? "Come on, Andrew! That's just semantics." No, it's a problem. The reason you keep praying, asking, and seeking God's blessing is because you don't truly believe you're already blessed.

SILENCE

While ministering to an audience, I often walk over and give my Bible to someone on the front row. Then I ask the people, "What do you think I'd do if that person who already has my Bible came up to me and asked, 'Can I have your Bible, please?'" How would you respond if someone asked you for something you knew you'd already given them? Personally, I wouldn't know how to answer. I'd probably just look at them and think, *You've already got it—so what are you asking for? What am I supposed to do that I haven't already done?*

If you asked someone for something they knew you already had, how would they respond to you? There'd probably be an awkward silence. Sounds a lot like how God often responds to us!

You pray "O God, please heal my body" but don't hear a thing, so you wonder, *Lord, what's going on? Why haven't You answered my prayer?* God's probably in heaven scratching His head and thinking, *Now, wait a minute. Doesn't 1 Peter 2:24 say that by My stripes, you were (past tense) healed? It's already done! I've already placed the same power that raised Christ from the dead inside you (Eph. 1:19-21).* If God could be confused, I believe He would be, saying, "I know I already gave this to them, but here they are asking Me for it." That's not the way to approach God.

We pray other stupid prayers, too, like, "God, we ask You to come and be with us in our church service today. O Lord, meet with us!" The Word plainly says, *"I will never leave thee, nor forsake thee"* (Heb. 13:5) and *"Where two or three are gathered together in my name, there am I in the midst of them"* (Matt. 18:20). God's always with us, but still we pray, "O Lord, come and be with us" and "Lord, go with us as we leave this place." How is God going to answer prayers like that? Do you know what we're doing? We're letting our senses dominate us. Since we don't see Him or feel anything and nobody's jumped a pew yet, we ask Him to come, when the Word says He's already there.

BEGIN TO RECEIVE

An appropriate way to pray is, "Father, Your Word promises that You'll never leave us nor forsake us, and when two or three gather together in Your name, there is a special presence of the Holy Spirit. Father, we thank You that You're here. We believe it and we want it to manifest. We don't want You to just be here in the spirit realm. We desire to yield to You to the point that You can manifest Yourself in healings, deliverance, joy, peace, salvation, and Holy Spirit baptism. We want You to be free to manifest Yourself and do what You want to do." That's a proper way to pray because you're praying in agreement with God's Word. You're saying, "We believe Your promises, but we want them to manifest. We desire for You to come from the spirit world into physical manifestation."

Praying "O God, come and be with us" is incorrect. It means you don't believe that God is there until you can see or feel Him. Then, when someone starts shouting "I feel the Holy Ghost," you say, "God's here now!" It wasn't that He just showed up; He was there the whole time. You just began to receive.

Wherever you are right now, there are television signals all around you. It doesn't matter if you're at home, in a car, at work, on a bus, or sitting under a tree somewhere, television signals are there. Just because you can't perceive them with your five natural senses doesn't mean they're not present. Even in the physical realm, an unbeliever—someone with zero faith—can prove that there are television signals surrounding you. All they have to do is take a television set, plug it in, turn it on, and tune it in.

When you first see the signal on the screen is not when the station started broadcasting. The signals were there before the television set was turned on. When you turned on and tuned in your set is when you started receiving, but it's not when the station began broadcasting.

What would you do if your television set went blank all of a sudden? Would you call the station and ask them to start broadcasting again? No! You'd check your receiver by turning it to another station. If other channels were still coming in, but that one wasn't, then you might think the station is not broadcasting. Maybe they're having a problem with their transmitter. But if your television went totally blank and no channels came in, you wouldn't call the station. You'd know, *My receiver's the problem.* Since 99 percent of the time the issue is with your receiver—not the station's transmitter—the first thing to do is check your receiver.

PRAY IN FAITH

God's the One with the transmitter. He's the Giver of all earthly and spiritual blessings (Eph. 1:3), and He's already transmitted them to you. Everything comes from God, but He's already transmitted. If you aren't seeing them manifest in your life, the problem isn't with God's transmitter; you need to fix your receiver.

Yet, when most Christians don't feel joy, they go to the Lord and ask, "O God, where's my joy? What's wrong? Restore unto me the joy of my salvation!" Have you sung that song? It's a great tune, but the words are actually taken from an Old Testament scripture.

Create in me a clean heart, O God; and renew a right spirit within me. [11] Cast me not away from thy presence; and take not thy holy spirit from me. [12] Restore unto me the joy of thy salvation; and uphold me with thy free spirit.

PSALM 51:10-12

David prayed this in repentance of his sin with Bathsheba.

However, for a New Testament believer to say "O God, cast me not away from Your presence. Please, don't leave me!" is an insult against what Jesus came to do. David didn't have a covenant that promised God would stick with him through everything. The Old Covenant was based upon performance, so God did come and go. Old Testament people weren't born again. They didn't have an eternal redemption the way it's spoken of in the New Covenant (Heb. 9:12 and 14). However, Jesus promised, *"I will never leave thee, nor forsake thee"* (Heb. 13:5) and *"Lo, I am with you alway, even unto the end of the world"* (Matt. 28:20). If you've been born again and don't feel the presence of God, for you to pray this prayer that David prayed and say "Cast me not away from Your presence, renew a right spirit within me, and take not Your Holy Spirit from me" means that you don't understand what benefits you have in your covenant. You're in unbelief—not believing the New Covenant.

Instead of praying in unbelief and then wondering why you aren't seeing better results, you need to pray in faith. It's the prayer of faith that will save the sick (James 5:15). It's the prayer of faith that will bring you deliverance and joy.

Say, "Father, I don't feel like You're here. There's simply no tangible indication of Your presence in my life right now. Everything's gone south. But, Father, Your Word says that You'll never leave me nor forsake me, so I know that You're here. Whatever is causing these problems in my life is not You. I know that You haven't forsaken me. I ask You now to help me see what I've done to turn away from You. As I seek You, please help me make the connection and release this life You've placed inside me. I know Your Holy Spirit's still here. I know Your blessings are still here. I'm believing that they'll be released. I refuse to have these other things." That's praying a prayer of faith!

DEFEND YOUR POSITION

There's still a fight. But the fight is to stand in the victory that God has already purchased for you—not to go out and win one. There's a big difference!

While in the army, I discovered that defending a position that is already held is much easier than trying to take a new one. If you are on top of a hill and have the advantage of a defensive position, you can hold it with five men. But a hundred men would be required to take that same position. Much more effort is needed to go conquer something you don't yet have than to defend something that's already yours.

You need to believe that you're already blessed (Eph. 1:3). God has already given you healing, wisdom, revelation, prosperity, joy, peace—everything you'll ever need.

One-third of your salvation is over. Your spirit is completely saved. It's identical to Jesus. It has His joy, His peace, His knowledge, His love, and His fruit. Everything that's true of Jesus is true of your born-again spirit. There's no inadequacy. Your spirit is not in the process of growing up into these things. It's not that these things are in your spirit in seed form and have to mature. No, they are already complete and full-grown in the spirit. All you have to do is renew your mind and let these things manifest themselves through you. If this isn't a revelation to you, you need this revelation to fully understand what I'm sharing.

God has already done it. This isn't just "in principle." It's not just written on a piece of paper somewhere. There was an actual transformation that took place in your spirit the very moment you were born again. Now you have love, joy, peace, long-suffering, gentleness, goodness, faith, meekness, and temperance (Gal. 5:22-23). You are—right now in your spirit—identical to Jesus (1 John 4:17 and 1 Cor. 6:17). The same power that raised Christ from the dead now lives inside of you (Eph. 1:19-21). It's infinitely easier to release something you know and believe you already have than to try to go get something you don't.

If you're not absolutely convinced that you've already got it, you'll either submit to, or have to battle, thoughts that you won't get it. However, once you know it's yours, how could you doubt you'd get it? This is simple, but so profound.

DRAWING THE LINE

When my wife and I first started out in ministry, we were so poor, we couldn't even pay attention. The Lord had already blessed us with financial prosperity, but I wasn't cooperating with His laws for releasing it. In fact, I was violating a number of instructions in God's Word. Therefore, we really struggled until I learned some things and adjusted accordingly. God loved us and we didn't starve to death, but we didn't prosper until we understood how His kingdom works and began to cooperate with it.

During that period of time, I didn't even have a complete Bible. It had gone through Vietnam with me. It was so beat up and marked up that most passages could hardly be read. Also, entire books had fallen out and been lost. Here I was, pastoring this little church in Segoville, Texas, without a full Bible!

Right or wrong, I made a decision: "Father, I have to start seeing Your power manifest somewhere. If I can't believe You for enough money to buy a new Bible, how am I going to believe You for enough money to lead people into salvation and see them healed, delivered, and baptized in the Holy Spirit?" I just made an issue out of it, saying, "God, this faith either works, or I'm going to die right here. The outcome of this battle determines whether or not I'm going on." To me, this was nonnegotiable.

So, I started believing God for a new Bible. All told, it took me six months to get enough money to buy it. It's not that this wasn't my priority; it's just that finances for us were tight. My wife and I would go two or three weeks without food—even when she was eight months' pregnant—because we just didn't have money. I'm not exaggerating when I say that it took me six months to believe for the extra twenty-five dollars to go buy a Bible.

To some people, financial "trouble" is having $1,000 in the bank and $1,100 worth of bills. We didn't even have a bank account—much less any money to put in it! There were days when we'd go without a penny in our pockets. I'd even pick up soda bottles just to get gas money.

DEALING WITH DOUBT

Satan plagued me that entire time. I fought doubt constantly. There probably wasn't a ten-minute period of time during my waking hours for six months that I didn't have some thought like, *It's not going to work. You'll never get it. You don't even have a Bible. Some man of God you are!* I'd have to throw down those thoughts and say, "No! In the name of Jesus, I do have my Bible!" I fought these constant, unrelenting thoughts for six whole months.

Finally, I had enough money. So, I went to a bookstore, bought a Bible, and had my name engraved on it. It was mine! After I walked out the door with that new Bible under my arm, I never again doubted that I'd get it.

"Well, of course," you might say. "Why would you doubt that you'd get something you've already got?" My point exactly!

Do you know why you have to counter the thought *I'm going to die* immediately after praying "O Lord, please heal me"? It's because you don't believe you've already been healed. You believe God can heal you, but you're waiting on Him to do so. That's wrong. God has already released His healing power. You aren't waiting on God to heal you; God is waiting on you to appropriate what He's already done.

BELIEVE AND RECEIVE!

It's like that television signal. The signal is already being broadcast. If you aren't seeing the picture, it's not God who isn't transmitting; it's your receiver that isn't working right. You need to get into the owner's manual—God's Word—and start studying. Find out how to turn that thing on, tune it in, eliminate the static, and deal with things to get the best reception.

Don't say, "I'm waiting on God." That's not how it works. *"By whose stripes ye **were** healed"* (1 Pet. 2:24, emphasis mine). God is waiting on you to believe and receive.

Since I've begun teaching this, I've seen a tremendous increase in the amount of people receiving their healing. They are no longer just asking and waiting on God to do it. Instead, they're believing what the Lord has already done. They're taking their authority and commanding what's already been provided to come into manifestation. The results have been awesome!

When my oldest son, Joshua, was young, he became sick and looked like he was going to die. Jamie and I fought it, stood against it, and finally he got better. This happened several years in a row. Finally, I saw this coming back on him again and sought the Lord about it. I prayed, "Lord, what's wrong?" He answered, "The problem is that you are fighting to *get* healed instead of fighting because you've *been* healed. You're trying to obtain healing instead of defending the healing you already have." Once I understood this, things turned around.

Don't fight to *get* healed; fight because you've *been* healed. Don't fight in an attempt to obtain healing; fight to defend the healing that's already been provided for you in Christ.

Allow this revelation to sink in and change your attitude toward everything you receive from the Lord!

LESSON 2 – ADDITIONAL INFORMATION

My *Spirit, Soul & Body* teaching goes into much more depth on these truths. It reveals from God's Word how your born-again spirit is already as perfect, complete, and full of God's blessing and power as it ever will be throughout all eternity.

Spirit, Soul & Body was one of the first revelations I received through studying the Bible. It has served as a foundation for almost everything the Lord has shown me since. These important truths freed me from the bondage of much wrong thinking and enabled me to consistently experience God's supernatural power. Personally, I cannot comprehend how anyone can truly prosper in their relationship with God apart from understanding this basic revelation. I've seen the Lord set more people free through *Spirit, Soul & Body* than almost anything else I've ever ministered. Check it out!

CHECK YOUR RECEIVER
LESSON 2 – OUTLINE

I. Ephesians was written from the perspective of what has already taken place.

Paul, an apostle of Jesus Christ by the will of God, to the saints which are at Ephesus, and to the faithful in Christ Jesus: [2] Grace be to you, and peace, from God our Father, and from the Lord Jesus Christ. [3] Blessed be the God and Father of our Lord Jesus Christ, who hath blessed us with all spiritual blessings in heavenly places in Christ.

EPHESIANS 1:1-3, EMPHASIS MINE

A. Notice the terminology here: "Blessed be God who *has*—past tense, it's already . been done—blessed us with all spiritual blessings."

B. Really, *"all spiritual blessings in heavenly places in Christ"* is just an old English way of expressing the truth that God has already blessed you with everything—and it's in the spiritual realm.

C. Everything that God has done for you has already been deposited into your born-again spirit.

D. Although it's already there, you must draw it out of the spirit and into the physical realm.

II. If we asked someone for something they knew we already had, how would they respond to us?

A. There'd probably be an awkward silence, which sounds a lot like how God often responds to us!

I will never leave thee, nor forsake thee.

HEBREWS 13:5

Where two or three are gathered together in my name, there am I in the midst of them.

MATTHEW 18:20

B. When we ask God for what He has already given us, we're letting our senses dominate us.

III. Wherever you are right now, there are television signals all around you.

    A. Just because you can't perceive them with your five natural senses doesn't mean they're not present.

    B. When you turned on and tuned in your television set is when you started receiving, but it's not when the station began broadcasting.

    C. God is the Giver of all earthly and spiritual blessings (Eph. 1:3), and He's already transmitted them to you.

    D. If you aren't seeing them manifest in your life, the problem isn't with God's transmitter.

    E. You need to fix your receiver.

Lo, I am with you alway, even unto the end of the world.

MATTHEW 28:20

IV. You need to believe that you're already blessed (Eph. 1:3).

    A. God has already given you healing, wisdom, revelation, prosperity, joy, peace everything you'll ever need.

    B. All you have to do is renew your mind and let these things manifest themselves through you.

V. There was an actual transformation that took place in your spirit the very moment you were born again.

    A. Now you have love, joy, peace, long-suffering, gentleness, goodness, faith, meekness, and temperance (Gal. 5:22-23).

    B. You are—right now in your spirit—identical to Jesus (1 John 4:17 and 1 Cor. 6:17).

    C. The same power that raised Christ from the dead now lives inside of you (Eph. 1:19-20).

VI. It's infinitely easier to release something you know and believe you already have than it is to try and go get something you don't.

    A. If you're not absolutely convinced that you've already got it, you'll either submit to or have to battle thoughts that you won't get it.

    B. However, once you know it's yours, how could you doubt you'd get it?

    C. This is simple, but so profound.

VII.   It's like that television signal.

    A. If you aren't seeing the picture, it's not God who isn't transmitting; it's your receiver that isn't working right.

    B. You need to get into the owner's manual—God's Word—and start studying.

    C. Find out how to turn that thing on, tune it in, eliminate the static, and deal with things to get the best reception.

    D. God is waiting on you to believe and receive.

VIII.   Once Andrew understood this, things turned around.

By whose stripes ye were *healed.*

1 PETER 2:24, EMPHASIS MINE

    A. Don't fight to *get* healed; fight because you've *been* healed.

    B. Don't fight in an attempt to obtain healing; fight to defend the healing that's already been provided for you in Christ.

    C. Allow this revelation to sink in and change your attitude toward everything you receive from the Lord!

LESSON 2 – ADDITIONAL INFORMATION

My *Spirit, Soul & Body* teaching goes into much more depth on these truths. It reveals from God's Word how your born-again spirit is already as perfect, complete, and full of God's blessing and power as it ever will be throughout all eternity.

Spirit, Soul & Body was one of the first revelations I received through studying the Bible. It has served as a foundation for almost everything the Lord has shown me since. These important truths freed me from the bondage of much wrong thinking and enabled me to consistently experience God's supernatural power. Personally, I cannot comprehend how anyone can truly prosper in their relationship with God apart from understanding this basic revelation. I've seen the Lord set more people free through *Spirit, Soul & Body* than almost anything else I've ever ministered. Check it out!

CHECK YOUR RECEIVER
LESSON 2 – TEACHER'S GUIDE

1.　Ephesians was written from the perspective of what has already taken place. Notice the terminology in Ephesians 1:1-3: "Blessed be God who *has*—past tense, it's already been done—blessed us with all spiritual blessings." Really, *"all spiritual blessings in heavenly places in Christ"* is just an old English way of expressing the truth that God has already blessed us with everything—and it's in the spiritual realm. Everything that God has done for us has already been deposited into our born-again spirits. Although it's already there, we must draw it out of the spirit and into the physical realm.

2.　If someone asked us for something we knew they already had, how would we respond to them? There'd probably be an awkward silence, which sounds a lot like how God often responds to us (Heb. 13:5 and Matt. 18:20). When we ask God for what He has already given us, we're letting our senses dominate us.

3.　Wherever we are right now, there are television signals all around us. Just because we can't perceive them with our five natural senses doesn't mean they're not present. When we turned on and tuned in our television sets is when we started receiving, but it's not when the station began broadcasting. God is the Giver of all earthly and spiritual blessings (Eph. 1:3), and He's already transmitted them to us. If we aren't seeing them manifest in our lives, the problem isn't with God's transmitter. We need to fix our receivers (Matt. 28:20).

4.　We need to believe that we're already blessed (Eph. 1:3). God has already given us healing, wisdom, revelation, prosperity, joy, peace—everything we'll ever need. All we have to do is renew our minds and let these things manifest themselves through us.

1.　A.　Read Ephesians 1:1-3. Where is everything that God has already blessed us with? (In the spiritual realm)
　　B.　What has already been deposited into our born-again spirits? (Everything that God has done for us)
　　C.　Although it's already there, we must draw it out of the spirit and into where? (The physical realm)
2.　A.　Read Hebrews 13:5 and Matthew 18:20. How would we respond to someone who asked us for something we knew they already had? (There'd probably be an awkward silence)
　　B.　What are we letting dominate us? (Our senses)
3.　A.　Read Ephesians 1:3 and Matthew 28:20. Who is the Giver of all earthly and spiritual blessings? (God)
　　B.　If we aren't seeing them manifest in our lives, is the problem with God's transmitter or our receivers? (We need to fix our receivers)
4.　A.　According to Ephesians 1:3, what do we need to believe? (That we're already blessed)
　　B.　What has God already given us? (Healing, wisdom, revelation, prosperity, joy, peace—everything we'll ever need)

5.   An actual transformation took place in our spirits the very moment we were born again. Now we have love, joy, peace, long-suffering, gentleness, goodness, faith, meekness, and temperance (Gal. 5:22-23). We are—right now in our spirits—identical to Jesus (1 John 4:17 and 1 Cor. 6:17). The same power that raised Christ from the dead now lives inside of us (Eph. 1:19-20).

6.   It's infinitely easier to release something we know and believe we already have than it is to try and go get something we don't. If we're not absolutely convinced that we've already got it, we'll either submit to or have to battle thoughts that we won't get it. However, once we know it's ours, how could we doubt we'd get it? This is simple, but so profound.

7.   It's like that television signal. If we aren't seeing the picture, it's not God who isn't transmitting; it's our receivers that aren't working right. We need to get into the owner's manual—God's Word—and start studying so we can find out how to turn that thing on, tune it in, eliminate the static, and deal with things to get the best reception. God is waiting on us to believe and receive.

8.   Once we understand this, things will start to turn around (1 Pet. 2:24). We don't fight to *get* healed; we fight because we've *been* healed. We don't fight in an attempt to obtain healing; we fight to defend the healing that's already been provided for us in Christ. Let's allow this revelation to sink in and change our attitudes toward everything we receive from the Lord!

5. A. Read Galatians 5:22-23, 1 John 4:17, 1 Corinthians 6:17, and Ephesians 1:19-20. Where did the actual transformation take place the very moment we were born again? (In our spirits)

    B. What power now lives inside of us? (The same power that raised Christ from the dead)

6. A. Is it easier to release something we know and believe we already have or to try and go get something we don't? (It's infinitely easier to release something we know and believe we already have)

    B. What will we either submit to or have to battle if we're not absolutely convinced that we've already got it? (Thoughts that we won't get it)

7. A. What do we need to get into and start studying so we can find out how to turn on and tune in our receivers? (The owner's manual—God's Word)

    B. Who is God waiting on? (Us to believe and receive)

8. A. According to 1 Peter 2:24, do we fight to get healed or because we've been healed? (Because we've been healed)

    B. Do we fight in an attempt to obtain healing or to defend the healing that's already been provided for us in Christ? (To defend the healing that's already been provided for us in Christ)

    C. As we allow this revelation to sink in, what will it change? (Our attitudes toward everything we receive from the Lord)

CHECK YOUR RECEIVER
LESSON 2 – DISCIPLESHIP QUESTIONS

1. According to Ephesians 1:1-3, we have (past tense) been blessed with what?

2. According to 1 Peter 2:24, we were (past tense) healed by what?

3. Read Ephesians 1:19-21. The power that raised Christ from the dead and set Him at the right hand of the Father is to _____.

4. Hebrews 13:5 tells us two things God will never do. What are they?

5. According to Matthew 18:20, Jesus promised to be there in the midst of whom?

6. As an Old Testament saint, David asked God in Psalm 51:10-12 to create in him a what?

7. And to renew what?

8. David asked God not to cast him away from His presence nor take His _____ from him.

9. What did David ask Him to restore unto him?

10. Read Hebrews 9:12 and 14. How many times did Jesus enter in the holy place?

11. What did Jesus obtain for us?

12. What purges our consciences from dead works?

13. Matthew 28:20 tells us that Jesus is with us for how long?

14. Even to what?

15. According to James 5:15, what shall save the sick?

16. Who shall raise them up?

17. What will happen if they have committed sins?

18. Read Galatians 5:22-23. Is there any law against the fruit of the Spirit?

19. First John 4:17 says that as Jesus is, so are _____ in this world.

20. According to 1 Corinthians 6:17, those who are joined to the Lord are what?

CHECK YOUR RECEIVER
LESSON 2 – ANSWER KEY

1. *"All spiritual blessings in heavenly places in Christ"*

2. Jesus' stripes

3. Us-ward who believe

4. He will never leave us nor forsake us

5. Two or three gathered together in His name

6. Clean heart

7. A right spirit within him

8. Holy Spirit

9. The joy of his salvation

10. Once

11. Eternal redemption

12. The blood of Christ

13. Always

14. The end of the world

15. The prayer of faith

16. The Lord

17. They shall be forgiven them

18. No

19. We

20. One spirit

CHECK YOUR RECEIVER
LESSON 2 – SCRIPTURES

EPHESIANS 1:1-3
Paul, an apostle of Jesus Christ by the will of God, to the saints which are at Ephesus, and to the faithful in Christ Jesus: **[2]** Grace be to you, and peace, from God our Father, and from the Lord Jesus Christ. **[3]** Blessed be the God and Father of our Lord Jesus Christ, who hath blessed us with all spiritual blessings in heavenly places in Christ.

1 PETER 2:24
Who his own self bare our sins in his own body on the tree, that we, being dead to sins, should live unto righteousness: by whose stripes ye were healed.

EPHESIANS 1:19-21
And what is the exceeding greatness of his power to us-ward who believe, according to the working of his mighty power, **[20]** Which he wrought in Christ, when he raised him from the dead, and set him at his own right hand in the heavenly places, **[21]** Far above all principality, and power, and might, and dominion, and every name that is named, not only in this world, but also in that which is to come.

HEBREWS 13:5
Let your conversation be without covetousness; and be content with such things as ye have: for he hath said, I will never leave thee, nor forsake thee.

MATTHEW 18:20
For where two or three are gathered together in my name, there am I in the midst of them.

PSALM 51:10-12
Create in me a clean heart, O God; and renew a right spirit within me. **[11]** Cast me not away from thy presence; and take not thy holy spirit from me. **[12]** Restore unto me the joy of thy salvation; and uphold me with thy free spirit.

HEBREWS 9:12
Neither by the blood of goats and calves, but by his own blood he entered in once into the holy place, having obtained eternal redemption for us.

HEBREWS 9:14
How much more shall the blood of Christ, who through the eternal Spirit offered himself without spot to God, purge your conscience from dead works to serve the living God?

MATTHEW 28:20

Teaching them to observe all things whatsoever I have commanded you: and, lo, I am with you alway, even unto the end of the world. Amen.

JAMES 5:15

And the prayer of faith shall save the sick, and the Lord shall raise him up; and if he have committed sins, they shall be forgiven him.

GALATIANS 5:22-23

But the fruit of the Spirit is love, joy, peace, longsuffering, gentleness, goodness, faith, [23] Meekness, temperance: against such there is no law.

1 JOHN 4:17

Herein is our love made perfect, that we may have boldness in the day of judgment: because as he is, so are we in this world.

1 CORINTHIANS 6:17

But he that is joined unto the Lord is one spirit.

ACCEPTED AND ENLIGHTENED
LESSON 3

According as he hath [past tense] *chosen us in him before the foundation of the world.*

EPHESIANS 1:4, BRACKETS MINE

When you cried out to the Lord for salvation is not when He first set His desire upon you. God didn't hear you and all of a sudden say, "Okay, I think I'll respond and send My Son." No, He already chose you. The provision had already been made. Atonement is already an accomplished work. Salvation was just waiting for you to reach out in faith and appropriate it. Although you had to choose to believe and receive, God had already made the provision before you ever had the need, before you were even born, and before you had ever sinned.

That we should be holy and without blame before him in love: [5] Having predestinated us unto the adoption of children by Jesus Christ to himself, according to the good pleasure of his will, [6] To the praise of the glory of his grace, wherein he hath [past tense] *made us accepted in the beloved.*

EPHESIANS 1:4-6, EMPHASIS & BRACKETS MINE

Most Christians are trying to do things (live holy, read the Word, tithe, fast, etc.) to make themselves acceptable to God. That's like a person with a stick tied to their back and a carrot dangling out in front of them. They're on a treadmill going nowhere. Every time they reach out and strain toward their goal—it moves! Religion has these Christians constantly looking forward to a time when they'll be accepted by God. They're blinded to the truth that He's already made them *"accepted in the beloved"* (Eph. 1:6).

The Greek word translated here *"accepted"* is the exact same word rendered *"highly favoured"* in Luke 1:28: *"And the angel* [Gabriel] *came in unto her, and said, Hail, thou that art highly favoured, the Lord is with thee* [Mary]: *blessed art thou among women"* (brackets mine). These are the only two times this Greek word is used in the New Testament. Therefore, being *"accepted"* means you are *"highly favoured"* of God!

AN ACCOMPLISHED FACT

Most Christians don't believe the Lord's acceptance, favor, and love toward them is an accomplished fact. It's something they long for and hope to obtain, but they don't understand that they already have it. The truth is, God loves you, and He can't love you any more than He already does. There's absolutely nothing you can do to make Him love you more—or less. Now, that's contrary to most religious teaching today.

Religion says, "God loves you proportional to your performance." That's not true. You're accepted because of what Jesus did. Ephesians 1:6 declares that you are "accepted *in the beloved*" (emphasis mine). Who's the beloved? Jesus! *"In whom we have redemption through his blood, the forgiveness of sins, according to the riches of his grace"* (Eph. 1:7).

You have already been forgiven—completely. Jesus didn't only deal with your past sins, which you've confessed; at the cross, He paid for all of your past-, present-, and even future-tense sins. This is the *"eternal redemption"* that Hebrews 9:12 reveals.

If you were asked to write a prayer that believers 2,000 years from now would be able to read and benefit from, what would you pray? Based on my experience with thousands of people, the average Christian today would say "O God, I ask You to pour out Your Spirit on that generation. Send revival and move in a mighty way! O Lord, do a new thing on the earth in that day!" Basically, their whole prayer would be, "God, do something!"

Paul prayed just the opposite.

That the God of our Lord Jesus Christ, the Father of glory, may give unto you the spirit of wisdom and revelation in the knowledge of him: [18] The eyes of your understanding being enlightened; that ye may know what is the hope of his calling, and what the riches of the glory of his inheritance in the saints, [19] And what is the exceeding greatness of his power to us-ward who believe, according to the working of his mighty power.

EPHESIANS 1:17-19

There's a huge difference between what we pray: "O God, go and touch this person" and what Paul prayed: "Lord, please help them to see and understand what You've already done."

When you know what God has already done, you'll pray with confidence.

WHO'S RESPONDING TO WHOM?

Jesus loves the people you're interceding for much more than you do. It's not your prayer that's making Him love them and move in their lives. He loves them millions of times more than you possibly could! You can't even approach the love God has for the people you're interceding for, but how many times have you prayed for someone and felt, *Lord, if You love this person half as much as I do, You'd touch their life!*

I prayed that way over thirty years ago. While interceding for our city, I literally wept, wailed, begged, and pleaded, thinking God had to do something to send revival. I worked myself up into such a frenzy that I pounded the wall and cried out "God, if You love the people of Arlington, Texas, half as much as I do, there'd be revival!" However, as soon as that came out of my mouth, I knew something was terribly wrong with my theology.

I thought God was responding to my prayer. I believed my intercession motivated and moved Him to do something. I pictured the Lord in heaven with His arms folded, upset with us over how ungodly we were. It seemed to me that He had withdrawn His Spirit and His blessings, and we had to plead with Him to turn His heart back toward us. Many people believe this is the way to pray for revival, but it's absolutely wrong.

Don't misunderstand me—I'm for revival and all of its benefits. I just disagree on how we get there.

DIP IN, DRAW OUT, AND RELEASE

Revival doesn't come by begging the Lord to pour out His Spirit. Neither does it come by pleading with Him to move and do a new thing. Revival comes by starting to believe what God has already done and beginning to walk in His dynamic, supernatural life.

If you want to see revival, go raise someone from the dead, open up some blind eyes, and minister to people and see them set free. Then you'll have all the revival you can handle!

Jesus didn't come asking God to pour out His Spirit. After being filled with the Holy Ghost, He simply dipped in, drew out, released, and gave of the Spirit to people. Everything we'd call "revival" happened in Christ's ministry, but not through begging and pleading with God to do something. Jesus simply did what His Father told Him to do.

Yes, we need revival in our land. But how does it come? By recruiting another million Christians to pray, agree, and fast one day a week asking God for it? No! Revival comes when we seek the Lord wholeheartedly and begin to believe, draw out, and flow in what He's already done. If you catch on fire for God, people will come and watch you burn!

SEE AND UNDERSTAND

Paul didn't pray for God to do something new. Instead, he said, *"Wherefore I also, after I heard of your faith in the Lord Jesus, and love unto all the saints, Cease not to give thanks for you, making mention of you in my prayers; That the God of our Lord Jesus Christ, the Father of glory, may give unto you…"* (Eph. 1:15-17). What? A new thing? Another outpouring? A brand-new wave? No. *"The spirit of wisdom and revelation in the knowledge of him"* (Eph. 1:17).

Paul wasn't asking for something new but that the revelation of what God has already done and is now resident within us would begin to come out.

Wherein he hath [already] abounded toward us in all wisdom and prudence; [9] Having made known unto us the mystery of his will.

In other words, this wisdom and revelation Paul was praying for have already been given to every believer. It's just that not every Christian is receiving it. They don't have their set plugged in, turned on, and tuned in to it.

Paul prayed, *"The eyes of your understanding being enlightened; that ye may know what is the hope of his calling, and what the riches of the glory of his inheritance in the saints"* (Eph. 1:18). You don't need God to do something new. What you need is to see and understand what He's already done.

As a born-again believer, you are now more than a conqueror through Christ (Rom. 8:37). You have already been transformed from sinful, unrighteous, and unholy to righteous and holy in Him (2 Cor. 5:17, 21; and Eph. 4:24). You were delivered out of the kingdom of darkness and translated into the kingdom of God's own dear Son (Col. 1:13). The same power (Eph. 1:19-20), life (Gal. 2:20), wisdom (1 Cor. 1:30), victory (1 Cor. 15:57), anointing (1 John 2:20), and faith (Gal. 2:20) that Jesus had now resides in you. You don't need more of anything!

You just need a revelation of what you already have. That's what Paul was praying: that the eyes of your understanding would be enlightened, that you would know what is the hope of His calling, that you would have a full revelation of your potential in Christ, and that you would see what the riches of the glory of His inheritance are in you—a saint!

FOCUS YOUR ATTENTION!

Most people imagine the glory of God as being far off. They picture the splendor of heaven—gates of pearl, streets of gold, mansions, etc.—but Ephesians 1:18 reveals that the riches of the glory of God's inheritance are in the saints. What's in heaven pales in comparison to what's already inside of you.

You're probably thinking, *That can't be right!* Why? You look in a mirror, you see the natural—you see zits, gray hairs, bulges, etc. You survey your emotional realm and notice that you don't feel peace or joy, so you conclude, *This can't be where God's glory is. Surely, it's not here.* But it is there; God's glory is in your born-again spirit, not your body or soul.

Your five natural senses cannot perceive your spirit. Neither can you "feel" it with your soul (your personality—mind, will, emotions, and conscience). You must see who you are and what you have in the spirit realm through God's Word and then believe it by faith. Most Christians don't know this, but God's glory is already inside their spirits.

If you had a revelation of this, depression would have no power over you. How could you stay down in the dumps when you truly know the hope of your calling and what are the riches of the glory of His inheritance in you right now? In order to stay depressed, you'd have to shut that revelation off and look only in the physical realm at your circumstances and other negative things. But if you focus your attention on who you are and what you have in Christ—recognizing that it's a done deal and that the glory you'll experience throughout all eternity is already inside you—depression would leave, and you'd start enjoying victory. That'll put a shout in a fence post!

LESSON 3 – ADDITIONAL INFORMATION

You have already been forgiven—completely! Jesus didn't only deal with your past sins at the cross, which you've confessed, He paid for all of your past-, present-, and even future-tense sins. This is the *"eternal redemption"* that Hebrews 9:12 reveals.

My message entitled "Eternal Redemption" deals with Hebrews 9 in depth. It's the second part of *Spirit, Soul & Body*. Also, "Complete Forgiveness," *Redemption*, and *The War Is Over* all expand upon these truths.

ACCEPTED AND ENLIGHTENED
LESSON 3 – OUTLINE

I.   Atonement is already an accomplished work.

According as he hath [past tense] *chosen us in him before the foundation of the world.*

EPHESIANS 1:4, BRACKETS MINE

   A.   Salvation was just waiting for you to reach out in faith and appropriate it.

   B.   Although you had to choose to believe and receive, God had already made the provision before you ever had the need, before you were even born, and before you had ever sinned.

That we should be holy and without blame before him in love: [5] Having predestinated us unto the adoption of children by Jesus Christ to himself, according to the good pleasure of his will, [6] To the praise of the glory of his grace, wherein he hath [past tense] *made us accepted in the beloved.*

EPHESIANS 1:4-6, EMPHASIS & BRACKETS MINE

II. Most Christians are trying to do things (live holy, read the Word, tithe, fast, etc.) to make themselves acceptable to God.

   A.   They're blinded to the truth that He has already made them *"accepted in the beloved"* (Eph. 1:6).

And the angel [Gabriel] *came in unto her, and said, Hail, thou that art highly favoured, the Lord is with thee* [Mary]: *blessed art thou among women.*

LUKE 1:28, BRACKETS MINE

   B.   Being *"accepted"* means you are *"highly favoured"* of God!

   C.   You're accepted because of what Jesus did.

In whom we have redemption through his blood, the forgiveness of sins, according to the riches of his grace.

EPHESIANS 1:7

   D.   At the cross, Jesus paid for all of your past-, present-, and even future-tense sins.

E. This is the *"eternal redemption"* that Hebrews 9:12 reveals.

III. There's a huge difference between what we pray: "O God, go and touch this person" and what Paul prayed: "Lord, please help them to see and understand what You've already done."

That the God of our Lord Jesus Christ, the Father of glory, may give unto you the spirit of wisdom and revelation in the knowledge of him: [18] The eyes of your understanding being enlightened; that ye may know what is the hope of his calling, and what the riches of the glory of his inheritance in the saints, [19] And what is the exceeding greatness of his power to us-ward who believe, according to the working of his mighty power.

EPHESIANS 1:17-19

A. When we know what God has already done, we'll pray with confidence.

B. Revival doesn't come by begging the Lord to pour out His Spirit.

C. Revival comes when we seek the Lord wholeheartedly and begin to believe, draw out, and flow in what He's already done.

IV. Paul didn't pray for God to do something new.

Wherefore I also, after I heard of your faith in the Lord Jesus, and love unto all the saints, [16] Cease not to give thanks for you, making mention of you in my prayers; [17] That the God of our Lord Jesus Christ, the Father of glory, may give unto you the spirit of wisdom and revelation in the knowledge of him.

EPHESIANS 1:15-17

A. Paul wasn't asking for something new but that the revelation of what God has already done and is now resident within us would begin to come out.

Wherein he hath [already] abounded toward us in all wisdom and prudence; [9] Having made known unto us the mystery of his will.

EPHESIANS 1:8-9, BRACKETS MINE

B. In other words, this wisdom and revelation Paul was praying for have already been given to every believer.

C. It's just that not every Christian is receiving it—they don't have their sets plugged in, turned on, and tuned in to it.

That the eyes of your understanding being enlightened; that ye may know what is the hope of his calling, and what the riches of the glory of his inheritance in the saints.

EPHESIANS 1:18

    D. We just need a revelation of what we already have.

V.   Ephesians 1:18 reveals that the riches of the glory of God's inheritance are in the saints.

    A. What's in heaven pales in comparison to what's already inside of you.

    B. Your five natural senses cannot perceive your spirit. Neither can you "feel" it with your soul (your personality—mind, will, emotions, and conscience).

    C. You must see who you are and what you have in the spirit realm through God's Word and then believe it by faith.

    D. If you focus your attention on who you are and what you have in Christ—recognizing that it's a done deal and that the glory you'll experience throughout all eternity is already inside you—depression would leave, and you'd start enjoying victory.

LESSON 3 – ADDITIONAL INFORMATION

You have already been forgiven—completely! Jesus didn't only deal with your past sins at the cross, which you've confessed, He paid for all of your past-, present-, and even future-tense sins. This is the *"eternal redemption"* that Hebrews 9:12 reveals.

My message entitled "Eternal Redemption" deals with Hebrews 9 in depth. It's the second part of *Spirit, Soul & Body*. Also, "Complete Forgiveness," *Redemption*, and *The War Is Over* all expand upon these truths.

ACCEPTED AND ENLIGHTENED
LESSON 3 – TEACHER'S GUIDE

1.   Atonement is already an accomplished work (Eph. 1:4-6). Salvation was just waiting for us to reach out in faith and appropriate it. Although we had to choose to believe and receive, God already made the provision before we ever had the need, before we were even born, and before we had ever sinned.

2.   Most Christians are trying to do things (live holy, read the Word, tithe, fast, etc.) to make themselves acceptable to God. They're blinded to the truth that He has already made them *"accepted in the beloved"* (Eph. 1:6 and Luke 1:28). Being *"accepted"* means we are *"highly favoured"* of God! We're accepted because of what Jesus did (Eph. 1:7). At the cross, Jesus paid for all of our past-, present-, and even future-tense sins. This is the *"eternal redemption"* that Hebrews 9:12 reveals.

3.   There's a huge difference between what we pray: "O God, go and touch this person" and what Paul prayed: "Lord, please help them to see and understand what You've already done" (Eph. 1:17-19). When we know what God has already done, we'll pray with confidence. Revival doesn't come by begging the Lord to pour out His Spirit; revival comes when we seek the Lord wholeheartedly and begin to believe, draw out, and flow in what He's already done.

1.   A.   Read Ephesians 1:4-6. What was an already accomplished work? (Atonement)
     B.   Salvation was just waiting for us to what? (Reach out in faith and appropriate it)
     C.   When had God made the provision? (Before we ever had the need, before we were even born, and before we had ever sinned)
2.   A.   Read Ephesians 1:6-7 and Luke 1:28. What does our being accepted mean? (We are highly favored of God)
     B.   Read Hebrews 9:12. At the cross, what did Jesus pay for? (All of our past-, present-, and even future-tense sins)
3.   A.   Read Ephesians 1:17-19. When will we pray with confidence? (When we know what God has already done)
     B.   How does revival come? (When we seek the Lord wholeheartedly and begin to believe, draw out, and flow in what He's already done)

4.   Paul didn't pray for God to do something new (Eph. 1:15-17). Paul wasn't asking for something new but that the revelation of what God has already done and is now resident within us would begin to come out (Eph. 1:8-9). In other words, the wisdom and revelation Paul was praying for have already been given to every believer. It's just that not every Christian is receiving—they don't have their sets plugged in, turned on, and tuned in (Eph. 1:18). We just need a revelation of what we already have.

5.   Ephesians 1:18 reveals that the riches of the glory of God's inheritance are in the saints. What's in heaven pales in comparison to what's already inside of us. Our five natural senses cannot perceive our spirits. Neither can we "feel" them with our souls (our personalities—minds, wills, emotions, and consciences). We must see who we are and what we have in the spirit realm through God's Word and then believe it by faith. If we focus our attention on who we are and what we have in Christ—recognizing that it's a done deal and that the glory we'll experience throughout all eternity is already inside us—depression will leave, and we will start enjoying victory.

4. A.   Read Ephesians 1:8-9 and 15-18. Was Paul asking for something new? (No)
    B.   What do we need a revelation of? (What we already have—what God has already done and is now resident within us)
5. A.   How must we see who we are and what we have in the spirit realm? (Through God's Word)
    B.   In order for depression to leave and us to start enjoying victory, what must we focus our attention on? (Who we are and what we have in Christ, recognizing that it's a done deal and that the glory we'll experience throughout all eternity is already inside us)

ACCEPTED AND ENLIGHTENED
LESSON 3 – DISCIPLESHIP QUESTIONS

1. According to Ephesians 1:4-6, the Father chose us in Him before the foundation of the world that we should be what?

2. What has (past tense) God made us in His grace?

3. Ephesians 1:7 reveals that we have what?

4. According to Hebrews 9:12, Jesus obtained eternal redemption for _____.

5. Ephesians 1:8-9 says that God has abounded toward us in all what?

6. Read Ephesians 1:15-20. What spirit did Paul pray that the Lord would give us?

7. What being enlightened?

8. That we may know what?

9. According to Romans 8:37, we are more than _____ through Him who loved us.

10. Second Corinthians 5:17 reveals that anyone in Christ is a what?

11. What has passed away?

12. All things have become what?

13. According to 2 Corinthians 5:21, Jesus was made sin that we might be made_____ in Him.

14. Ephesians 4:24 exhorts us to put on the new man, which after God is created in _____.

15. According to Colossians 1:13, the Father delivered us from the power of darkness and translated us into _____.

16. Read 1 Corinthians 1:30. What has Christ Jesus been made unto us?

    A. Wisdom
    B. Righteousness
    C. Sanctification
    D. Redemption
    E. All of the above
    F. None of the above

17. According to 1 Corinthians 15:57, what has God given us through our Lord Jesus Christ?

18. What does 1 John 2:20 reveal that we have from the Holy One?

19. According to Galatians 2:20, who now lives in us?

20. The life we now live in the flesh, we live by the faith of whom?

ACCEPTED AND ENLIGHTENED
LESSON 3 – ANSWER KEY

1. Holy and without blame before Him in love

2. Accepted in the beloved

3. Redemption through His blood, the forgiveness of sins

4. Us

5. Wisdom and prudence

6. The spirit of wisdom and revelation in the knowledge of Him

7. The eyes of our understanding

8. *"The hope of his calling, and what the riches of the glory of his inheritance in the saints, And what is the exceeding greatness of his power to us-ward who believe, according to the working of his mighty power, Which he wrought in Christ, when he raised him from the dead, and set him at his own right hand in the heavenly places"*

9. Conquerors

10. New creature

11. Old things

12. New

13. The righteousness of God

14. Righteousness and true holiness

15. The kingdom of His dear Son

16. E.   All of the above

17. The victory

18. An unction

19. Christ

20. The Son of God

ACCEPTED AND ENLIGHTENED
LESSON 3 – SCRIPTURES

EPHESIANS 1:4-9

According as he hath chosen us in him before the foundation of the world, that we should be holy and without blame before him in love: [5] Having predestinated us unto the adoption of children by Jesus Christ to himself, according to the good pleasure of his will, [6] To the praise of the glory of his grace, wherein he hath made us accepted in the beloved. [7] In whom we have redemption through his blood, the forgiveness of sins, according to the riches of his grace. [8] Wherein he hath abounded toward us in all wisdom and prudence; [9] Having made known unto us the mystery of his will, according to his good pleasure which he hath purposed in himself.

LUKE 1:28

And the angel came in unto her, and said, Hail, thou that art highly favoured, the Lord is with thee: blessed art thou among women.

HEBREWS 9:12

Neither by the blood of goats and calves, but by his own blood he entered in once into the holy place, having obtained eternal redemption for us.

EPHESIANS 1:15-20

Wherefore I also, after I heard of your faith in the Lord Jesus, and love unto all the saints, [16] Cease not to give thanks for you, making mention of you in my prayers; [17] That the God of our Lord Jesus Christ, the Father of glory, may give unto you the spirit of wisdom and revelation in the knowledge of him: [18] The eyes of your understanding being enlightened; that ye may know what is the hope of his calling, and what the riches of the glory of his inheritance in the saints, [19] And what is the exceeding greatness of his power to us-ward who believe, according to the working of his mighty power, [20] Which he wrought in Christ, when he raised him from the dead, and set him at his own right hand in the heavenly places.

ROMANS 8:37

Nay, in all these things we are more than conquerors through him that loved us.

2 CORINTHIANS 5:17

Therefore if any man be in Christ, he is a new creature: old things are passed away; behold, all things are become new.

2 CORINTHIANS 5:21

For he hath made him to be sin for us, who knew no sin; that we might be made the righteousness of God in him.

EPHESIANS 4:24

And that ye put on the new man, which after God is created in righteousness and true holiness.

COLOSSIANS 1:13

Who hath delivered us from the power of darkness, and hath translated us into the kingdom of his dear Son.

GALATIANS 2:20

I am crucified with Christ: nevertheless I live; yet not I, but Christ liveth in me: and the life which I now live in the flesh I live by the faith of the Son of God, who loved me, and gave himself for me.

1 CORINTHIANS 1:30

But of him are ye in Christ Jesus, who of God is made unto us wisdom, and righteousness, and sanctification, and redemption.

1 CORINTHIANS 15:57

But thanks be to God, which giveth us the victory through our Lord Jesus Christ.

1 JOHN 2:20

But ye have an unction from the Holy One, and ye know all things.

HIS POWER IN YOU
LESSON 4

Paul prayed that you'd understand...

What is the exceeding greatness of his power to us-ward who believe, according to the working of his mighty power, [20] Which he wrought in Christ, when he raised him from the dead, and set him at his own right hand in the heavenly places, [21] Far above all principality, and power, and might, and dominion, and every name that is named, not only in this world, but also in that which is to come: [22] And hath put all things under his feet, and gave him to be the head over all things to the church, [23] Which is his body, the fulness of him that filleth all in all.

EPHESIANS 1:19-23

God wants you to see the exceeding greatness of His power toward those who believe. It's the very same power He used to raise Jesus Christ from the dead.

Have you ever prayed and asked the Lord for more power? Where do you think He'd get it? Ephesians 1:19-20 declares that you already have within you the same power that raised Jesus Christ from the dead. That's the greatest manifestation of God's power ever!

Raising Jesus from the dead required more power than creating the universe, parting the Red Sea, or anything else God has ever done. If you could put God's power on some kind of meter that would show how much power is released, I guarantee the power indicators would have all pegged out over the max when Christ arose from the dead. Why? Satan and all his demons did everything they possibly could to prevent the resurrection—but they failed!

RUINED!

The large church I attend puts on an elaborate Easter pageant. In it, the devil heckles Jesus on the Mount of Temptation. He also shows up in the crowd as they shout "Crucify Him!" again and again. Then, once Jesus is dead and buried, Satan and all of his demons stay outside the tomb pushing on the stone. Even though they try with all of their might to keep the resurrection from happening, they can't. All of a sudden there is an explosion. Smoke billows out as the stone falls on top of the devil. Then Jesus triumphantly walks out of the tomb and stands victoriously on top of the stone.

Although this dramatization isn't literally how it happened, it accurately and symbolically illustrates what's spiritually true. Satan did everything he could, but his power was nothing compared to God's. The resurrection of Jesus Christ is the greatest demonstration of God's power ever.

You have that same raising-from-the-dead power on the inside of you. It's not out there in heaven somewhere. It's within you—in your born-again spirit (Rom. 8:11). You don't need more power; you just need to believe that you already have it and begin to discover how it operates. Find out the laws that govern how the power of God works, and then put them into practice.

If you receive this revelation, it'll ruin you for most of the religious tradition floating around and masquerading as Christianity today.

COMMANDERS, NOT BEGGARS

Having a revelation of God's power within you will definitely change the way you pray! You'll stop begging God and saying, "O Lord, I'm nothing. I have nothing, but I believe that You can do anything. Come and move!" Instead, a bold New Testament attitude will cause you to say, "In myself, I am nothing. I don't have any virtue or worth based on my own human ability. But I'm in covenant with You, Father. I am a brand-new creature, and in my born-again spirit, I have the same power that raised Jesus from the dead. You said in Your Word that whomever I lay my hands on will be healed—and I believe it!" Then you'll get up, take your authority, and start commanding and releasing God's power.

This is what Peter did when he looked upon the lame man by the gate of the temple. Realizing God's power within him, Peter declared, *"Such as I have give I thee: In the name of Jesus Christ of Nazareth rise up and walk"* (Acts 3:6). Then he reached down, grabbed the man by the hand, and lifted him up. The man's feet and ankle bones immediately received strength, and he walked, leaped, and praised God (Acts 3:7-8).

Peter said, *"Such as I have."* It wasn't his own human strength he was referring to but God's raising-from-the-dead power within his born-again spirit. Most churches today would kick you out for saying something like that. They'd argue, "You can't do anything!" Of course not—in your physical self. But in the real you—your born-again spirit—you've been given the resurrection life of God.

This understanding will transform you into a commander. No longer will you beg God, saying "The doctor told me I'm going to die, and I can't do anything about it. O God, please heal me!" and then just sit there as a helpless nothing pleading with the Lord to do something. Praying like that shows that you don't yet have the revelation that the same power that raised Jesus Christ is now living on the inside of you. This understanding will change you from being a murmurer, complainer, whiner, and griper into a believer who takes authority, stands, and demands Satan not to steal what God has given. It's a totally different attitude.

Instead of being petrified and hiding in a corner, praying "God, please get the devil off my back," you'll stand there and say, "Where is he? I just dare Satan to show his ugly face. I'm going to fight him to the death because I have authority and power!" The difference isn't just emotional; it will manifest in your results as well.

SUPERIOR FIREPOWER

When I first arrived as a soldier in Vietnam, we came under heavy attack from the enemy. These weren't guerilla fighters but well-equipped, communist-trained, national troops. Five thousand of them surrounded the mountaintop where only 120 of us U.S. soldiers were stationed. Therefore, we were on "red alert." That meant all troops were supposed to stay awake all night and pull bunker guard together instead of taking turns the way we normally did.

That first night, I pulled guard all by myself. The other men assigned to that bunker with me fell asleep. I mentioned the red alert, but they ignored it. So, I stayed up all night by myself. The next night I was too sleepy to do it again, so I became a little more insistent that they stay up with me.

Finally, one of them said, "You must be new." When I responded that I was, they began to laugh. Then they told me how superior our firepower was compared to what the enemy had. If they ever came out of their holes, we would literally wipe them out in minutes. They described to me all the different weapons we had and how powerful they were. During this red alert, a "Huey" combat helicopter circled us overhead throughout the night. Just one fifty-caliber minigun on that helicopter could spray an area the size of a football field with a round every six inches—and the concussion from a fifty-caliber bullet can kill a person if it comes within six inches of their head! The vast superiority of our weapons overwhelmed me. And in a short period of time, I was asleep with the others.

My lack of knowledge is what caused my anxiety in that situation. Once I learned what we had, fear left and confidence came. Of course, I still exercised my alertness, prudence, and wisdom, but now I could rest. Although I wasn't what you'd call "gung-ho" for the war, I thought, *If we must fight, then let's do it on our terms*. I was daring the enemy to just try and attack us.

So, stop whining, griping, complaining, and begging God. Find out what Jesus has already done, and learn how to release it. Then confidence will replace fear, as you begin acting like the commander you were born again to be.

MAJORITY RULES

Make Paul's prayer your very own, saying, "Father, I have a glimpse of this, but I need a revelation. Open up the eyes of my understanding and help me see the hope of my calling in You. Enlighten me to understand the riches of the glory and the exceeding greatness of Your raising-from-the-dead power that You've placed within my born-again spirit. Father, please give me a revelation of what I already have."

Not "O God, give me more than I've already got. I don't have enough. I know You can do anything, but I can do nothing." In your carnal self—apart from your born-again spirit—that's true. But you aren't only carnal. Part of you has been born again and now has all of Christ's life, victory, and power already in it.

You are, in your spirit, as Jesus is right now. In your spirit, you are—right at this moment—the same as you'll be throughout all eternity. You don't need God to do something new; you just need a revelation of what He's already done.

You're made up of three distinct parts—spirit, soul, and body (1 Thess. 5:23). Your born-again spirit is exactly like God and is always for Him (Eph. 4:24, 1 Cor. 6:17, and 1 John 4:17). If your soul—your mental, emotional part—becomes renewed and believes what God's Word says is in your spirit, you'll experience the life and power of God within (spirit + soul = 2 against 1). On the other hand, if your soul agrees with your physical body, the life and power of God within you won't be able to manifest in the natural realm (soul + body = 2 against 1). The simple majority always rules.

If you let your sense knowledge dominate you, your soul will agree with your body, and it'll shut off the flow of God's life and power in you. When you let only what you can see, taste, hear, smell, and feel control your thoughts, you'll say, "If I really had the resurrection power of God on the inside of me, I'd feel it. Since I don't feel anything, I must not have it." That's how the supernatural power of God in your resurrected spirit stays cut off from manifestation.

WIPE AWAY THE TEARS

For I reckon that the sufferings of this present time are not worthy to be compared with the glory which shall be revealed in us.

ROMANS 8:18, EMPHASIS MINE

Notice that the glory isn't going to be revealed *to* us, but rather *in* us. It's not like we arrive in heaven and then all of a sudden God imparts His glory to us. No, what happens when we arrive in heaven is we'll no longer think carnally. We'll be able to completely see what was already in us.

That's why God will have to wipe the tears away from our eyes. It's not because so many people will just barely make it to heaven. No, it's because when we arrive and receive the full revelation of what we already had, we'll weep, wail, and gnash our teeth over the way we let the devil steal from us. Intimidated by his lies, we begged and pleaded with God to do something He'd already done. Since we didn't believe that He had already done it, we lived far below our privileges in Christ and let the devil beat up on us for no good reason. That's why there'll be weeping and wailing at first in heaven. The Lord will have to supernaturally comfort us to enable us to enjoy being there!

This is a totally different mindset. I constantly meet people who are so depressed, discouraged, and defeated that they take offense at what I'm sharing. They think I'm insensitive, uncompassionate, and don't know what it's like to hurt. I'm not going to glorify the devil by listing all of my problems, but I've had things hurt me so bad that I honestly didn't think I could live through the night. I've experienced many things that were beyond my ability to cope with, but here I am, alive and well today. These truths I'm sharing with you are what brought me through.

The touchy-feely, feel-good philosophy of the world has permeated into "Christianity" today. Many people would rather sit there and wallow in their pain than get over it. They prefer to receive other people's pity, have arms wrapped around them, and get pats on the back, affirming "Oh, yes, it's really miserable" than to come out of it. Some people look more for such momentary "comfort" than they do for the solution that would set them free long term.

THE ANSWER

What I'm sharing isn't insensitive; it's the answer. It's only the truth you know that will set you free (John 8:32). Your ignorance of God's Word is what Satan uses to keep you in bondage. *"My people are destroyed for lack of knowledge"* (Hos. 4:6). What you don't know is killing you!

I understand that people have problems. Not everyone believes perfectly or always operates in this. I can have compassion on someone who has fallen into a problem. However, the right reaction when you hear this is: "Father, that's true. Through the death, burial, and resurrection of Jesus Christ, You have already provided everything I need. Right now, it's in my born-again spirit. Therefore, I'm going to get up in the name of Jesus and believe You. I determine in my heart to appropriate what is rightfully mine and to come out of this junk!" Now that's the correct response!

You can keep on hurting and receiving other people's pity, or you can pull your thumb out of your mouth and grow up. You don't have to just sit there with a sad look on your face. Start recognizing what Jesus has already done for you!

My purpose is to help, not offend. But our passive so-called Christianity today runs so contrary to this truth that many people will be offended by these things I'm saying. However, I challenge you to carefully consider what I'm communicating. Understanding this reality has set me free and enabled me to walk in a higher level of victory than ever before.

I've done things far beyond my mere human ability. I haven't been depressed, discouraged, or defeated in more than forty years. I've seen people raised from the dead, blind eyes opened, and terminal illnesses healed. All of this came through cooperating with the power of God inside me.

DIRECT FROM GOD TO YOU!

What I'm preaching works. It keeps me stable when everything around me seems to be falling apart. If you receive this revelation, it'll work for you too.

Therefore, I encourage you to take the prayer in Ephesians 1:17-23, combine it with the prayer in Ephesians 3:16-21, and make them your own. Pray them and pray them and pray them—not to make God do something but to open up the eyes of your understanding so that you might see the fullness of what He has already done. Believe me, God wants you to have this revelation even more than you do. Simply open up your heart, start seeking, and become hungry in a positive way, saying, "God, I can't live any longer without a revelation of what You've already done. I refuse to keep asking, begging, and pleading with You to do what You've already done. I must have this understanding!" As you seek Him with all your heart, these truths will totally change your life.

This isn't a revelation you receive once and then never have to revisit. It's the kind of understanding that must become part of your everyday Christian life. The rest of this study will begin to expand and expound on this even further. I believe it'll really help you. But, ultimately, you need the Holy Spirit to make this real to you personally. This needs to go beyond mere intellectual knowledge and become revelation knowledge—directly from God to you.

I agree with you now in prayer that the Lord will use these things I've shared to help you receive the revelation that you've already got it!

HIS POWER IN YOU
LESSON 4 – OUTLINE

I.   God wants you to see the exceeding greatness of His power toward those who believe.

What is the exceeding greatness of his power to us-ward who believe, according to the working of his mighty power, [20] Which he wrought in Christ, when he raised him from the dead, and set him at his own right hand in the heavenly places, [21] Far above all principality, and power, and might, and dominion, and every name that is named, not only in this world, but also in that which is to come: [22] And hath put all things under his feet, and gave him to be the head over all things to the church, [23] Which is his body, the fulness of him that filleth all in all.

EPHESIANS 1:19-23

    A.   It's the very same power He used to raise Jesus Christ from the dead.

    B.   That's the greatest manifestation of God's power ever!

II. You have that same raising-from-the-dead power on the inside of you (Eph. 1:19-20).

    A.   It's not out there in heaven somewhere.

    B.   It's within you—in your born-again spirit (Rom. 8:11).

    C.   You just need to believe that you already have it and begin to discover how it operates.

    D.   Find out the laws that govern how the power of God works, and then put them into practice.

    E.   If you receive this revelation, it'll ruin you for most of the religious tradition floating around and masquerading as Christianity today.

III. Having a revelation of God's power within you will definitely change the way you pray!

Such as I have give I thee: In the name of Jesus Christ of Nazareth rise up and walk.

ACTS 3:6

    A.   When Peter said *"Such as I have,"* he wasn't referring to his own human strength but God's raising-from-the-dead power within his born-again spirit (Acts 3:6-8).

    B.   This understanding will transform you into a commander.

    C.   Find out what Jesus has already done, and learn how to release it.

D. Then confidence will replace fear, as you begin acting like the commander you were born again to be.

IV. You're made up of three distinct parts—spirit, soul, and body (1 Thess. 5:23).

    A. Your born-again spirit is exactly like God and is always for Him (Eph. 4:24, 1 Cor. 6:17, and 1 John 4:17).

    B. If your soul—your mental, emotional part—becomes renewed and believes what God's Word says is in your spirit, you'll experience the life and power of God within (spirit + soul = 2 against 1).

    C. On the other hand, if your soul agrees with your physical body, the life and power of God within you won't be able to manifest in the natural realm (soul + body = 2 against 1).

    D. The simple majority always rules.

V. When we arrive in heaven, we'll no longer think carnally, but we'll be able to completely see what was already in us.

For I reckon that the sufferings of this present time are not worthy to be compared with the glory which shall be revealed in us.

ROMANS 8:18, EMPHASIS MINE

    A. That's why God will have to wipe the tears away from our eyes.

    B. Since we didn't believe that He had already done it, we lived far below our privileges in Christ and let the devil beat up on us for no good reason.

    C. It's only the truth we know that will set us free (John 8:32).

    D. Our ignorance of God's Word is what Satan uses to keep us in bondage.

My people are destroyed for lack of knowledge.

HOSEA 4:6

VI. Understanding this reality has set me free and enabled me to walk in a higher level of victory than ever before.

    A. If you receive this revelation, it'll work for you too.

    B. Take the prayer in Ephesians 1:17-23, combine it with the prayer in Ephesians 3:16-21, and make them your own.

C. Pray them and pray them and pray them—not to make God do something but to open up the eyes of your understanding so that you might see the fullness of what He has already done.

D. This is the kind of understanding that must become part of your everyday Christian life.

E. It needs to go beyond mere intellectual knowledge and become revelation knowledge—directly from God to you.

HIS POWER IN YOU
LESSON 4 – TEACHER'S GUIDE

1.   God wants us to see the exceeding greatness of His power toward those who believe (Eph. 1:19-23). It's the very same power He used to raise Jesus Christ from the dead. That's the greatest manifestation of God's power ever!

2.   We have that same raising-from-the-dead power on the inside of us (Eph. 1:19-20). It's not out there in heaven somewhere. It's within us—in our born-again spirits (Rom. 8:11). We just need to believe that we already have it and begin to discover how it operates. We need to find out the laws that govern how the power of God works and then put them into practice. If we receive this revelation, it'll ruin us for most of the religious tradition floating around and masquerading as Christianity today.

3.   Having a revelation of God's power within us will definitely change the way we pray! When Peter said *"Such as I have,"* he wasn't referring to his own human strength but God's raising-from-the-dead power within his born-again spirit (Acts 3:6-8). This understanding will transform us into commanders. Let's find out what Jesus has already done and learn how to release it. Then confidence will replace fear, as we begin acting like the commanders we were born again to be.

1.   A.   Read Ephesians 1:19-23. What does God want us to see? (The exceeding greatness of His power toward those who believe)
     B.   What was the greatest manifestation of God's power ever? (Raising Jesus Christ from the dead)
2.   A.   Read Romans 8:11. Where is that same raising-from-the-dead power? (On the inside of us—in our born-again spirits)
     B.   What do we need to find out and then put into practice? (The laws that govern how the power of God works)
3.   A.   Read Acts 3:6-8. This understanding will transform us into what? (Commanders)
     B.   What will replace fear as we begin acting like the commanders we were born again to be? (Confidence)

4.   We're made up of three distinct parts—spirit, soul, and body (1 Thess. 5:23). Our born-again spirits are exactly like God and are always for Him (Eph. 4:24, 1 Cor. 6:17, and 1 John 4:17). If our souls—our mental, emotional part—become renewed and believe what God's Word says is in our spirits, we'll experience the life and power of God within (spirit + soul = 2 against 1). On the other hand, if our souls agree with our physical bodies, the life and power of God within us won't be able to manifest in the natural realm (soul + body = 2 against 1). The simple majority always rules.

5.   When we arrive in heaven, we'll no longer think carnally, but we'll be able to completely see what was already in us (Rom. 8:18). That's why God will have to wipe the tears away from our eyes. Since we didn't believe that He had already done it, we lived far below our privileges in Christ and let the devil beat up on us for no good reason. It's only the truth we know that will set us free (John 8:32). Our ignorance of God's Word is what Satan uses to keep us in bondage (Hos. 4:6).

6.   Understanding this reality will set us free and enable us to walk in a higher level of victory than ever before. Let's take this prayer in Ephesians 1:17-23, combine it with the prayer in Ephesians 3:16-21, and make them our own. Let's pray them and pray them and pray them—not to make God do something but to open up the eyes of our understanding so that we might see the fullness of what He has already done. This is the kind of understanding that must become part of our everyday Christian lives. It needs to go beyond mere intellectual knowledge and become revelation knowledge—directly from God to us.

4. A. Read 1 Thessalonians 5:23, Ephesians 4:24, 1 Corinthians 6:17, and 1 John 4:17. Name the three distinct parts we're made up of. (Spirit, soul, and body)
    B. What part of us is exactly like God and is always for Him? (Our born-again spirits)
    C. When will we experience the life and power of God within—spirit + soul or soul + body? (Spirit + soul. When our souls—mental, emotional part—become renewed and believe what God's Word says is in our spirits)
5. A. Read Romans 8:18. When we arrive in heaven, what will we be able to completely see? (What was already in us)
    B. Read John 8:32 and Hosea 4:6. What is it that sets us free? (Only the truth we know)
    C. What does Satan use to keep us in bondage? (Our ignorance of God's Word)
6. A. As we pray Ephesians 1:17-23 and 3:16-21, are we praying them to make God do something or to open up the eyes of our understanding so that we might see the fullness of what He's already done? (To open up the eyes of our understanding so that we might see the fullness of what He's already done)
    B. What must this understanding become part of? (Our everyday Christian lives)

HIS POWER IN YOU
LESSON 4 – DISCIPLESHIP QUESTIONS

1. According to Ephesians 1:17-23, the riches of the glory of His inheritance are where?

2. What is to us-ward who believe?

3. According to Romans 8:11, what does the Spirit that raised Jesus from the dead do?

    A. Grows in us
    B. Gives us strength
    C. Will quicken our mortal bodies
    D. All of the above
    E. None of the above

4. Read Acts 3:6-8. Did Peter give something he didn't have to the lame man?

5. According to 1 Thessalonians 5:23, what does the very God of peace do?

6. What does Paul want our spirits, souls, and bodies to be?

7. What does Ephesians 4:24 tell us to do with the new man?

8. Who was this new man created after in righteousness and true holiness?

9. According to 1 Corinthians 6:17, who is one spirit?

10. According to 1 John 4:17, what is made perfect?

11. How are we in this world?

12. Romans 8:18 says that *"the sufferings of this present time are not worthy to be compared"* with what?

13. Read John 8:32. What does the truth we know make us?

14. According to Hosea 4:6, God's people are destroyed for what?

15. In Ephesians 3:16-21, Paul prayed that we'd be strengthened with might by His Spirit where?

16. That Christ may dwell where by faith?

17. What are we to be filled with?

18. How is He able to do exceeding abundantly above all that we ask or think?

HIS POWER IN YOU
LESSON 4 – ANSWER KEY

1. In the saints

2. The exceeding greatness of His power

3. C. Will quicken our mortal bodies

4. No

5. Sanctifies us wholly

6. Preserved blameless

7. Put him on

8. God

9. He that is joined to the Lord

10. Our love

11. As He is

12. *"The glory which shall be revealed in us"*

13. Free

14. Lack of knowledge

15. In the inner man

16. In our hearts

17. All the fullness of God

18. According to the power that works in us

HIS POWER IN YOU
LESSON 4 – SCRIPTURES

EPHESIANS 1:17-23

That the God of our Lord Jesus Christ, the Father of glory, may give unto you the spirit of wisdom and revelation in the knowledge of him: [18] The eyes of your understanding being enlightened; that ye may know what is the hope of his calling, and what the riches of the glory of his inheritance in the saints, [19] And what is the exceeding greatness of his power to us-ward who believe, according to the working of his mighty power, [20] Which he wrought in Christ, when he raised him from the dead, and set him at his own right hand in the heavenly places, [21] Far above all principality, and power, and might, and dominion, and every name that is named, not only in this world, but also in that which is to come: [22] And hath put all things under his feet, and gave him to be the head over all things to the church, [23] Which is his body, the fulness of him that filleth all in all.

ROMANS 8:11

But if the Spirit of him that raised up Jesus from the dead dwell in you, he that raised up Christ from the dead shall also quicken your mortal bodies by his Spirit that dwelleth in you.

ACTS 3:6-8

Then Peter said, Silver and gold have I none; but such as I have give I thee: In the name of Jesus Christ of Nazareth rise up and walk. [7] And he took him by the right hand, and lifted him up: and immediately his feet and ankle bones received strength. [8] And he leaping up stood, and walked, and entered with them into the temple, walking, and leaping, and praising God.

1 THESSALONIANS 5:23

And the very God of peace sanctify you wholly; and I pray God your whole spirit and soul and body be preserved blameless unto the coming of our Lord Jesus Christ.

EPHESIANS 4:24

And that ye put on the new man, which after God is created in righteousness and true holiness.

1 CORINTHIANS 6:17

But he that is joined unto the Lord is one spirit.

1 JOHN 4:17

Herein is our love made perfect, that we may have boldness in the day of judgment: because as he is, so are we in this world.

ROMANS 8:18

For I reckon that the sufferings of this present time are not worthy to be compared with the glory which shall be revealed in us.

JOHN 8:32

And ye shall know the truth, and the truth shall make you free.

HOSEA 4:6

My people are destroyed for lack of knowledge: because thou hast rejected knowledge, I will also reject thee, that thou shalt be no priest to me: seeing thou hast forgotten the law of thy God, I will also forget thy children.

EPHESIANS 3:16-21

That he would grant you, according to the riches of his glory, to be strengthened with might by his Spirit in the inner man; [17] That Christ may dwell in your hearts by faith; that ye, being rooted and grounded in love, [18] May be able to comprehend with all saints what is the breadth, and length, and depth, and height; [19] And to know the love of Christ, which passeth knowledge, that ye might be filled with all the fulness of God. [20] Now unto him that is able to do exceeding abundantly above all that we ask or think, according to the power that worketh in us, [21] Unto him be glory in the church by Christ Jesus throughout all ages, world without end. Amen.

BY GRACE THROUGH FAITH
LESSON 5

The book of Ephesians was written to show you what God has already done. Its prayers don't petition Him for something new, but that the eyes of your understanding might be enlightened to see what you already have (Eph. 1:17-18).

Notice how everything is in the past tense:

And you hath he quickened [made alive]*, who were dead in trespasses and sins.*

EPHESIANS 2:1, BRACKETS MINE

It's not, "You can He quicken if you believe, if you will seek, if you will petition God." No! It's all written from this same "done-deal" perspective. You've already got it. God has already quickened you.

ALIVE!

If you've received Christ, you've been made alive. Although the quickening power of the Lord has been purchased for everyone—Christian and non-Christian alike—the non-Christian hasn't received it yet and been made alive. But as a born-again believer, you have been quickened.

You may not have manifested the life of God in you, but your spirit is as alive as it will ever be. Even though your physical body may be hurting and your soul is still wrestling with depression, your born-again spirit is alive the way Jesus is alive. You have God's resurrection power inside you. You aren't trying to be made alive; you were already made alive in the spirit realm. Through faith, you can draw that life out of your spirit and into your soul and body.

Pray according to God's Word, understanding who you are and what you have in Christ. Don't start petitioning Him from a place of unbelief, opposite the Word, saying, "Lord, I'm dead. There's nothing good in my life. I'm lifeless." Instead say, "Father, I thank You that I do have resurrection life inside of me. The doctor says I'm dying. There's death working in my body, so I'm drawing out Your life, which is in me. I thank You that it's done. Now I take my authority and speak. I command sickness to leave and healing to manifest, in Jesus' name." That's the proper attitude. You've already been quickened!

Wherein in time past ye walked according to the course of this world, according to the prince of the power of the air, the spirit that now worketh in the children of disobedience.

EPHESIANS 2:2

Notice how following and being dominated by Satan was something in the past. You might think, *I'm a Christian, but I'm still dominated by the devil.* If that's so, it's because Ephesians 2:1 isn't reality for you. You don't understand how you've already been quickened and delivered from the death that was in trespasses and sin. When you truly understand that you've been made alive, it breaks the power of sin, and you live in victory.

Your life will be characterized by victory instead of defeat. It's not that you reach sinless perfection and never make a mistake; it's just that when you understand and acknowledge that Christ has already done it—that you already have resurrection life and you are as Jesus is in the spirit—victory is an inevitable byproduct.

That the communication of thy faith may become effectual [begin to work] *by the acknowledging of every good thing which is in you in Christ Jesus.*

PHILEMON 6, BRACKETS MINE

Your faith works and you'll see victory manifest—physically, financially, emotionally, etc.—as you acknowledge every good thing in you in Christ.

NEW NATURE/NEW SEAT

Among whom also we all had our conversation in times past in the lusts of our flesh, fulfilling the desires of the flesh and of the mind; and were by nature the children of wrath, even as others.

EPHESIANS 2:3

Again, everything is in the past tense. Some say, "But this is still working in me." If so, it's because you haven't understood that in the spirit, you already have everything. You are as complete as you'll ever be. Since you haven't understood and acknowledged the good things that are in you in Christ, you're still being dominated by the flesh.

The truth is, your nature has been changed. You don't have an old nature anymore that compels you to live in sin. It died and was buried the moment you accepted Christ. Your new nature—your born-again spirit—was created in righteousness and true holiness (Eph. 4:24). The only reason you still struggle with those old desires toward sin is your un-renewed mind. As God's Word transforms your mind, you'll experience those old desires less, and you'll experience more of your new nature.

But God, who is rich in mercy, for his great love wherewith he loved us, [5] Even when we were dead in sins, hath quickened us together with Christ, (by grace ye are saved).

EPHESIANS 2:4-5

Notice again, it is in the past tense. You've already been quickened. God loved you. He has already done this.

And hath [past tense] *raised us up together, and made us sit together in heavenly places in Christ Jesus.*

EPHESIANS 2:6, BRACKETS MINE

This isn't something to seek after or to try to attain unto; it's something to be received as a gift. It is already done. You are already in relationship with God. You are already raised from the dead spiritually, and you are now seated with Christ in heavenly places.

SODIUM & CHLORINE

That in the ages to come he might shew the exceeding riches of his grace in his kindness toward us through Christ Jesus. [8] For by grace are ye saved through faith; and that not of yourselves: it is the gift of God: [9] Not of works, lest any man should boast.

EPHESIANS 2:7-9

That's a powerful passage of Scripture. It's also very familiar. Therefore, many people think they already know what it says. They just skip over it and don't really give it much time or effort, which is why they don't receive its full benefit.

You were saved by grace through faith. You weren't saved by grace alone. Neither were you saved by faith alone. You were saved by grace *through* faith. In order to make a point to someone, sometimes I'll emphasize one over the other. For instance, if someone argues "I believe you have to be holy, pay your tithes, be baptized, etc.," then I'll respond, "No, you're saved by faith. It's your faith in what Jesus did that saves you, not what you do for the Lord." So, it's not absolutely wrong to emphasize "you were saved by grace" or "you were saved by faith" in order to make a point, but technically speaking, you weren't saved by grace alone or by faith alone; it was a combination of the two. You were saved by grace through faith!

Grace and faith are like sodium and chlorine. If you ingest either one of them alone, it's poisonous. Alone, either one would kill you if taken in a sufficient quantity. However, if you mix them together, you get sodium chloride (table salt). Together they become something you cannot live without—salt. That's how grace and faith are.

Grace alone (apart from faith) won't save you. In His grace, God has provided salvation for everyone through the death, burial, and resurrection of Jesus Christ. God's grace is the same to everyone. However, not every person is saved. Why? Although the provision for salvation has already been made (grace), each individual must appropriate (faith) God's grace for themselves.

Faith alone (apart from grace) won't save you either. You must put your faith in Jesus Christ and what He accomplished in the Atonement (grace). If your faith is in anything else (living holy, paying tithes, reading the Bible, attending church, etc.), it won't produce salvation. Your faith is either in Jesus and what He did (grace) or in yourself and what you do (works). It truly comes down to that. Biblical faith always believes on Jesus and appropriates what God's grace has already provided.

GRACE VS. FAITH

I'm a grace teacher. I emphasize what God has done for us. Due to this, I've been rejected by many "faith" people. They think I overemphasize God's grace and underemphasize what we must do for God.

I'm also a faith teacher. I emphasize our responsibility to respond positively to what God has already done. That's why I'm rejected by the strong "grace" crowd. They think I put too much emphasis on what we must do.

Overall, the body of Christ is divided primarily into two different camps: grace or faith. Grace people misunderstand and criticize faith people, and vice versa. Both tend to take their positions to the extreme.

Grace people don't like to hear preaching on faith. Why? They look at it as something they must do. Therefore—to them—it compromises God's grace. They teach that the Christian life is based totally on God's grace. Your faith—what you believe—has nothing to do with it. That's why grace, by itself, will kill you.

On the other hand, faith people don't like to hear preaching on grace. Why? Their focus is all wrapped up in what they must do. They discuss how to build yourself up in faith, what faith will accomplish, etc. Faith preachers don't like to mention God's grace, because they feel it weakens people's motivation to be aggressive and make things happen. However, faith, by itself, will also kill you.

All error stems from a truth in God's Word being overemphasized at the expense of other complementary truths. Just take one truth and exalt it to the exclusion of other necessary truths (either through neglect or on purpose), and it will be error.

There must be a balance. All truths from God's Word fit together and harmonize. When understood properly, grace and faith complement each other. You were saved by grace through faith (Eph. 2:8). It took both, not just one or the other.

UNEARNED, UNDESERVED, UNMERITED

Grace is multifaceted. First Peter 4:10 speaks of *"the manifold* [many-fold, multifaceted] *grace of God"* (brackets mine). Therefore, grace can be defined in several different ways.

Most people define *grace* as unmerited favor. While that's certainly true, it's incomplete. This definition focuses on the truth that grace is unearned and undeserved. It is a gift. If you work for it, pay for it, or meet some minimum requirement in order to receive it, then it isn't grace. Grace is unearned, undeserved, unmerited favor.

Another important facet of grace is that it's something God did for you, independent of you. By grace, Jesus died for the sins of the entire world. He didn't wait until you'd already lived and sinned before responding to you. No, God accomplished salvation prior to, and independent of, you. He had predetermined that He would send His Son to the cross even before He created the world, before He made people, and before they sinned. Redemption beat in the heart of God long before you came along.

God's grace made the provision for your salvation before you ever needed it. Jesus died for your sins 2,000 years ago—before you were born, before you ever sinned. Prior to, and independent of, you or anything you could do to earn or deserve it, God provided for your salvation. That's unmerited favor!

CONSISTENT

Grace is also consistent. Since it is not based on our performance and it's done prior to, and independent of, any worth, value, or merit on our part, God—by grace—is the same toward everyone. Christian and non-Christian, God-hater and God-lover, His grace is exactly the same.

For the grace of God that bringeth salvation hath appeared to all men.

TITUS 2:11

Grace includes everything Jesus did for us in the atonement. The Word says His grace has appeared to *"all men,"* not just those who have received it or will receive it. Therefore, God's grace is the same to everyone.

If grace alone was enough for salvation, then everyone would be saved. God's grace is consistent toward all people and has come to all people, but not everyone is saved. Jesus made it very clear that more people will choose the wide gate and broad way leading to destruction than will find the narrow gate leading to life (Matt. 7:13). Why? You aren't saved by grace alone; you're saved by grace through faith. You must respond to God's grace with faith in order to receive it.

God extended as much grace toward Adolf Hitler as He has to you or me. But as far as we know, Hitler didn't receive God's grace. Unless Adolf changed his heart at the very last minute, which only God knows, he ended his life resisting the Lord. Even though he was an apparent God-hater, God's grace always remained consistent toward him. But according to our knowledge, Hitler refused to receive it.

God's grace alone doesn't save you. God's grace doesn't heal you by itself. Neither does it bless you. God's grace, by itself, doesn't do anything for you. However, when you receive that grace and mix it with faith, God's power is released to make salvation a reality in your life.

YOUR POSITIVE RESPONSE

Faith is not something you do that makes God move. Studying the Bible, confessing the Word, acting on the Word, etc., are all involved in the faith process, but in themselves, they aren't "faith." Faith doesn't make God do anything.

One of the major reasons people aren't receiving more from the Lord is because they think "faith" is God responding to something they do. This puts the burden on them to perform and produce. They may be motivated for a period of time, thinking, *Oh, I'm going to be perfect and do all these things. Then God will heal me.* Ultimately, nobody can measure up to that. No one's good enough to move God. Faith doesn't move God; He's not stuck. He's not the one who needs to move. Faith is not something you do to make God do something. The Bible calls such "faith" works and legalism. You're doing something to try to make God do something for you. That's flesh.

You can take the Word, confess it, pray, get up, act healed, and throw your medicine away, but your actions will never make God heal you. In fact, what God has already provided will be prevented from coming into physical manifestation because of works and legalism. Why? God will not be coerced into anything. Everything from God must come by grace through faith.

Faith is simply your positive response to what God has already provided by grace. If what you're calling "faith" is not a response to what God has already done, then it's not true faith. Faith doesn't try to get God to positively respond to you. True faith is your positive response to what God has already done by grace.

Faith only appropriates what God has already provided by grace. If you're trying to make God do something new, then it's not faith. True faith only receives—reaches out and takes—what God has already done.

LESSON 5 – ADDITIONAL INFORMATION

Your un-renewed mind is the only reason you still struggle with those old desires toward sin. As God's Word transforms your mind, you will experience fewer of those old desires and more of your new nature. Again, this is covered in much greater detail in my teaching *Spirit, Soul & Body.*

BY GRACE THROUGH FAITH
LESSON 5 – OUTLINE

I.   If you have received Christ, you've been made alive.

And you hath he quickened [made alive], *who were dead in trespasses and sins.*

EPHESIANS 2:1, BRACKETS MINE

    A. You may not have manifested the life of God in you, but your spirit is as alive as it will ever be.

    B. You have God's resurrection power inside you.

    C. Through faith, you can draw that life out of your spirit and into your soul and body.

II. When you truly understand that you have been made alive, it breaks the power of sin, and you live in victory.

Wherein in time past ye walked according to the course of this world, according to the prince of the power of the air, the spirit that now worketh in the children of disobedience.

EPHESIANS 2:2

    A. When you understand and acknowledge that Christ has already done it—that you already have resurrection life and you are as Jesus is in the spirit—victory is an inevitable byproduct.

That the communication of thy faith may become effectual [begin to work] *by the acknowledging of every good thing which is in you in Christ Jesus.*

PHILEMON 6, BRACKETS MINE

    B. Your faith works and you'll see victory manifest—physically, financially, emotionally, etc.—as you acknowledge every good thing in you in Christ.

III. The truth is, your nature has been changed.

Among whom also we all had our conversation in times past in the lusts of our flesh, fulfilling the desires of the flesh and of the mind; and were by nature the children of wrath, even as others.

EPHESIANS 2:3

A. Your new nature—your born-again spirit—was created in righteousness and true holiness (Eph. 4:24).

B. As God's Word transforms your mind, you'll experience those old desires less, and you'll experience more of your new nature.

But God, who is rich in mercy, for his great love wherewith he loved us, [5] Even when we were dead in sins, hath quickened us together with Christ, (by grace ye are saved;) [6] And hath [past tense] raised us up together, and made us sit together in heavenly places in Christ Jesus.

EPHESIANS 2:4-6, BRACKETS MINE

C. You are already in relationship with God, raised from the dead spiritually, and you are now seated with Christ in heavenly places.

IV. You were saved by grace through faith.

That in the ages to come he might shew the exceeding riches of his grace in his kindness toward us through Christ Jesus. [8] For by grace are ye saved through faith; and that not of yourselves: it is the gift of God: [9] Not of works, lest any man should boast.

EPHESIANS 2:7-9

A. Grace alone (apart from faith) won't save you.

B. Faith alone (apart from grace) won't save you either.

C. Biblical faith always believes on Jesus and appropriates what God's grace has already provided.

D. When understood properly, grace and faith complement each other.

E. It takes both grace and faith, not just one or the other.

V. Grace is multifaceted (1 Pet. 4:10).

A. Grace is unearned, undeserved, unmerited favor.

B. Grace is something God did for you, independent of you.

C. Grace is also consistent—it is the same toward everyone.

For the grace of God that bringeth salvation hath appeared to all men.

TITUS 2:11

D. Grace includes everything Jesus did in the atonement.

VI. You must respond to God's grace with faith in order to receive it.

 A. When you receive God's grace and mix it with faith, His power is released to make salvation a reality in your life.

 B. Faith is not something you do to make God do something.

 C. God will not be coerced into anything.

 D. Everything from God must come by grace through faith.

 E. Faith is simply your positive response to what God has already provided by grace.

 F. Faith only appropriates what God has already provided by grace.

 G. True faith only receives—reaches out and takes—what God has already done.

LESSON 5 – ADDITIONAL INFORMATION

Your un-renewed mind is the only reason you still struggle with those old desires toward sin. As God's Word transforms your mind, you will experience fewer of those old desires and more of your new nature. Again, this is covered in much greater detail in my teaching *Spirit, Soul & Body*.

BY GRACE THROUGH FAITH
LESSON 5 – TEACHER'S GUIDE

1.   If we have received Christ, we've been made alive (Eph. 2:1). We may not have manifested the life of God in us, but our spirits are as alive as they will ever be. We have God's resurrection power inside us. Through faith, we can draw that life out of our spirits and into our souls and bodies.

2.   When we truly understand that we have been made alive, it breaks the power of sin, and we live in victory (Eph. 2:2). When we understand and acknowledge that Christ has already done it—that we already have resurrection life and we are as Jesus is in the spirit—victory is an inevitable byproduct (Philem. 6). Our faith works and we'll see victory manifest—physically, financially, emotionally, etc.—as we acknowledge every good thing in us in Christ!

3.   The truth is, our nature has been changed (Eph. 2:3). Our new nature—our born-again spirits—was created in righteousness and true holiness (Eph. 4:24). As God's Word transforms our minds, we'll experience those old desires less, and we'll experience more of our new nature (Eph. 2:4-6). We are already in relationship with God, raised from the dead spiritually, and we are now seated with Christ in heavenly places.

1.   A.   Read Ephesians 2:1. What has happened if we have received Christ? (We've been made alive)
      B.   How can we draw that life out of our spirits and into our souls and bodies? (Through faith)
2.   A.   Read Ephesians 2:2 and Philemon 6. When we truly understand that we've been made alive, it breaks what? (The power of sin)
      B.   What happens as we acknowledge every good thing in us in Christ? (Our faith works and we'll see victory manifest—physically, financially, emotionally, etc.)
3.   A.   Read Ephesians 2:3-6 and 4:24. What was our new nature—born-again spirit—created in? (Righteousness and true holiness)
      B.   As God's Word transforms our minds, what will we experience less of and more of? (Less of those old desires and more of our new nature)

4.   We were saved by grace through faith (Eph. 2:7-9). Grace alone (apart from faith) won't save us. Faith alone (apart from grace) won't save us either. Biblical faith always believes on Jesus and appropriates what God's grace has already provided. When understood properly, grace and faith complement each other. It takes both grace and faith, not just one or the other.

5.   Grace is multifaceted (1 Pet. 4:10). Grace is unearned, undeserved, unmerited favor. Grace is something God did for us, independent of us. Grace is also consistent—it is the same toward everyone (Titus 2:11). Grace includes everything Jesus did for us in the atonement.

6.   We must respond to God's grace with faith in order to receive it. When we receive God's grace and mix it with faith, His power is released to make salvation a reality in our lives. Faith is not something we do to make God do something. God will not be coerced into anything. Everything from God must come by grace through faith. Faith is simply our positive response to what God has already provided by grace. Faith only appropriates what God has already provided by grace. True faith only receives—reaches out and takes—what God has already done.

4.   A.   Read Ephesians 2:7-9. How were we saved? (By grace through faith)
     B.   Who does biblical faith always believe on? (Jesus)
     C.   What does biblical faith always appropriate? (What God's grace has already provided)
5.   A.   Read 1 Peter 4:10 and Titus 2:11. Grace is what? (Multifaceted; unearned, undeserved, unmerited favor; something God did for us—independent of us; consistent—it's the same toward everyone)
     B.   What does grace include? (Everything Jesus did for us in the Atonement)
6.   A.   What must we do in order to receive God's grace? (Respond with faith)
     B.   What is faith? (Faith is simply our positive response to what God has already provided by grace)
     C.   Everything from God must come how? (By grace through faith)

BY GRACE THROUGH FAITH
LESSON 5 – DISCIPLESHIP QUESTIONS

1. According to Ephesians 1:17-18, what did Paul pray for us?

    A. That we may have the spirit of wisdom and revelation in the knowledge of Him
    B. The eyes of our understanding being enlightened
    C. That we may know what is the hope of His calling
    D. That we may know what the riches of the glory of His inheritance in the saints
    E. All of the above

2. Ephesians 2:1-2 reveals that God has quickened—made alive—us who were what?

3. According to Philemon 6, how does the communication of our faith become effectual?

4. Ephesians 2:3 reveals that we were fulfilling the desires of the flesh and of the what?

5. What were we by nature?

6. What does Ephesians 4:24 reveal our new man to be created in?

7. Ephesians 2:4-9 shows that God is rich in what?

8. God loved us even when we were what?

9. How are we saved?

10. According to 1 Peter 4:10, what are we to minister to one another?

11. If we do so, we'll be good stewards of what?

12. Read Titus 2:11. To whom has this grace appeared?

13. According to Matthew 7:13, where does Jesus tell us to enter in?

14. Those who go to destruction are what?

BY GRACE THROUGH FAITH
LESSON 5 – ANSWER KEY

1.   E.   All of the above

2.   Dead in trespasses and sins

3.   By the acknowledging of every good thing that is in us in Christ Jesus

4.   Mind

5.   The children of wrath

6.   Righteousness and true holiness

7.   Mercy

8.   Dead in sins

9.   By grace—through faith

10.   The gift we've received

11.   The manifold grace of God

12.   All men

13.   *"The strait gate"*

14.   Many

BY GRACE THROUGH FAITH
LESSON 5 – SCRIPTURES

EPHESIANS 1:17-18
That the God of our Lord Jesus Christ, the Father of glory, may give unto you the spirit of wisdom and revelation in the knowledge of him: [18] The eyes of your understanding being enlightened; that ye may know what is the hope of his calling, and what the riches of the glory of his inheritance in the saints.

EPHESIANS 2:1-9
And you hath he quickened, who were dead in trespasses and sins; [2] Wherein in time past ye walked according to the course of this world, according to the prince of the power of the air, the spirit that now worketh in the children of disobedience: [3] Among whom also we all had our conversation in times past in the lusts of our flesh, fulfilling the desires of the flesh and of the mind; and were by nature the children of wrath, even as others. [4] But God, who is rich in mercy, for his great love wherewith he loved us, [5] Even when we were dead in sins, hath quickened us together with Christ, (by grace ye are saved;) [6] And hath raised us up together, and made us sit together in heavenly places in Christ Jesus: [7] That in the ages to come he might shew the exceeding riches of his grace in his kindness toward us through Christ Jesus. [8] For by grace are ye saved through faith; and that not of yourselves: it is the gift of God: [9] Not of works, lest any man should boast.

PHILEMON 6
That the communication of thy faith may become effectual by the acknowledging of every good thing which is in you in Christ Jesus.

EPHESIANS 4:24
And that ye put on the new man, which after God is created in righteousness and true holiness.

1 PETER 4:10
As every man hath received the gift, even so minister the same one to another, as good stewards of the manifold grace of God.

TITUS 2:11
For the grace of God that bringeth salvation hath appeared to all men.

MATTHEW 7:13
Enter ye in at the strait gate: for wide is the gate, and broad is the way, that leadeth to destruction, and many there be which go in thereat.

"SUCH AS I HAVE"
LESSON 6

The early days of the charismatic movement were wild! People met in Bible studies, home groups, and prayer breakfasts because there weren't very many Spirit-filled churches established yet. Mature spiritual oversight was lacking because most of the people involved had just been touched within the last year or two, including the ministers. Therefore, immaturity abounded. Many glorious things happened in the early 1970s, but there was plenty of wildfire too.

Several outstanding scriptures became very popular in those days:

Have faith in God. [23] For verily I say unto you, That whosoever shall say unto this mountain, Be thou removed, and be thou cast into the sea; and shall not doubt in his heart, but shall believe that those things which he saith shall come to pass; he shall have whatsoever he saith. [24] Therefore I say unto you, What things soever ye desire, when ye pray, believe that ye receive them, and ye shall have them.

MARK 11:22-24

And:

All things are possible to him that believeth.

MARK 9:23

According to these verses, whosoever can ask God for whatsoever they desire—and anything's possible! Can you see how easy it would be to slip into error if you didn't know that faith only appropriates what God has already provided by grace?

WHAT THINGS SOEVER YOU DESIRE?

In my hometown of Arlington, Texas, a woman started a Bible school with twenty or thirty students. She took Mark 11:22-24 and applied it to her desire to be married to Kenneth Copeland. Then she released her faith and began confessing, "I believe I receive, and I shall have it."

However, Kenneth was already married to Gloria. So this lady viewed Gloria as her "mountain" and began praying for her to "be removed" and "be cast into the sea." She actually commanded Gloria to die and get out of the way so she could then marry Kenneth. As an act of her faith, this lady had a wedding ceremony with these Bible college students in attendance where she "married" Kenneth Copeland "in the spirit." Then she just continued waiting for Gloria Copeland to die, so God could put Kenneth and her together.

Forty years have passed, and it hasn't happened yet—and it's not going to either. "How come? God's Word plainly says, *'What things soever ye desire.'* Can't you just curse somebody, command them to die, and then marry their spouse? Can't you plan a bank robbery, pray for the money, and then say, 'I believe in my heart and confess with my mouth that I'm going to steal a million dollars and not get caught. I believe and receive. It's mine!' Why can't you do those things?" It's very simple once you see it. God—by grace—didn't provide murder, adultery, or thievery in Christ's atonement. Therefore, since Jesus didn't provide it, your "faith" can't make it happen.

RECEIVE WHAT'S ALREADY BEEN GIVEN

Faith doesn't move God. He doesn't respond to what we do "in faith" and then move. By grace, God has already provided everything. The Lord doesn't look at your praying, confessing, begging, fasting, agreeing with others, and the other things you do as adding up to "enough" to make Him move. Those things aren't like a pry bar that once enough pressure is applied—BOOM—you can make God's power work. The Lord doesn't respond to your faith.

Your faith, if it's a true faith, is simply a response to what He has already done. God—by grace—has already healed everybody. He took upon Himself all of the sins and sicknesses of the entire world at the cross. He has already dealt with it. It's a done deal. It's over. That's why 1 Peter 2:24 says, *"By whose stripes ye* were [past tense] *healed"* (emphasis and brackets mine). It's already done. The Lord isn't healing people today. He provided healing 2,000 years ago in the death, burial, and resurrection of Christ. People are drawing on that healing by faith and receiving the manifestation of it today. But God already did the necessary work to provide it a long time ago.

Healing was released, transmitted, and broadcast 2,000 years ago in the atonement of the Lord Jesus Christ. Once you're born again, He places within you the same resurrection power that raised Jesus from the dead. It's not a matter of getting God to give you healing; He already has. The issue is whether or not you will—by faith—reach out and take it.

When you need healing, God doesn't even have to lift His little finger. People pray, "O God, put forth Your mighty hand." Wrong! The Lord has already accomplished healing and placed it inside your born-again spirit. In order for healing to manifest, you must receive it. You don't have to make God give it; you just have to receive in the physical realm what He has already given you in the spirit. Appropriate—by faith—what God has already provided by grace.

ACTIVE WAITING

When you understand what I'm sharing, it will totally revolutionize the way you receive from God. Most people I minister to are trying to get God to heal them. So, they pray, do all these other things, and then passively sit back and wait on Him to move. To justify themselves, they quote scriptures like Psalm 27:14, which says,

> *Wait on the Lord: be of good courage, and he shall strengthen thine heart: wait, I say, on the Lord.*

They just twiddle their thumbs and sigh, "Well, it's God's turn!" This kind of "waiting" is not how to effectively receive from God.

"Waiting on the Lord" means being like a waiter or a waitress in a restaurant. They aren't just sitting down somewhere, waiting for you to do something. No! When they're waiting on you, they are attentive to you. A good waiter sees when your beverage glass starts getting low and comes right over to fill it. They are sensitive to and in tune with who they're waiting on, constantly asking, "Is there anything else I can do for you? Are you all right? Do you need anything?" That's the kind of "waiting" the Bible is talking about.

God's Word doesn't advocate waiting on the Lord the way you wait on a bus. It's not a scriptural principle for you to pray and then say, "Well, it's in God's court now. Que sera, sera—whatever will be, will be. It's up to Him. God has seen what I've done, and now we'll see what He'll do." No, God doesn't respond to you.

When a problem comes up in your life, it's nothing new to the Lord. He knew what your problems would be long before you ever had them. By grace, He provided the solution in advance—before you were even born! He provided healing before you ever became sick. He provided joy before tragedy, grief, and sorrow came into your life. God has already made your way of escape. He's already accomplished everything. By grace, it's a done deal! You aren't waiting for God to do something new; He's waiting on you to respond positively to what He's already done.

If you've been believing "God, I've done this, I'm doing that, and I'm confessing these things and waiting for You to heal me," then that's precisely the reason you aren't seeing healing manifest. It's the wrong attitude. Instead, change your thinking, and start saying, "Father, I thank You that You have already healed me. By Your stripes, I was healed. The same power that raised Jesus from the dead is already in me. By faith, I receive what You have already provided."

"YOU COMMAND ME!"

Peter didn't even pray a prayer to ask God to heal that man at the temple gate; he just said, "Such as I have, I give it to you." How could he do that? Peter knew that God had already done it. He understood that God's healing power had already been released. The Lamb had been slain, and the perfect sacrifice had already been made. God—by grace—had already produced healing. Peter didn't wonder *Will the Lord heal him?* because he knew in his heart that God had already done it.

The only question today is, "Are you ready to believe and receive?" If you're praying for someone else, there needs to be a degree of faith on their part. It's not like it has to be fifty-fifty or something like that. If you're strong in faith, you can carry someone. If they're in neutral, you can at least push them. But if they're in park with the emergency brake on or in reverse, fighting against you, saying "I don't believe God wants it," then you won't be able to make it happen.

When Peter ministered to this man, first he fastened his eyes upon him (Acts 3:4). This means he looked at him with a penetrating stare. Paul did the same thing when he ministered to a crippled man in Acts 14:8-10. As he did, he perceived that the man had faith to be healed (Acts 14:9). That's exactly what Peter was doing. He perceived that this man had enough faith to receive healing.

So, Peter said, *"Such as I have give I thee"* (Acts 3:6). When you understand grace—that God has already done everything—you'll become bold and authoritative. You can literally command the power of God to come into manifestation because you aren't commanding God Himself to go and do something. Instead, you're commanding what He has already done to manifest in the physical realm.

When you understand how grace and faith work together, you'll become a commander instead of a beggar. The difference is huge!

Thus saith the Lord, *the Holy One of Israel, and his Maker, Ask me of things to come* concerning *my sons, and* concerning *the work of my hands command ye me.*

ISAIAH 45:11, EMPHASIS MINE

Concerning the work of His hands, God says to His children, "You command Me!"

FLIP THE SWITCH

The power company generates electricity at the power station. Then the electricity is delivered to your house. However, whether your living room light comes on or not has nothing to do with the power company generating electricity. The power is there, but it has been placed at your command. You must go over and flip the switch on the wall. When you do, you're commanding that power to flow.

Since you are the one commanding the power to flow, does that make you stronger than the power company? No. They *want* you to do it! They've already done their part by generating the electricity, delivering it to your house, and placing it at your command. Flipping the switch doesn't mean you are "forcing" them to do something. All you can "make" them do is what they've agreed to already. You can't make that electricity do something that it's not already wired to do.

Likewise, you can't force God to do anything that He hasn't—by grace—already done. God (Father & Son Power Company) has already done His part. Through Christ's atonement (the power station), everything you'll ever need has already been generated. In fact, the power has already been delivered to your house (born-again spirit). All you have to do is flip the switch. *"Concerning the work of my hands command ye me"* (Is. 45:11). When you believe what He has done and reach out in faith to appropriate it, you're commanding what God has already provided to come into manifestation.

You're the one responsible to flip the switch! If you want your living room light turned on, you can't call the power company and say, "I have people coming over for a party this evening. Could you please turn my living room light on?" They'll answer, "No. The power has already been generated and delivered to your house. We're not going to send someone all the way over there just to turn your living room light on. That's not in our agreement. The power is at your command; you flip the switch!"

God is the power source, not you. It's His power, not yours. But He has put that power inside your born-again spirit. You didn't produce the power, but it has been placed at your command.

God has already provided everything you need by grace—but it's at your command. Faith positively responds to what God has already done and appropriates it. Faith reaches over into the spiritual realm and draws out into the physical realm what God has already supplied. If you understand this, it'll revolutionize your life!

EXCUSES, EXCUSES

Most people are asking God to do for them what He has already done. They're pleading with Him to give them what He has already given. Then, after praying this way in unbelief, they wonder why they aren't seeing the physical manifestation of their healing. Since they think the Lord can do anything He desires, they wonder, *Why isn't He healing me? If God wanted me well, He could heal me right now.* So they come up with all kinds of excuses like, "God is perfecting me through this trial." Wrong!

People come up with wrong conclusions like that in order to make sense of their disappointing experiences. They pray for healing, thinking that faith is something they do to move God. They believe He evaluates their "faith"—whether they're sincere enough and have done enough—and then responds to them accordingly. Since there's no apparent response, they wonder, *Why isn't God answering my prayer?* Then they start coming up with different excuses like: "Maybe He's trying to teach me something. Maybe I'm not holy enough. Maybe I haven't prayed enough. Maybe I have sin in my life. Maybe I need to do this and that and all these other things." No—God has already done His part!

When you understand that God has already done it, condemnation is defused. How could you think that you're not holy enough if He has already done it? God provided everything you would ever need before you were born again, before you did anything good or bad, before you were even born. He provided it independent of you—by grace. All you have to do is—by faith—reach over and get it. That's how you were saved.

CAN YOU RECEIVE?

What would have happened if someone had told you that if you'd pray and seek God, beg and plead for mercy, fast and live holy, tithe, and be earnest, sincere, and desperate enough, then Jesus would come and die for your sins? If salvation had been presented as something that could happen but hasn't happened yet, the devil could easily have convinced you that "Maybe God can do it and maybe He's done it for others, but He'll never do it for you, because you're just too _____ (fill in the blank)."

It's mind-boggling to think that Almighty God would become a human being, take our sicknesses and sin, suffer our punishment, go to hell, and then turn around and give us—as a free gift—salvation. That's too wild! The only way someone could believe that is if it had already happened and the Holy Spirit bore them witness saying, "Yes, I did it! You just have to receive what I've already done for you." If you thought your salvation had yet to be accomplished and was based upon whether or not you were good enough, you'd be convinced, "It won't work for me." But since forgiveness of sins was presented as an already done deal, you were able to receive it.

The same is true of every other salvation benefit, including healing. It's already been provided. At the cross, Jesus bore all your sicknesses, diseases, and infirmities at the same time as He bore all your sin. You don't have to wonder, *Will God heal me?* Like forgiveness, healing is a done deal. It's just a matter of whether you can reach out by faith and receive. If you can get this attitude that healing has already been done, it will manifest. Praise the Lord!

LESSON 6 – ADDITIONAL INFORMATION

For additional light on these important issues, I'd like to recommend to you some teaching materials. *Spiritual Authority* will really help you sort these things out. Also, "The Book of Job," "God's Not Guilty," and "The Sovereignty of God" all soundly debunk the false idea that the Lord puts suffering in your life to teach you things. It's simply not true!

"SUCH AS I HAVE"
LESSON 6 – OUTLINE

I.   The early days of the charismatic movement were wild!

   A.   Several outstanding scriptures became very popular in those days.

Have faith in God. [23] For verily I say unto you, That whosoever shall say unto this mountain, Be thou removed, and be thou cast into the sea; and shall not doubt in his heart, but shall believe that those things which he saith shall come to pass; he shall have whatsoever he saith. [24] Therefore I say unto you, What things soever ye desire, when ye pray, believe that ye receive them, and ye shall have them.

MARK 11:22-24

All things are possible to him that believeth.

MARK 9:23

   B.   According to these verses, whosoever can ask God for whatsoever they desire—and anything's possible!

   C.   Can you see how easy it would be to slip into error if you didn't know that faith only appropriates what God has already provided by grace?

   D.   God—by grace—didn't provide murder, adultery, or thievery in Christ's atonement.

   E.   Therefore, since Jesus didn't provide it, your "faith" can't make it happen!

II.   True faith is simply a response to what God has already done by grace.

   A.   The Lord provided healing 2,000 years ago in the death, burial, and resurrection of Christ.

By whose stripes ye were [past tense] *healed.*

1 PETER 2:24, EMPHASIS & BRACKETS MINE

   B.   People are drawing on that healing by faith and receiving the manifestation of it today—but God already did the necessary work to provide it a long time ago.

   C.   The Lord has already accomplished healing and placed it inside your born-again spirit.

   D.   In order for healing to manifest, you must receive it.

E.   Appropriate—by faith—what God has already provided by grace.

III.   When you understand what I'm sharing, it will totally revolutionize the way you receive from God.

A.   "Waiting on the Lord" means being like a waiter or a waitress in a restaurant.

Wait on the Lord: be of good courage, and he shall strengthen thine heart: wait, I say, on the Lord.

PSALM 27:14

B.   You aren't waiting for God to do something new—He's waiting on you to respond positively to what He's already done.

C.   The only question today is, "Are you ready to believe and receive?"

IV.   When you understand grace—that God has already done everything—you'll become bold and authoritative (Acts 3:4-6 and 14:8-10).

A.   You can literally command the power of God to come into manifestation because you aren't commanding God Himself to go and do something.

B.   Instead, you're commanding what He has already done to manifest in the physical realm.

C.   When you understand how grace and faith work together, you'll become a commander instead of a beggar.

V.   Concerning the work of His hands, God says to His children, "You command Me!"

Thus saith the Lord, the Holy One of Israel, and his Maker, Ask me of things to come concerning my sons, and concerning the work of my hands command ye me.

ISAIAH 45:11, EMPHASIS MINE

A.   God (Father & Son Power Company) has already done His part.

B.   Through Christ's atonement (the power station), everything you'll ever need has already been generated.

C.   In fact, the power has already been delivered to your house (born-again spirit).

D.   When you believe what He has done and reach out in faith to appropriate it, you're commanding what God has already provided to come into manifestation.

E.   You didn't produce the power, but it has been placed at your command.

VI. Faith reaches over into the spiritual realm and draws out into the physical realm what God has already supplied.

    A. Most people are asking God to do for them what He has already done.

    B. When you understand that God has already done it, condemnation is defused.

    C. God provided everything you would ever need before you were born again, before you did anything good or bad, before you were even born.

    D. Every salvation benefit—including forgiveness of sins, healing, etc.—has already been provided.

    E. It's just a matter of whether you can reach out by faith and receive.

LESSON 6 – ADDITIONAL INFORMATION

For additional light on these important issues, I'd like to recommend to you some teaching materials. *Spiritual Authority* will really help you sort these things out. Also, "The Book of Job," "God's Not Guilty," and "The Sovereignty of God" all soundly debunk the false idea that the Lord puts suffering in your life to teach you things. It's simply not true!

"SUCH AS I HAVE"
LESSON 6 – TEACHER'S GUIDE

1.   The early days of the charismatic movement were wild! Several outstanding scriptures became very popular in those days (Mark 11:22-24 and 9:23). According to these verses, whosoever can ask God for whatsoever they desire—and anything is possible! We can see how easy it would be to slip into error if we didn't know that faith only appropriates what God has already provided by grace. God—by grace—didn't provide murder, adultery, or thievery in Christ's atonement. Therefore, since Jesus didn't provide it, our "faith" can't make it happen.

2.   True faith is simply a response to what God has already done by grace. The Lord provided healing 2,000 years ago in the death, burial, and resurrection of Christ (1 Pet. 2:24). People are drawing on that healing by faith and receiving the manifestation of it today—but God already did the necessary work to provide it a long time ago. The Lord has already accomplished healing and placed it inside our born-again spirits. In order for healing to manifest, we must receive it. We must appropriate—by faith—what God has already provided by grace.

3.   When we understand these truths, it'll totally revolutionize the way we receive from God. "Waiting on the Lord" means being like a waiter or a waitress in a restaurant (Ps. 27:14). We aren't waiting for God to do something new—He's waiting on us to respond positively to what He has already done. The only question today is, "Are we ready to believe and receive?"

1. A. Read Mark 11:22-24 and 9:23. Why can't we appropriate by faith murder, adultery, or thievery? (Because God—by grace—didn't provide them in Christ's atonement)
    B. If Jesus didn't provide it, can our "faith" make it happen? (No)
2. A. Read 1 Peter 2:24. What is true faith? (True faith is simply a response to what God has already done by grace)
    B. The Lord has already accomplished healing and placed it where? (Inside our born-again spirits)
    C. In order for healing to manifest, what must we do? (Receive it, appropriate it—draw on that healing by faith)
3. A. Read Psalm 27:14. Are we waiting on God to do something new? (No)
    B. God is waiting on us to do what? (Respond positively to what He has already done)

4.   When we understand grace—that God has already done everything—we'll become bold and authoritative (Acts 3:4-6 and 14:8-10). We can literally command the power of God to come into manifestation because we aren't commanding God Himself to go and do something. Instead, we're commanding what He has already done to manifest in the physical realm. When we understand how grace and faith work together, we'll become commanders instead of beggars.

5.   Concerning the work of His hands, God says to His children, "You command Me" (Is. 45:11)! God (Father & Son Power Company) has already done His part. Through Christ's atonement (the power station), everything we will ever need has already been generated. In fact, the power has already been delivered to our houses (born-again spirits). When we believe what He has done and reach out in faith to appropriate it, we're commanding to come into manifestation what God has already provided. We didn't produce the power, but it has been placed at our command.

6.   Faith reaches over into the spiritual realm and draws out into the physical realm what God has already supplied. Most people are asking God to do for them what He has already done. When we understand that God has already done it, condemnation is defused. God provided everything we would ever need before we were born again, before we did anything good or bad, before we were even born. Every salvation benefit—including forgiveness of sins, healing, etc.—has already been provided. It's just a matter of whether we can reach out by faith and receive.

4.   A.   Read Acts 3:4-6 and 14:8-10. What will we become when we understand grace, that God has already done everything? (Bold and authoritative)
     B.   When we understand how grace and faith work together, what will we become—commanders or beggars? (Commanders)
5.   A.   Read Isaiah 45:11. What does God say to His children concerning the work of His hands? ("You command Me")
     B.   What are we doing when we believe what He has done and reach out in faith to appropriate it? (We're commanding what God has already provided to come into manifestation)
     C.   Did we produce the power? (No, but it has been placed at our command)
6.   A.   What does faith do? (It reaches over into the spiritual realm and draws out into the physical realm what God has already supplied)
     B.   When we understand that God has already done it, what is defused? (Condemnation)
     C.   What did God provide before we were born again, before we did anything good or bad, before we were even born? (Everything we would ever need, every salvation benefit—including forgiveness of sins, healing, etc.)

"SUCH AS I HAVE"
LESSON 6 – DISCIPLESHIP QUESTIONS

1. Who was speaking in Mark 11:22-24?

2. Who should we have faith in?

3. What shall we say to the mountain?

4. Where should we not doubt?

5. What should we believe shall come to pass?

6. What shall we have?

7. When should we believe that we receive what things soever we desire?

8. According to Mark 9:23, to whom are all things possible?

9. According to 1 Peter 2:24, by Jesus' stripes, we _____ healed.

    A. Are
    B. Were
    C. Will be
    D. All of the above
    E. None of the above

10. Who does Psalm 27:14 instruct us to wait on?

11. Read Acts 3:4 and 6. What did Peter give the lame man?

12. What did Peter command him in the name of Jesus?

13. In Acts 14:8-10, had this man Paul ministered to ever walked before?

14. What did Paul perceive that the crippled man had?

15. What did Paul say to him with a loud voice?

16. Then what happened?

17. What does the Lord tell us to ask of Him in Isaiah 45:11?

18. What does He instruct us concerning the work of His hands?

"SUCH AS I HAVE"
LESSON 6 – ANSWER KEY

1.   Jesus

2.   God

3.   Be removed and be cast into the sea

4.   In our hearts

5.   Those things that we say

6.   Whatsoever we say

7.   When we pray

8.   Them that believe

9.   B. Were

10. The Lord

11. Such as he had

12. *"Rise up and walk"*

13. No

14. Faith to be healed

15. *"Stand upright on thy feet"*

16. The crippled man leaped and walked

17. Things to come concerning His sons

18. *"Command ye me"*

"SUCH AS I HAVE"
LESSON 6 – SCRIPTURES

MARK 11:22-24
And Jesus answering saith unto them, Have faith in God. [23] For verily I say unto you, That whosoever shall say unto this mountain, Be thou removed, and be thou cast into the sea; and shall not doubt in his heart, but shall believe that those things which he saith shall come to pass; he shall have whatsoever he saith. [24] Therefore I say unto you, What things soever ye desire, when ye pray, believe that ye receive them, and ye shall have them.

MARK 9:23
Jesus said unto him, If thou canst believe, all things are possible to him that believeth.

1 PETER 2:24
Who his own self bare our sins in his own body on the tree, that we, being dead to sins, should live unto righteousness: by whose stripes ye were healed.

PSALM 27:14
Wait on the LORD: be of good courage, and he shall strengthen thine heart: wait, I say, on the LORD.

ACTS 3:4
And Peter, fastening his eyes upon him with John, said, Look on us.

ACTS 3:6
Then Peter said, Silver and gold have I none; but such as I have give I thee: In the name of Jesus Christ of Nazareth rise up and walk.

ACTS 14:8-10
And there sat a certain man at Lystra, impotent in his feet, being a cripple from his mother's womb, who never had walked: [9] The same heard Paul speak: who stedfastly beholding him, and perceiving that he had faith to be healed, [10] Said with a loud voice, Stand upright on thy feet. And he leaped and walked.

ISAIAH 45:11
Thus saith the LORD, the Holy One of Israel, and his Maker, Ask me of things to come concerning my sons, and concerning the work of my hands command ye me.

GOD'S BEST
LESSON 7

Niki (Ochenski) Weller was believing God for her healing, but hadn't received the manifestation yet. She'd seen visions of the Lord, and in them He told her that she would be healed. Because of this, she had faith and was happy. Niki was praising God even though her doctor—who kept a weekly appointment with her—never expected to see her alive again. Niki was nearly gone!

Although she had faith, it was misdirected. Niki believed God was going—future tense—to heal her. She was passively waiting on the Lord to do something. Then she listened to my message on cassette about how God has already done it and faith just reaches over to appropriate what has already been provided. My statement that "progressive miracles aren't God's best" really upset her at first.

I'm not against progressive miracles, and there's no "bad" way to be healed. However, some ways are definitely better than others—and God's best for everyone is always an instantaneous miracle. The only reason progressive miracles come is because of the way people believe. Their theology—the way they think—only lets it manifest a little at a time.

Since the Lord had told her that she would have a progressive miracle, Niki took offense at my remark. But because she had such a good relationship with God, she just asked Him about it. While listening to the tape, she said in her heart, "Now, God, what about that? You told me I was going to be healed progressively." He answered, saying, "Niki, that's according to your faith. That's what you were believing for. It was all you could receive, so I was meeting you where you were. But My best is instantaneous."

Once she understood, Niki saw that she could've been healed five years before. She'd been passively "waiting" on God, and her faith wasn't out there for an instantaneous healing. She hadn't understood how grace and faith work together to bring into manifestation what God has already provided. This became a revelation to her as she recognized that her healing was already done.

REDIRECTED FAITH

The next day, I went over to the Ochenskis' house. I was praying that Niki would become so angry that she'd reach out in aggressive, violent faith and take her healing (Matt. 11:12). Up until then, she hadn't been able to feed herself, go to the bathroom on her own, or even brush her hair. Niki wasn't paralyzed, but she was so weak and frail that she couldn't even lift her hand—much less move, walk, or do anything. However, after I arrived, she became so riled up that she put her arm across my chest, pushed me out of the way, stood up, and walked!

All I did was redirect her faith. Niki had thought that "faith" was something she did, and sooner or later God would respond and grant healing. I simply told her, "No, that's not Bible faith. You must believe that God has already done it. Then—by faith—reach over into the spirit realm and take what's rightfully yours." Healing manifested—BOOM—just as soon as Niki received the revelation.

This ministered to me too! I saw how this understanding could effectively redirect a person's faith. Therefore, I've been trying to share it with as many people as I can.

I've seen more individuals healed in the past few years than I have in a long, long time. It's simply because people are understanding and saying, "I'm no longer asking God to heal me; I am receiving my healing, which He has already provided. When I pray for people, I'm no longer asking God to heal them. Instead, I'm ministering healing. I'm giving them healing—the same healing virtue that God has placed in me." I am seeing infinitely better results, and so are others—glory to God!

REACH OUT AND RECEIVE!

All of this applies to your financial prosperity too. God has already commanded upon you blessing and the power to get wealth. You just have to learn how to reach out in faith and receive it.

God doesn't give you wealth directly; He gives you power to get it instead.

But thou shalt remember the LORD thy God: for it is he that giveth thee power to get wealth, that he may establish his covenant.

DEUTERONOMY 8:18

As a born-again believer, you already have God's wealth anointing and prosperity power. However, you must believe in your heart that you already have it and then put it to work by faith.

Many things are involved in the process of putting this power to work and seeing wealth manifest. You need to wholeheartedly seek God and His kingdom first (Matt. 6:33). You must trust in Him and start giving. It's important to understand that there's always a period of time between sowing and reaping. Also, you must go out and work. There are many, many practical things you can do to actively cooperate with God's laws of faith concerning prosperity.

The Lord has worked these truths deep into my life. My wife and I have gone from nearly starving to death on several occasions as impoverished young ministers to seeing God provide an average of $1,200 every hour of every day of the year for the purpose of preaching the Gospel. Prosperity is simply having enough of God's supply to fully accomplish His will for your life. I pray that you get a hold of this revelation and fully accomplish your destiny in Him.

Once you believe that God—by grace—has already provided prosperity, you'll begin to reach out in faith and take it. You'll start cooperating with the power and anointing to get wealth that is already in your born-again spirit. Instead of just praying and asking God to dump a bunch of money in your lap while you sit at home watching "As the Stomach Turns" on television, you'll get up, go out, and start touching things. Why? Because you know that God has promised to bless all the work of your hands (Deut. 28:8 and 12).

When you start doing things—believing for that anointing to manifest and prosperity to come—then you'll start seeing it. If you just sit at home, pray, and wait for God to magically put money in your wallet, you'll never receive it. God said He'd bless the work of your hands. One hundred times zero is zero (100 x 0 = 0). You need to believe that God has already done His part, and then do something. It's not, "God, did You see that I worked? Now release Your power!" No! You're working because you believe that God has already given you this anointing to get wealth, and you're acting in faith to release that power to manifest the prosperity the Lord has already provided. Can you see the difference?

GOD HAS ALREADY MOVED

Confession doesn't make God move. You're wrong if you think reciting "By His stripes, I am healed" 599 times will force God to heal you. You can't make God do anything. Faith doesn't move Him. God—by grace—has already moved as much as He's going to. He's already provided everything. Your need was abundantly supplied before you even had it. Since the Lord has already done it, you confess God's Word to encourage your own heart and to drive off the devil. It might take you confessing that Word 599 times before you actually believe (Rom. 10:17), but God is not the one who needs to move; He already has. Confession moves you into faith and the devil out of the way so your manifestation can come (Rev. 12:11).

You don't have to read the Bible to make God love you. He won't love you any more than He already does if you read the Word, and neither will He love you any less if you don't. However, *you'll* love God more if you read the Bible, and *you'll* love Him less if you don't. His love doesn't change; yours does. God has put things in His Word that draw out this love and everything else He has already placed in your life.

Living holy doesn't make God love you more. Neither does a lack of holiness cause Him to love you less. God—by grace—is the same toward everyone. However, if you don't live holy, you won't love God as much. Through sin, your heart will become hardened, and you'll deaden yourself to the things of God (Heb. 3:13).

You need to study the Word, fellowship with believers, and do good things—but not in order to move God. He has already moved, but you have to recognize that you must, by faith, reach over into the spiritual realm and receive. Attending church, reading the Word, and listening to good Bible teaching don't cause God to move in your life; they help your faith.

Even doing this study won't make God love you more. He isn't going to look down on you and say, "You did Andrew's study! I'm giving you three stars. At six stars, you'll get one answered prayer!" No, that's not how He works. The Lord loves you, and His grace is the same toward you whether or not you do this study. However, you won't be the same toward God and His grace without this understanding. Apart from this revelation, you won't have the same degree of faith operating in your life. This teaching is helping your faith—your positive response to what God has already done.

Reading the Bible and going to church help you. Studying the Word and fellowshipping with other believers stirs your love for God (Heb. 10:23-25). However, the Lord would love you exactly the same if you never went to church or read the Word again. But it's stupid not to do these things. Why would you cut yourself off from the very things God has given to help you walk by faith?

FAITH RESPONDS TO GRACE

Although you need to do those things, don't ever think that your actions make God react. He never reacts to you. God has already done everything by grace, and faith is your reaction to Him. Flesh, works, and legalism all try to do things in order to solicit a positive response from God. But the Lord said He'd never share His glory with anyone. You didn't "make" God save, heal, or prosper you; He had already done it. All you did was respond positively in faith to reach out and appropriate what He had already provided.

Don't confuse trying to "make" God do something, with your faith causing to manifest what He has already done. You can't force God to do anything. But—by faith—you can make manifest what He has already provided. That's a big difference!

Faith is simply your positive response to what God has already done. You don't get the glory. You can't say that you made something happen. It was God's power, not yours. He wasn't reacting to you or anything you've done; you simply responded to His grace.

Faith or grace taken alone—either one apart from the other—will kill you. They must complement each other in order for you to experience the abundant life God intended for you to enjoy. Faith teaching, if it's just "Do something to move God," will kill you. You'll end up stuck in the flesh—frustrated, legalistic, and works-oriented. On the other hand, extreme grace will also kill you. If it's "God does everything and you have nothing to do with it," your subsequent passivity will prevent what the Lord has done from manifesting in your life. Then you'll have to make up all kinds of excuses for why you aren't experiencing the abundant life God provided by His grace and clearly promised in His Word. Grace and faith must work together.

"I LABOURED MORE ABUNDANTLY"

Paul understood and lived by this truth.

But by the grace of God I am what I am: and his grace which was bestowed upon me was not in vain; but I laboured more abundantly than they all: yet not I, but the grace of God which was with me.

1 CORINTHIANS 15:10

Paul cooperated with God's grace. He didn't labor in order to get it, but once grace came, he labored in faith to reach out and receive what God had already done. That's a powerful revelation.

I pray that God gives you understanding and wisdom as you begin to harmonize this revelation of grace and faith and apply it to your daily life. The rest of this study will build upon the foundation that has been laid so far. I'll be sharing some things that will really encourage and help you to successfully walk this out.

LESSON 7 – ADDITIONAL INFORMATION

In the early part of 2000, I ministered on grace and faith at a church in Lewisville, Texas. It was the same truth I've taught thousands of times (*Living in the Balance of Grace and Faith*). I emphasized how faith works and countered some common misconceptions (i.e., "faith" is believing that God will do something in the future). While sharing that true Bible faith is to believe what God has already done by grace, I used healing as my main example.

Since Niki's healing was so dramatic in illustrating this truth, we made a DVD out of it, called *Niki Ochenski: The Story of a Miracle!* This powerful story has already impacted tens of thousands of lives!

Several teachings that will help you better understand and receive the manifestation of prosperity include "Grace and Faith in Giving," *Financial Stewardship*, and *How to Receive God's Best*. Prosperity is simply having enough of God's supply to fully accomplish His will for your life. I pray that you get a hold of this revelation and fully accomplish your destiny in Him.

GOD'S BEST
LESSON 7 – OUTLINE

I.   Concerning healing, God's best for everyone is always an instantaneous miracle.

    A.   The only reason progressive miracles come is because of the way people believe.

    B.   Their theology—the way they think—only lets it manifest a little at a time.

    C.   Grace and faith work together to bring into manifestation what God has already provided.

    D.   "I'm no longer asking God to heal me; I am receiving my healing, which He has already provided. When I pray for people, I'm no longer asking God to heal them. Instead, I'm ministering healing. I'm giving them healing—the same healing virtue that God has placed in me."

II.   All of this applies to your financial prosperity too.

    A.   God has already commanded upon you blessing and the power to get wealth—you just have to learn how to reach out in faith and receive it.

But thou shalt remember the LORD thy God: for it is he that giveth thee power to get wealth, that he may establish his covenant.

DEUTERONOMY 8:18

    B.   Many things are involved in the process of putting this power to work and seeing wealth manifest (i.e., Matt. 6:33).

    C.   There are many, many practical things you can do to actively cooperate with God's laws of faith concerning prosperity.

    D.   Once you believe that God—by grace—has already provided prosperity, you'll begin to reach out in faith and take it; you'll start cooperating with the power and anointing to get wealth that is already in your born-again spirit.

    E.   When you start doing things—believing for that anointing to manifest and prosperity to come—then you'll start seeing it (Deut. 28:8 and 12).

    F.   You're working because you believe that God has already given you this anointing to get wealth, and you're acting in faith to release that power to manifest the prosperity the Lord has already provided.

III. God—by grace—has already moved as much as He's going to. He's already provided everything.

    A. Confession moves you into faith and the devil out of the way so your manifestation can come (Rom. 10:17 and Rev. 12:11).

    B. God has put things in His Word that draw out His love and everything else He has already placed in your life.

    C. Attending church, reading the Word, and listening to good Bible teaching don't cause God to move in your life; they help your faith.

    D. Although you need to do those things, don't ever think that your actions make God react.

    E. God has already done everything by grace, and faith is your reaction to Him.

    F. Don't confuse trying to "make" God do something, with your faith causing to manifest what He has already done.

    G. Faith is simply your positive response to what God has already done.

IV. Faith or grace taken alone—either one apart from the other—will kill you.

    A. They must complement each other in order for you to experience the abundant life God intended for you to enjoy.

    B. Grace and faith must work together.

V. Paul understood and lived by this truth.

But by the grace of God I am what I am: and his grace which was bestowed upon me was not in vain; but I laboured more abundantly than they all: yet not I, but the grace of God which was with me.

1 CORINTHIANS 15:10

    A. Paul cooperated with God's grace.

    B. He didn't labor in order to get it, but once grace came, he labored in faith to reach out and receive what God had already done.

    C. I pray that God gives you understanding and wisdom as you begin to harmonize this revelation of grace and faith and apply it to your daily life.

LESSON 7 – ADDITIONAL INFORMATION

In the early part of 2000, I ministered on grace and faith at a church in Lewisville, Texas. It was the same truth I've taught thousands of times (*Living in the Balance of Grace and Faith*). I emphasized how faith works and countered some common misconceptions (i.e., "faith" is believing that God will do something in the future). While sharing that true Bible faith is to believe what God has already done by grace, I used healing as my main example.

Since Niki's healing was so dramatic in illustrating this truth, we made a DVD out of it, called *Niki Ochenski: The Story of a Miracle!* This powerful story has already impacted tens of thousands of lives!

Several teachings that will help you better understand and receive the manifestation of prosperity include "Grace and Faith in Giving," *Financial Stewardship*, and *How to Receive God's Best*. Prosperity is simply having enough of God's supply to fully accomplish His will for your life. I pray that you get a hold of this revelation and fully accomplish your destiny in Him.

GOD'S BEST
LESSON 7 – TEACHER'S GUIDE

1.   Concerning healing, God's best for everyone is always an instantaneous miracle. The only reason progressive miracles come is because of the way people believe. Their theology—the way they think—only lets it manifest a little at a time. Grace and faith work together to bring into manifestation what God has already provided. "We're no longer asking God to heal us; we are receiving our healing, which He has already provided. When we pray for people, we're no longer asking God to heal them. Instead, we are ministering healing. We are giving them healing—the same healing virtue that God has placed in us."

2.   All of this applies to our financial prosperity too. God has already commanded upon us blessing and the power to get wealth—we just have to learn how to reach out in faith and receive it (Deut. 8:18). Many things are involved in the process of putting this power to work and seeing wealth manifest (i.e., Matt. 6:33). There are many, many practical things we can do to actively cooperate with God's laws of faith concerning prosperity. Once we believe that God—by grace—has already provided prosperity, we'll begin to reach out in faith and take it. We'll start cooperating with the power and anointing to get wealth that is already in our born-again spirits. When we start doing things—believing for that anointing to manifest and prosperity to come—then we'll start seeing it (Deut. 28:8 and 12). We're working because we believe that God has already given us this anointing to get wealth, and we're acting in faith to release that power to manifest the prosperity the Lord has already provided.

1. A. Concerning healing, what is always God's best for everyone? (An instantaneous miracle)

     B. When we pray for people and minister healing, what are we doing? (We're no longer asking God to heal them, but we are giving them healing—the same healing virtue that God has placed in us)

2. A. Read Deuteronomy 8:18 and Matthew 6:33. What has God already commanded upon us? (The blessing and power to get wealth)

     B. Once we believe that God—by grace—has already provided prosperity, what must we do? (Begin to reach out in faith and take it, start cooperating with the power and anointing to get wealth that is already in our born-again spirits)

     C. Read Deuteronomy 28:8 and 12. Why are we working? (Because we believe that God has already given us this anointing to get wealth, and we're acting in faith to release that power to manifest the prosperity the Lord has already provided)

3. God—by grace—has already moved as much as He's going to. He's already provided everything. Confession moves us into faith and the devil out of the way so our manifestation can come (Rom. 10:17 and Rev. 12:11). God has put things in His Word that draw out His love and everything else He has already placed in our lives. Attending church, reading the Word, and listening to good Bible teaching don't cause God to move in our lives; they help our faith. Although we need to do those things, we shouldn't ever think that our actions make God react. God has already done everything by grace, and faith is our reaction to Him. We shouldn't confuse trying to "make" God do something, with our faith causing to manifest what He has already done. Faith is simply our positive response to what God has already done.

4. Faith or grace taken alone—either one apart from the other—will kill us. They must complement each other in order for us to experience the abundant life God intended for us to enjoy. Grace and faith must work together.

5. Paul understood and lived by this truth (1 Cor. 15:10). He cooperated with God's grace. He didn't labor in order to get it, but once grace came, he labored in faith to reach out and receive what God had already done. May God give us understanding and wisdom as we begin to harmonize this revelation of grace and faith and apply it to our daily lives.

3. A. Read Romans 10:17 and Revelation 12:11. What moves us into faith and the devil out of the way so our manifestation can come? (Confession)

   B. Where has God put things that draw out His love and everything else He has already placed in our lives? (In His Word)

   C. We shouldn't confuse trying to "make" God do something with what? (Our faith causing to manifest what He has already done)

4. A. What will happen if we take faith or grace alone—either one apart from the other? (It'll kill us)

   B. What must complement each other—work together—in order for us to experience the abundant life God intended for us to enjoy? (Grace and faith)

5. A. Read 1 Corinthians 15:10. What did Paul cooperate with? (God's grace)

   B. Once grace came, Paul labored in faith to reach out and receive what? (What God had already done)

GOD'S BEST
LESSON 7 – DISCIPLESHIP QUESTIONS

1. According to Matthew 11:12, the violent take _____ by force.

2. Deuteronomy 8:18 says that God has given us what power?

3. That He may establish what?

4. Read Matthew 6:33. All these things will be added to us when we seek first _____.

5. Deuteronomy 28:8 and 12 reveal that God has commanded the blessing on us where?

   A. In our storehouses
   B. In all that we set our hands to do
   C. In the land which He has given us
   D. All of the above
   E. None of the above

6. God said He would bless the work of _____.

7. We shall lend to many nations, but we shall not what?

8. According to Romans 10:17, what comes by hearing the Word of God?

9. Revelation 12:11 reveals that we overcome the devil by the blood of the Lamb and by what?

10. Hebrews 3:13 tells us to exhort one another how often, lest we become hardened through the deceitfulness of sin?

11. What does Hebrews 10:23-25 tell us to hold fast to?

12. Let us consider one another to provoke unto what?

13. As we see the day approaching, we should _____.

    A. Not forsake the assembling of ourselves
    B. Exhort one another
    C. Break bread
    D. A. and C.
    E. A. and B.

14. According to 1 Corinthians 15:10, _____ toward Paul was not in vain.

15. Even though Paul labored more abundantly, what was it because of?

GOD'S BEST
LESSON 7 – ANSWER KEY

1. It (the kingdom of heaven)

2. Power to get wealth

3. His covenant

4. The kingdom of God and His righteousness

5. D. All of the above

6. Our hands

7. Borrow

8. Faith

9. The word of our testimony

10. Daily

11. The profession of our faith

12. Love and good works

13. E. A. and B.

14. His grace

15. The grace of God that was with him

GOD'S BEST
LESSON 7 – SCRIPTURES

MATTHEW 11:12

And from the days of John the Baptist until now the kingdom of heaven suffereth violence, and the violent take it by force.

DEUTERONOMY 8:18

But thou shalt remember the LORD thy God: for it is he that giveth thee power to get wealth, that he may establish his covenant which he sware unto thy fathers, as it is this day.

MATTHEW 6:33

But seek ye first the kingdom of God, and his righteousness; and all these things shall be added unto you.

DEUTERONOMY 28:8

The LORD shall command the blessing upon thee in thy storehouses, and in all that thou settest thine hand unto; and he shall bless thee in the land which the LORD thy God giveth thee.

DEUTERONOMY 28:12

The LORD shall open unto thee his good treasure, the heaven to give the rain unto thy land in his season, and to bless all the work of thine hand: and thou shalt lend unto many nations, and thou shalt not borrow.

ROMANS 10:17

So then faith cometh by hearing, and hearing by the word of God.

REVELATION 12:11

And they overcame him by the blood of the Lamb, and by the word of their testimony; and they loved not their lives unto the death.

HEBREWS 3:13

But exhort one another daily, while it is called To day; lest any of you be hardened through the deceitfulness of sin.

HEBREWS 10:23-25

Let us hold fast the profession of our faith without wavering; (for he is faithful that promised;) **[24]** And let us consider one another to provoke unto love and to good works: **[25]** Not forsaking the assembling of ourselves together, as the manner of some is; but exhorting one another: and so much the more, as ye see the day approaching.

1 CORINTHIANS 15:10

But by the grace of God I am what I am: and his grace which was bestowed upon me was not in vain; but I laboured more abundantly than they all: yet not I, but the grace of God which was with me.

SEEING IN THE SPIRIT
LESSON 8

We're already blessed (Eph. 1). God has already done it. He has already blessed us with every spiritual blessing in Christ (Eph. 1:3). We have, living on the inside of us, the same power that raised Jesus Christ from the dead (Eph. 1:19-20). Everything we will ever need has already been provided. It's not a matter of asking God to do it; it's a matter of believing that it is already done and releasing it to manifest.

God—by grace—has already done everything. Faith isn't something we do to make God move. Rather, it's our positive response to what He has already done. Since God has already done it, faith is simple. It's not a struggle. We don't have to do all these things in order to twist God's arm. Faith is simply us responding in a positive way to what God has already done.

"HOW CAN THIS BE?"

Many people wonder, *How can this be?* It's like their circuits overload and start to blow. They say, "I'm miserable and fighting depression. I don't understand how you can say that the Lord has already done everything He's going to do and I'm already healed. That can't be right. Here's my doctor's report. This proves you wrong!" Or they feel pain and other symptoms in their bodies and conclude, "Nope, I'm not healed." For many people, these truths are simply beyond belief because they're so obviously contrary to what they're presently experiencing in the physical realm.

Yet the Bible clearly teaches that God has already blessed you. You have the same power that raised Jesus Christ from the dead. Everything's a done deal, and you've already got it. So you're probably wondering, *If all this is true, then where is it?* In the spirit realm!

God has already moved and blessed us with every spiritual blessing. Everything we'll ever need—joy, peace, wisdom, revelation knowledge, etc.—has already been provided. But it's all in the spirit realm.

If you can't understand that everything God has already provided for you is in the spirit realm, then you will lose this truth I'm communicating. Why? Because the physical realm does not exactly reflect what's true in the spirit realm. Faith acts like a bridge to bring what is true and real in the spiritual world into the physical world. The truth is, very few believers allow their faith to be that bridge for what God has already done to cross over into the natural realm. They just don't see very much manifestation of it.

MY NEW IDENTITY

One of the first things the Lord gave me a clear revelation of was the truth that I had become righteous. It wasn't a righteousness I had earned through my works, but rather a free gift He gave me based upon His work (2 Cor. 5:21). It didn't come from my holy living and doing everything right. When I was born again, Jesus Christ Himself became my righteousness (1 Cor. 1:30). My born-again spirit was *"created in righteousness and true holiness"* (Eph. 4:24). My new nature was created righteous. It's not something I'm becoming or evolving into. In my spirit, I am righteous. So is every other born-again believer!

I saw this truth in the Word and in my heart, but I couldn't perceive it in my experience. I looked in the mirror and saw zits, wrinkles, and bulges. My feelings and thoughts included anger, bitterness, lust, and many other nasty things at times. In considering all of this, I knew I wasn't being like Jesus. At the time, I thought that when the Bible spoke of being righteous—in right standing with God—it meant sinless perfection in my thoughts, feelings, and actions. So, I diligently searched my physical actions (body) and my thoughts and my feelings (mental-emotional realm, a.k.a. soul), but I still couldn't perceive this righteousness. I really struggled with this for a long period of time. Then the Lord gave me revelation concerning spirit, soul, and body.

Through this revelation of spirit, soul, and body, I realized that when the Bible calls me righteous, it's talking about my born-again spirit—not my thoughts, feelings, actions, and physical body. I began to understand that in my spirit, I was totally changed. I'm a new creature. There's a new me!

Therefore if any man be in Christ, he is a new creature: old things are passed away; behold, all things are become new.

2 CORINTHIANS 5:17

I started to recognize that in my spirit, I had become a totally brand-new person.

When I stopped going by what I saw in the mirror, thought in my mind, and observed in my actions, I began to experience victory in my Christian life. As I changed my identity to who the Word said I was in the spirit, I started enjoying the promised abundant life in manifestation (John 10:10). How did that happen? Through God's Word.

"SO ARE WE IN THIS WORLD"

God's Word is the only reliable, accurate representation of the spirit world. Jesus declared,

It is the spirit that quickeneth [makes alive]; *the flesh profiteth nothing: the words that I speak unto you, they are spirit, and they are life.*

JOHN 6:63, BRACKETS MINE

God's Word is spiritual. The Bible tells us what is truly going on in the spirit realm.

That's why some people struggle so much to understand God's Word. They're trying to perceive in the natural realm what the Bible is speaking of their spirits. Take, for instance, 1 John 4:17: *"As he [Jesus Christ] is, so are we in this world"* (brackets mine). It's not talking about your physical actions (body) or your thoughts and feelings (soul), because God's Word plainly reveals that someday (future—when you arrive in heaven), your body and soul (corruptible) will complete the process of change to perfection (will put on incorruption: 1 Cor. 13:9-12 and 15:50-54). However, Christ is perfect right now. So then, what part of you is already perfect—as Jesus is? Your born-again spirit.

As Jesus is—right at this moment—so are you in this world. It's not talking about when you get to heaven; it means right now here on earth. You can't say you're acting exactly as Jesus. You might be acting better than I do or better than you've ever acted before, but you are not manifesting everything physically, emotionally, and mentally exactly as Jesus is. The only way to understand 1 John 4:17 is to realize that it's talking about your born-again spirit. In the spirit, you are a totally brand-new person. The real you—who you'll be throughout eternity—is who you are in Christ. Living from who you are in Christ is what the Word calls "walking by the spirit" (Gal. 5:16). If you begin to do that, then you will find the power of God manifest in your life.

THE SPIRITUAL MIRROR

God's Word is a spiritual mirror. When you look into it, you see who you are in the spirit (2 Cor. 3:18). It always reflects *"Christ in you, the hope of glory"* (Col. 1:27). This shines additional light on James 1:22-25—

> *But be ye doers of the word, and not hearers only, deceiving your own selves. [23] For if any be a hearer of the word, and not a doer, he is like unto a man beholding his natural face in a glass* [mirror]: *[24] For he beholdeth himself, and goeth his way, and straightway forgetteth what manner of man he was. [25] But whoso looketh into the perfect law of liberty* [the Word, especially the New Testament], *and continueth therein, he being not a forgetful hearer, but a doer of the work, this man shall be blessed in his deed.*

BRACKETS MINE

As you look in the mirror (God's Word), discover your identity in Christ (who you are in the spirit), and act on that knowledge in faith, you will see the life of God within you manifest.

If I told you your hair was messed up, how would you know if it was or not? You can't go by how it feels. The only way you can know is to look in a mirror. Then you just believe it and act accordingly. If some hairs are out of place, you comb them. You trust the mirror to tell you the truth.

However, what you see in a mirror is only a reflection. It's not the real thing. You've never really seen your face before. It's true—think about it. You might have observed your reflection in a mirror, viewed a photograph, or seen a drawing, but you've never looked directly at your own face. How do you know that these representations of your face are accurate? Haven't you seen those funny mirrors at a circus or carnival? Everyone knows that they "doctor" those pictures of people in magazines at the grocery store, and drawing caricatures is even considered a form of art. Therefore, you have to trust that the image you're seeing in the mirror is true.

It's the same when you look into the spiritual mirror of God's Word. The Word tells you who you are and what you have in Christ. It reveals spiritual truths and what's happening in the spiritual world. If you want to experience life and peace, then you need to be spiritually minded.

For to be carnally [not necessarily sinfully, but naturally] *minded is death; but to be spiritually minded is life and peace.*

ROMANS 8:6, BRACKETS MINE

You will never move into the supernatural things of God while being dominated by the natural realm—what you can see, taste, hear, smell, and feel. If you can't believe anything beyond what your five senses can tell you or confirm, then you are carnally minded. If something must be proven in a test tube, scientifically, before you believe it exists, then you are trapped in the natural realm. God is a Spirit, and He moves in the spirit realm (John 4:24). In order to flow with God in the supernatural and enjoy life and peace, you need to become spiritually minded.

LESSON 8 – ADDITIONAL INFORMATION

For further study, refer to my teaching *Spirit, Soul & Body*.

SEEING IN THE SPIRIT
LESSON 8 – OUTLINE

I.   The Bible clearly teaches that God has already blessed you (Eph. 1:3).

   A.   You have the same power that raised Jesus Christ from the dead (Eph. 1:19-20).

   B.   Everything we will ever need—joy, peace, wisdom, revelation knowledge, etc.—has already been provided.

   C.   But it's all in the spirit realm.

   D.   The physical realm does not exactly reflect what's true in the spirit realm.

   E.   Faith acts like a bridge to bring what is true and real in the spiritual world into the physical world.

II. Through a revelation of spirit, soul, and body, I realized that when the Bible calls me righteous, it's talking about my born-again spirit—not my thoughts, feelings, actions, and physical body (2 Cor. 5:21, 1 Cor. 1:30, and Eph. 4:24).

   A.   I started to recognize that in my spirit, I had become a totally brand-new person.

Therefore if any man be in Christ, he is a new creature: old things are passed away; behold, all things are become new.

2 CORINTHIANS 5:17

   B.   When I stopped going by what I saw in the mirror, thought in my mind, and observed in my actions, I began to experience victory in my Christian life.

   C.   As I changed my identity to who the Word said I was in the spirit, I started enjoying the promised abundant life in manifestation (John 10:10).

III. God's Word is the only reliable, accurate representation of the spirit world.

It is the spirit that quickeneth [makes alive]; the flesh profiteth nothing: the words that I speak unto you, they are spirit, and they are life.

JOHN 6:63, BRACKETS MINE

   A.   The reason some people struggle so much to understand God's Word is because they're trying to perceive in the natural realm what the Bible is speaking of their spirits.

As he [Jesus Christ] *is, so are we in this world.*

1 JOHN 4:17, BRACKETS MINE

    B. As Jesus is—right at this moment—so are you in this world.

    C. The real you—who you will be throughout eternity—is who you are in Christ.

    D. Living from who you are in Christ is what the Word calls "walking by the spirit" (Gal. 5:16).

IV.   God's Word is a spiritual mirror.

    A. When you look into it, you see who you are in the spirit (2 Cor. 3:18).

    B. It always reflects *"Christ in you, the hope of glory"* (Col. 1:27).

But be ye doers of the word, and not hearers only, deceiving your own selves. [23] For if any be a hearer of the word, and not a doer, he is like unto a man beholding his natural face in a glass [mirror]: *[24] For he beholdeth himself, and goeth his way, and straightway forgetteth what manner of man he was. [25] But whoso looketh into the perfect law of liberty* [the Word, especially the New Testament]*, and continueth therein, he being not a forgetful hearer, but a doer of the work, this man shall be blessed in his deed.*

JAMES 1:22-25, BRACKETS MINE

    C. As you look in the mirror (God's Word), discover your identity in Christ (who you are in the spirit), and act on that knowledge in faith, you will see the life of God within you manifest.

V.   If you want to experience life and peace, then you need to be spiritually minded.

For to be carnally [not necessarily sinfully, but naturally] *minded is death; but to be spiritually minded is life and peace.*

ROMANS 8:6, BRACKETS MINE

    A. You will never move into the supernatural things of God while being dominated by the natural realm—what you can see, taste, hear, smell, and feel.

    B. If you can't believe anything beyond what your five senses can tell you or confirm, then you are carnally minded.

    C. God is a Spirit, and He moves in the spirit realm (John 4:24).

    D. In order to flow with God in the supernatural and enjoy life and peace, you need to become spiritually minded.

LESSON 8 – ADDITIONAL INFORMATION

For further study, refer to my teaching *Spirit, Soul & Body*.

SEEING IN THE SPIRIT
LESSON 8 – TEACHER'S GUIDE

1.   The Bible clearly teaches that God has already blessed us (Eph. 1:3). We have the same power that raised Jesus Christ from the dead (Eph. 1:19-20). Everything we will ever need—joy, peace, wisdom, revelation knowledge, etc.—has already been provided. But it's all in the spirit realm. The physical realm does not exactly reflect what's true in the spirit realm. Faith acts like a bridge to bring what is true and real in the spiritual world into the physical world.

2.   Through a revelation of spirit, soul, and body, we realize that when the Bible calls us righteous, it is talking about our born-again spirits—not our thoughts, feelings, actions, and physical bodies (2 Cor. 5:21, 1 Cor. 1:30, and Eph. 4:24). We start recognizing that in our spirits, we have become totally brand-new people (2 Cor. 5:17). When we stop going by what we see in the mirror, think in our minds, and observe in our actions, we will begin to experience victory in our Christian lives. As we change our identity to who the Word says we are in the spirit, we'll start enjoying the promised abundant life in manifestation (John 10:10).

3.   God's Word is the only reliable, accurate representation of the spirit world (John 6:63). The reason some people struggle so much to understand God's Word is because they're trying to perceive in the natural realm what the Bible is speaking of their spirits. As Jesus is—right at this moment—so are we in this world (1 John 4:17). The real us—who we will be throughout eternity—is who we are in Christ. Living from who we are in Christ is what the Word calls "walking by the spirit" (Gal. 5:16).

1. A. Read Ephesians 1:3 and 19-20. Does the physical realm exactly reflect what is true in the spirit realm? (No)
    B. What acts like a bridge to bring what is true and real in the spiritual world into the physical world? (Faith)
2. A. Read 2 Corinthians 5:21, 1 Corinthians 1:30, Ephesians 4:24, 2 Corinthians 5:17, and John 10:10. How do we realize that when the Bible calls us righteous, it's talking about our born-again spirits—not our thoughts, feelings, actions, and physical bodies? (Through a revelation of spirit, soul, and body)
    B. We will start enjoying the promised abundant life in manifestation as we change our identity to what? (Who the Word says we are in the spirit)
3. A. Read John 6:63, 1 John 4:17, and Galatians 5:16. What is the only reliable, accurate representation of the spirit world? (God's Word)
    B. Why do some people struggle so much to understand God's Word? (Because they're trying to perceive in the natural realm what the Bible is speaking of their spirits)
    C. What does the Word call "walking by the spirit"? (Living from who we are in Christ)

4.   God's Word is a spiritual mirror. When we look into it, we see who we are in the spirit (2 Cor. 3:18 and James 1:22-25). It always reflects *"Christ in you, the hope of glory"* (Col. 1:27). As we look in the mirror (God's Word), discover our identity in Christ (who we are in the spirit), and act on that knowledge in faith, we will see the life of God within us manifest.

5.   If we want to experience life and peace, then we need to be spiritually minded (Rom. 8:6). We will never move into the supernatural things of God while being dominated by the natural realm—what we can see, taste, hear, smell, and feel. If we can't believe anything beyond what our five senses can tell us or confirm, then we are carnally minded. God is a Spirit, and He moves in the spirit realm (John 4:24). In order to flow with God in the supernatural and enjoy life and peace, we need to become spiritually minded.

4. A. Read 2 Corinthians 3:18, James 1:22-25, and Colossians 1:27. What do we see when we look into the spiritual mirror of God's Word? (Who we are in the spirit)
    B. When will we see the life of God within us manifest? (As we look in the mirror [God's Word], discover our identity in Christ [who we are in the spirit], and act on that knowledge in faith)
5. A. Read Romans 8:6 and John 4:24. We will never move into the supernatural things of God while being dominated by what? (The natural realm—what we can see, taste, hear, smell, and feel)
    B. What do we need to become in order to flow with God in the supernatural and enjoy life and peace? (Spiritually minded)

SEEING IN THE SPIRIT
LESSON 8 – DISCIPLESHIP QUESTIONS

1. According to Ephesians 1:3, what have we been blessed with?

2. According to Ephesians 1:19-20, is the same power that raised Jesus from the dead toward us?

3. Second Corinthians 5:21 reveals that Jesus—who knew no sin—was made _____ that we might be made the righteousness of God in Him.

4. According to 1 Corinthians 1:30, what has God made unto us?

5. According to Ephesians 4:24, in my new man—born-again spirit—I am what?

6. Second Corinthians 5:17 reveals that anyone in Christ is a new what?

7. According to John 10:10, Jesus came that we might have _____ more abundantly.

8. According to John 6:63, what are spirit and life?

9. First John 4:17 declares that as _____ is, so are we—right now—in this world.

10. Read 1 Corinthians 13:9-12. How do we see now?

11. How will we see then?

12. According to 1 Corinthians 15:50-54, this corruptible shall put on what?

13. This mortal shall put on what?

14. How does Galatians 5:16 tell us to walk?

15. According to 2 Corinthians 3:18, we all, beholding as in a glass the glory of the Lord, are _____.

16. According to Colossians 1:27, Christ in us is our hope of what?

17. Read James 1:22-25. Those who hear the Word but don't do it deceive _____.

18. These people are like someone beholding their own face in a glass (mirror), going their way, and straightway forgetting what?

19. According to Romans 8:6, to be carnally minded is death, but to be spiritually minded is _____.

20. How must we worship God, according to John 4:24?

SEEING IN THE SPIRIT
LESSON 8 – ANSWER KEY

1. *"All spiritual blessings in heavenly places in Christ"*

2. Yes

3. Sin

4. Wisdom, righteousness, sanctification, and redemption

5. Righteous and truly holy

6. Creature

7. Life

8. The words Jesus speaks

9. He—Jesus

10. Through a glass, darkly

11. Face to face

12. Incorruption

13. Immortality

14. In the Spirit

15. Changed

16. Glory

17. Themselves

18. What manner of person they were

19. Life and peace

20. In spirit and truth

SEEING IN THE SPIRIT
LESSON 8 – SCRIPTURES

EPHESIANS 1:3

Blessed be the God and Father of our Lord Jesus Christ, who hath blessed us with all spiritual blessings in heavenly places in Christ.

EPHESIANS 1:19-20

And what is the exceeding greatness of his power to us-ward who believe, according to the working of his mighty power, [20] Which he wrought in Christ, when he raised him from the dead, and set him at his own right hand in the heavenly places.

2 CORINTHIANS 5:21

For he hath made him to be sin for us, who knew no sin; that we might be made the righteousness of God in him.

1 CORINTHIANS 1:30

But of him are ye in Christ Jesus, who of God is made unto us wisdom, and righteousness, and sanctification, and redemption.

EPHESIANS 4:24

And that ye put on the new man, which after God is created in righteousness and true holiness.

2 CORINTHIANS 5:17

Therefore if any man be in Christ, he is a new creature: old things are passed away; behold, all things are become new.

JOHN 10:10

The thief cometh not, but for to steal, and to kill, and to destroy: I am come that they might have life, and that they might have it more abundantly.

JOHN 6:63

It is the spirit that quickeneth; the flesh profiteth nothing: the words that I speak unto you, they are spirit, and they are life.

1 JOHN 4:17

Herein is our love made perfect, that we may have boldness in the day of judgment: because as he is, so are we in this world.

1 CORINTHIANS 13:9-12

For we know in part, and we prophesy in part. [10] But when that which is perfect is come, then that which is in part shall be done away. [11] When I was a child, I spake as a child, I understood as a child, I thought as a child: but when I became a man, I put away childish things. [12] For now we see through a glass, darkly; but then face to face: now I know in part; but then shall I know even as also I am known.

1 CORINTHIANS 15:50-54

Now this I say, brethren, that flesh and blood cannot inherit the kingdom of God; neither doth corruption inherit incorruption. [51] Behold, I shew you a mystery; We shall not all sleep, but we shall all be changed, [52] In a moment, in the twinkling of an eye, at the last trump: for the trumpet shall sound, and the dead shall be raised incorruptible, and we shall be changed. [53] For this corruptible must put on incorruption, and this mortal must put on immortality. [54] So when this corruptible shall have put on incorruption, and this mortal shall have put on immortality, then shall be brought to pass the saying that is written, Death is swallowed up in victory.

GALATIANS 5:16

This I say then, Walk in the Spirit, and ye shall not fulfil the lust of the flesh.

2 CORINTHIANS 3:18

But we all, with open face beholding as in a glass the glory of the Lord, are changed into the same image from glory to glory, even as by the Spirit of the Lord.

COLOSSIANS 1:27

To whom God would make known what is the riches of the glory of this mystery among the Gentiles; which is Christ in you, the hope of glory.

JAMES 1:22-25

But be ye doers of the word, and not hearers only, deceiving your own selves. [23] For if any be a hearer of the word, and not a doer, he is like unto a man beholding his natural face in a glass: [24] For he beholdeth himself, and goeth his way, and straightway forgetteth what manner of man he was. [25] But whoso looketh into the perfect law of liberty, and continueth therein, he being not a forgetful hearer, but a doer of the work, this man shall be blessed in his deed.

ROMANS 8:6

For to be carnally minded is death; but to be spiritually minded is life and peace.

JOHN 4:24

God is a Spirit: and they that worship him must worship him in spirit and in truth.

THE SPIRIT REALM IS REAL
LESSON 9

Some people see what God has done in the Scriptures, but then they run into this wall. "The Word says I already have everything, but I don't look blessed, I don't feel healed, and it sure doesn't seem like I have the power and anointing of God. There's no tingling in my hands or anything. How can you say that I can heal the sick, raise the dead, and so forth?" It's in the spirit, not the physical realm. There are two different worlds.

In 2 Kings 6, the king of Syria was warring against the king of Israel. He would send ambushes out to destroy the king of Israel's army. However, every time he did this, an ambush would be there waiting for him. It was as if the king of Israel knew the king of Syria's battle plans beforehand.

After this happened a number of times, the king of Syria was quite perplexed.

Therefore the heart of the king of Syria was sore troubled for this thing; and he called his servants, and said unto them, Will ye not shew me which of us is for the king of Israel?

2 KINGS 6:11

Basically, he said, "Who is the traitor? Someone here must be a spy."

And one of his servants said, None, my lord, O king: but Elisha, the prophet that is in Israel, telleth the king of Israel the words that thou speakest in thy bedchamber.

2 KINGS 6:12

Elisha, who was listening to God, kept telling the king of Israel what was going on. The king trusted what the prophet was seeing and hearing in the spirit, and he acted on his counsel. Therefore, he was able to defeat the Syrian army every single time.

SPIRITUAL TRUTH VS. PHYSICAL TRUTH

So the king of Syria decided to pursue Elisha:

Therefore sent he thither horses, and chariots, and a great host: and they came by night, and compassed the city about [where Elisha was]. [15] And when the servant of the man of God was risen early, and gone forth, behold, an host compassed the city both with horses and chariots. And his servant said unto him, Alas, my master! how shall we do?

2 KINGS 6:14-15, BRACKETS MINE

That's just an old English way of saying this servant panicked.

This man saw the armies, discerned why they were there, and panicked. He knew his master, Elisha, had been giving the king of Syria's battle plans to the king of Israel. But notice the prophet's response:

Fear not: for they that be with us are more than they that be with them.

2 KINGS 6:16

Now, people who don't understand that there's more to life than what you can see, taste, hear, smell, and feel would look at Elisha here and say, "He lied!" To them, there's simply no reality beyond the physical realm. Therefore, they don't understand people who are operating in faith. They think a believer is just saying that they're healed—when they really aren't—in the hope that it'll become so. I once heard a man preach, "You have to say it's so when it isn't so in order for it to become so." Not true. That's just lies, deception, and mind games. The faith person is simply describing what's true in the spirit but hasn't yet manifested in the physical realm.

You need to realize that spiritual truth and physical truth don't always agree. However, if you'll believe, speak, and act on spiritual truth, it will overcome the physical truth. Your unwavering faith in God's eternal Word causes the contrary temporal realm to change. That's how what's already true in the spirit becomes true in the physical.

People who are genuinely operating in faith confess what God has already done in the spirit. That's how they can tell the truth and say "I am blessed! I have everything I need. I'm a prosperous person" even though their checkbooks are in the red. That's how people can declare "By His stripes, I was healed. I've already been healed. Thank You, Jesus!" when their bodies are wracked with pain and other symptoms. They're not just "fakin' it till they make it"; as they continue to believe, what's true in the spirit will eventually manifest itself in the physical realm.

That's what Elisha did. He declared, *"Fear not: for they that be with us are more than they that be with them"* (2 Kin. 6:16). The prophet would have been lying if all there was to reality is just this physical world—what you can see, taste, hear, smell, and feel. But, of course, there is a real spiritual realm.

"LORD, OPEN HIS EYES"

However, Elisha's servant wasn't operating in faith the way his master was. Apparently, the prophet's confident answer shocked him. So, Elisha prayed,

LORD, I pray thee, open his eyes, that he may see. And the LORD opened the eyes of the young man; and he saw: and, behold, the mountain was full of horses and chariots of fire round about Elisha.

2 KINGS 6:17

The young man's physical eyes were already wide open. I'll bet they were as big as saucers, seeing all of those Syrians there to take them! But God opened the eyes of his heart so he could see in the spirit. That's what enabled him to perceive all of the horses and chariots of fire round about them.

You have the ability to see the unseen. Don't limit yourself only to what you can perceive with your natural eyes. Through God's Word, look beyond the mere physical world. With the eyes of your heart, you can see in the spirit.

Jesus used this same reasoning when He said, *"He that hath ears to hear, let him hear"* (Matt. 11:15). Every person listening had physical ears on their heads and heard what He was saying. But Jesus was referring to those who would hear Him with their hearts and receive His words into their innermost being.

In order to walk with God and do exploits, you need to be able to perceive things in your heart that you cannot perceive with your five natural senses. This is what Elisha prayed for his servant. God answered, and the man's spiritual eyes opened up to see the many angels surrounding them.

The moment the servant saw the angels was not when the angels arrived; they were already there. He just wasn't aware of them.

BELIEVING IS SEEING

The Word gives us no indication that Elisha's eyes were opened like his servant's. Elisha didn't see this, because he didn't need to. He believed it based on the promises of God.

God had already given many promises by that time. David was a prophet before then and had written many things, including:

> *For he shall give his angels charge over thee, to keep thee in all thy ways. [12] They shall bear thee up in their hands, lest thou dash thy foot against a stone.*

PSALM 91:11-12

God made many other promises about angels too. Plus, Elisha had physically seen the horses and chariots of God before (2 Kin. 2:11-12). Apparently, Elisha just believed. He didn't have to see.

As believers, we have many spiritual truths and realities in and around us that most of us have never perceived. Dominated by carnal-mindedness, we limit what we believe to what we can perceive with our five natural senses. We must go beyond the physical realm and begin to recognize that there is a real spiritual world.

In the spirit, God has already healed you. He has already commanded His blessing upon you. You have been given joy, peace, and love. All of these things and so much more are in you in abundance—in your born-again spirit. But before you see these things on the outside (physically manifest), you must see them on the inside (with the eyes of your heart).

The spiritual world is not fake. It's not a fantasy land. It is reality. In fact, the spiritual world actually created the physical world. Everything we can see and touch—the visible—was created by the invisible.

Through faith we understand that the worlds were framed by the word of God, so that things which are seen were not made of things which do appear.

HEBREWS 11:3

God took spiritual substance—things that were real in the spiritual realm—and made everything in the physical realm. The spiritual realm is the parent force, and the parent force is always greater. The Creator is always greater than the creation. From God's eternal point of view, the spiritual realm is more real than the natural realm.

Elisha understood this. Since he believed he had angelic protection surrounding him, he boldly walked out into the midst of the enemy, raised his hand, and smote them with blindness. They immediately began groping around in their darkness. Elisha commanded them to take each others' hands, and he led them single file directly to the king of Israel. Then he prayed and their eyes were opened (2 Kin. 6:18-20). Elisha took this entire Syrian army captive because he believed in the power that was available to him in the spirit realm. He knew it was there and drew upon it. Elisha didn't use a single natural weapon to accomplish this—only spiritual. The spirit realm is real.

THE SPIRIT REALM IS REAL
LESSON 9 – OUTLINE

I.   There are two different worlds.

    A. In 2 Kings 6, the king of Syria was warring against the king of Israel.

    B. It was as if the king of Israel knew the king of Syria's battle plans beforehand.

Therefore the heart of the king of Syria was sore troubled for this thing; and he called his servants, and said unto them, Will ye not show me which of us is for the king of Israel? [12] And one of his servants said, None, my lord, O king: but Elisha, the prophet that is in Israel, telleth the king of Israel the words that thou speakest in thy bedchamber.

2 KINGS 6:11-12

    C. So the king of Syria decided to pursue Elisha.

Therefore sent he thither horses, and chariots, and a great host: and they came by night, and compassed the city about [where Elisha was]. [15] And when the servant of the man of God was risen early, and gone forth, behold, an host compassed the city both with horses and chariots. And his servant said unto him, Alas, my master! how shall we do?

2 KINGS 6:14-15, BRACKETS MINE

    D. Elisha's servant saw the armies, discerned why they were there, and panicked.

Fear not: for they that be with us are more than they that be with them.

2 KINGS 6:16

II. The faith person is simply describing what's true in the spirit but hasn't yet manifested in the physical realm.

    A. You need to realize that spiritual truth and physical truth don't always agree.

    B. However, if you'll believe, speak, and act on spiritual truth, it will overcome the physical truth.

    C. Your unwavering faith in God's eternal Word causes the contrary temporal realm to change.

    D. That's how what's already true in the spirit becomes true in the physical.

E. As you continue to believe, what's true in the spirit will eventually manifest itself in the physical realm.

III. You have the ability to see the unseen.

LORD, I pray thee, open his eyes, that he may see. And the LORD opened the eyes of the young man; and he saw: and, behold, the mountain was full of horses and chariots of fire round about Elisha.

2 KINGS 6:17

A. Through God's Word, look beyond the mere physical world.

B. With the eyes of your heart, you can see in the spirit.

He that hath ears to hear, let him hear.

MATTHEW 11:15

C. Jesus was referring to those who would hear Him with their hearts and receive His words into their innermost being.

D. In order to walk with God and do exploits, you need to be able to perceive things in your heart that you cannot perceive with your five natural senses.

IV. As believers, we have many spiritual truths and realities in and around us that most of us have never perceived.

A. Before we see these things on the outside (physically manifest), we must see them on the inside (with the eyes of our hearts).

B. Everything we can see and touch—the visible—was created by the invisible.

Through faith we understand that the worlds were framed by the word of God, so that things which are seen were not made of things which do appear.

HEBREWS 11:3

C. God took spiritual substance—things that were real in the spiritual realm—and made everything in the physical realm.

D. The spiritual realm is the parent force, and the parent force is always greater.

E. From God's eternal point of view, the spiritual realm is more real than the natural.

F. The spirit realm is real.

THE SPIRIT REALM IS REAL
LESSON 9 – TEACHER'S GUIDE

1.   There are two different worlds. In 2 Kings 6, the king of Syria was warring against the king of Israel. It was as if the king of Israel knew the king of Syria's battle plans beforehand (2 Kin. 6:11-12). So the king of Syria decided to pursue Elisha (2 Kin. 6:14-16). Elisha's servant saw the armies, discerned why they were there, and panicked.

2.   The faith person is simply describing what's true in the spirit but hasn't yet manifested in the physical realm. We need to realize that spiritual truth and physical truth don't always agree. However, if we'll believe, speak, and act on spiritual truth, it will overcome the physical truth. Our unwavering faith in God's eternal Word causes the contrary temporal realm to change. That's how what's already true in the spirit becomes true in the physical. As we continue to believe, what's true in the spirit will eventually manifest itself in the physical realm.

3.   We have the ability to see the unseen (2 Kin. 6:17). Through God's Word, we can look beyond the mere physical world. With the eyes of our hearts, we can see in the spirit. In Matthew 11:15, Jesus was referring to those who would hear Him with their hearts and receive His words into their innermost being. In order to walk with God and do exploits, we need to be able to perceive things in our hearts that we cannot perceive with our five natural senses.

1.   A.   Read 2 Kings 6:11-16. How many different worlds are there? (Two)
     B.   What did Elisha's servant do when he saw the armies and discerned why they were there? (He panicked)
2.   A.   What happens if we'll believe, speak, and act on spiritual truth? (It will overcome the physical truth)
     B.   What causes the contrary temporal realm to change? (Our unwavering faith in God's eternal Word)
     C.   As we continue to believe, what's true in the spirit will eventually do what? (Manifest itself in the physical realm)
3.   A.   Read 2 Kings 6:17 and Matthew 11:15. With the eyes of our hearts—through God's Word—what ability do we have? (To see the unseen, to look beyond just the mere physical world, and to see in the spirit)
     B.   In order to walk with God and do exploits, what do we need to be able to perceive? (Things in our hearts that we cannot perceive with our five natural senses)

4.   As believers, we have many spiritual truths and realities in and around us that most of us have never perceived. Before we see these things on the outside (physically manifest), we must see them on the inside (with the eyes of our hearts). Everything we can see and touch—the visible—was created by the invisible (Heb. 11:3). God took spiritual substance—things that were real in the spiritual realm—and made everything in the physical realm. The spiritual realm is the parent force, and the parent force is always greater. From God's eternal point of view, the spiritual realm is more real than the natural. The spirit realm is real.

4.   A.   Read Hebrews 11:3. Before we see spiritual truths and realities on the outside (physically manifest), we must see them where? (On the inside—with the eyes of our hearts)
     B.   God took spiritual substance—things that were real in the spiritual realm—and did what in the physical realm? (Made everything)
     C.   From God's eternal point of view, what realm is more real—the spiritual or the natural? (The spiritual realm)

THE SPIRIT REALM IS REAL
LESSON 9 – DISCIPLESHIP QUESTIONS

1. According to 2 Kings 6:11-12, whose heart was sore troubled?

2. Who was telling the king of Israel the king of Syria's words?

3. According to 2 Kings 6:14-15, what did the king of Syria do?

4. According to 2 Kings 6:16-17, what was Elisha's answer?

5. What did Elisha pray?

6. What then did the young man see?

7. According to Matthew 11:15, what did Jesus say to those who have ears to hear?

8. According to Psalm 91:11-12, God gives His angels charge over us to keep us how?

9. They bear us up in their hands lest we what?

10. According to 2 Kings 2:11-12, what separated Elijah and Elisha?

11. What did Elijah go up by into heaven?

12. According to Hebrews 11:3, *"through faith we understand that the worlds were framed by the word of God, so that"* what?

13. According to 2 Kings 6:18-20, what did Elisha pray?

14. Who did he say he would bring them to if they followed him?

15. When they got to Samaria, what did Elisha pray?

THE SPIRIT REALM IS REAL
LESSON 9 – ANSWER KEY

1. The king of Syria

2. Elisha, the prophet

3. He sent horses, chariots, and a great host

4. *"Fear not: for they that be with us are more than they that be with them"*

5. *"Lord, I pray thee, open his eyes, that he may see"*

6. That the mountain was full of horses and chariots of fire round about Elisha

7. *"Let him hear"*

8. In all our ways

9. Dash our foot against a stone

10. A chariot of fire and horses of fire

11. A whirlwind

12. The *"things which are seen were not made of things which do appear"*

13. That God would smite this people—the Syrian army—with blindness

14. The man whom they sought

15. *"Lord, open the eyes of these men, that they may see"*

THE SPIRIT REALM IS REAL
LESSON 9 – SCRIPTURES

2 KINGS 6:11-12
Therefore the heart of the king of Syria was sore troubled for this thing; and he called his servants, and said unto them, Will ye not shew me which of us is for the king of Israel? [12] And one of his servants said, None, my lord, O king: but Elisha, the prophet that is in Israel, telleth the king of Israel the words that thou speakest in thy bedchamber.

2 KINGS 6:14-20
Therefore sent he thither horses, and chariots, and a great host: and they came by night, and compassed the city about. [15] And when the servant of the man of God was risen early, and gone forth, behold, an host compassed the city both with horses and chariots. And his servant said unto him, Alas, my master! how shall we do? [16] And he answered, Fear not: for they that be with us are more than they that be with them. [17] And Elisha prayed, and said, Lord, I pray thee, open his eyes, that he may see. And the Lord opened the eyes of the young man; and he saw: and, behold, the mountain was full of horses and chariots of fire round about Elisha. [18] And when they came down to him, Elisha prayed unto the Lord, and said, Smite this people, I pray thee, with blindness. And he smote them with blindness according to the word of Elisha. [19] And Elisha said unto them, This is not the way, neither is this the city: follow me, and I will bring you to the man whom ye seek. But he led them to Samaria. [20] And it came to pass, when they were come into Samaria, that Elisha said, Lord, open the eyes of these men, that they may see. And the Lord opened their eyes, and they saw; and, behold, they were in the midst of Samaria.

MATTHEW 11:15
He that hath ears to hear, let him hear.

PSALM 91:11-12
For he shall give his angels charge over thee, to keep thee in all thy ways. [12] They shall bear thee up in their hands, lest thou dash thy foot against a stone.

2 KINGS 2:11-12
And it came to pass, as they still went on, and talked, that, behold, there appeared a chariot of fire, and horses of fire, and parted them both asunder; and Elijah went up by a whirlwind into heaven. [12] And Elisha saw it, and he cried, My father, my father, the chariot of Israel, and the horsemen thereof. And he saw him no more: and he took hold of his own clothes, and rent them in two pieces.

HEBREWS 11:3

Through faith we understand that the worlds were framed by the word of God, so that things which are seen were not made of things which do appear.

WHERE GOD MOVES
LESSON 10

Daniel clearly exemplifies the reality of the spiritual realm. He prayed to receive revelation knowledge concerning Jeremiah's prophecy, which at the time appeared to not be coming to pass (Dan. 9:2).

And this whole land shall be a desolation, and an astonishment; and these nations shall serve the king of Babylon seventy years.

JEREMIAH 25:11

More than seventy years had already come and gone. However, the Lord showed Daniel later in Daniel 10 that this was really seventy weeks of years (490 years), not seventy years (Dan. 9:24).

So, Daniel asked for this revelation and began to pray.

And I set my face unto the Lord God, to seek by prayer and supplications, with fasting, and sackcloth, and ashes: [4] And I prayed unto the Lord my God, and made my confession, and said…

DANIEL 9:3-4

His prayer continues down through verse 19:

O Lord, hear; O Lord, forgive; O Lord, hearken and do; defer not, for thine own sake, O my God: for thy city and thy people are called by thy name.

THREE MINUTES

And whiles I was speaking, and praying, and confessing my sin and the sin of my people Israel, and presenting my supplication before the Lord my God for the holy mountain of my God; [21] Yea, whiles I was speaking in prayer, even the man Gabriel [the same angel who appeared to Zacharias and Mary in Luke 1:19 and 26-28], whom I had seen in the vision at the beginning, being caused to fly swiftly, touched me about the time of the evening oblation. [22] And he informed me, and talked with me, and said, O Daniel, I am now come forth to give thee skill and understanding.

DANIEL 9:20-22, BRACKETS MINE

It took Daniel about three minutes to pray this prayer (Dan. 9:4-19). While he was still praying, the angel Gabriel showed up and announced, "I've come with your answer." Wouldn't it be wonderful if everything you prayed for manifested itself in three minutes?

Notice when it was that God actually answered:

At the beginning of thy supplications the commandment came forth, and I am come to shew thee; for thou art greatly beloved: therefore understand the matter, and consider the vision.

DANIEL 9:23, EMPHASIS MINE

God moved in the spiritual world and gave the commandment at the very beginning of Daniel's prayer, yet it took approximately three minutes for Gabriel to show up.

WHY NOT INSTANTANEOUS MANIFESTATION?

Most people assume that God doesn't have to deal with such things as time, space, or distance. However, this is a clear biblical example where God gave a command to one of His angels, and it took approximately three minutes for him to show up. That's not a long period of time, but it plainly reveals that God moved in the spiritual realm before there was any physical evidence of it.

Most people believe that when God wills something to happen, the very moment He thinks it—BOOM—there's instantaneous manifestation in the natural realm. They don't think the Lord has to deal with any restrictions or limits. However, this example shows God giving the command and it taking approximately three minutes.

The Bible doesn't explain what was happening during that brief period of time. Maybe Gabriel needed to pack. Maybe he was on the other side of the universe, and it took him three minutes to cover a hundred billion light years. Who knows what was going on? But it establishes the principle that God commanded it in the spirit realm before there was physical manifestation.

Daniel prayed again in Daniel 10. If anything, his heart should have been encouraged and his faith strengthened after receiving such a powerful and relatively quick answer in chapter 9. Although the same man prayed, the results were much different.

DEMONIC OPPOSITION

I like using Daniel as an example of how God answers prayer. If I illustrated this point with an example from my life, you'd be tempted to dismiss it, saying, "Well, Andrew, you're different from me. You must be one of God's favorites. Some people He just responds to better than others." You can't say that about Daniel. This same man prayed and received two totally different results.

This time, it took three weeks—not three minutes—before Daniel saw the manifestation of what he prayed for.

In those days I Daniel was mourning three full weeks. [3] I ate no pleasant bread, neither came flesh nor wine in my mouth, neither did I anoint myself at all, till three whole weeks were fulfilled.

DANIEL 10:2-3

Daniel fasted and prayed again, but the results were worse, not better.

And, behold, an hand touched me, which set me upon my knees and upon the palms of my hands. [11] And he said unto me, O Daniel, a man greatly beloved, understand the words that I speak unto thee, and stand upright: for unto thee am I now sent. And when he had spoken this word unto me, I stood trembling.

DANIEL 10:10-11

Why does God answer some prayers in three minutes and others in three weeks? Have you ever wondered about this? Have you ever seen God do something quickly for you and on other occasions take weeks, months, or even years? Through all that time, you stood, believed, and wondered, *God, why are You doing this? What's taking You so long to answer my prayer?* That's actually an invalid question. The next verse shows why.

Then said he unto me, Fear not, Daniel: for from the first day *that thou didst set thine heart to understand, and to chasten thyself before thy God,* thy words were heard, *and I am come for thy words.*

DANIEL 10:12, EMPHASIS MINE

God gave the command and answered on the very first day, but it didn't manifest until three weeks later. Why? There was demonic opposition.

But the prince of the kingdom of Persia [a demonic power] *withstood me one and twenty days* [three weeks]*: but, lo, Michael, one of the chief princes* [another angel, see Jude 9 and Rev. 12:7]*, came to help me; and I remained there with the kings of Persia.*

DANIEL 10:13, BRACKETS MINE

Three weeks and additional help were required for this angelic messenger to break through the demonic opposition and manifest Daniel's answer.

THINGS THAT HINDER

God moved instantly both times. It wasn't that He answered in three minutes the first time and three weeks the second; God answered Daniel's prayer immediately on both occasions. God wasn't the variable. He didn't change. God remained constant. In the Old Covenant, Daniel was looking forward in faith to what Jesus would do. Today, as New Testament believers, we look back to what God has already done through Christ. It's a done deal.

God doesn't answer some prayers in three minutes and others in three weeks. The Lord answers everything immediately. The supply is already there. It has already been done. The provision was made before you ever had the need. It's not God moving differently for different people. Rather, it's people who receive differently. God has already done His part, but there are things that hinder what He's done in the spiritual realm from coming into the physical world.

Many people wrongly assume that the devil is all-powerful and all-knowing. Functionally, they believe that Satan is more faithful than God! They aren't sure if the Lord will answer their prayers, even if they do everything just right. But they're absolutely convinced that the devil will devour them if they do even one little thing wrong. They think the devil is always there and never misses a trick: "The Enemy's doing this and Satan's doing that. He's saying this and saying that. Blah, blah, blah!"

You need to recognize that there is only one devil, and he's not omnipresent. He can only be in one place at a time. So, for every believer to say that Satan has personally spoken to and tempted us each and every day is absolutely incorrect. Sure, the kingdom of darkness is against us, but we give the devil too much credit. He's not all-powerful. He doesn't always do things right.

It's very possible that the devil missed it in Daniel 9. Perhaps he was out licking his wounds, sulking and pouting, and misjudged how dangerous Daniel was. Maybe Satan was on vacation. Maybe he was tired and sleeping. We give the devil too much recognition. Anyone who fights against God sure isn't bright. I'm not saying he's stupid, just that he misses it sometimes.

THE VARIABLE

So, in Daniel 9, Daniel's prayer got through to God, and Gabriel appeared with the answer in three minutes. Satan wasn't even a factor! But after Daniel received such a powerful revelation and prophesied several important elements concerning the Messiah, the devil marshaled his forces to make sure Daniel didn't pray unopposed ever again.

Satan—not God or Daniel—was the variable. Sometimes he fights us, sometimes he doesn't. I don't know all the reasons for this, but we give the devil way too much credit when we think he's consistent and always does things right. Satan blows it lots of times.

Scripture gives no indication that demons reproduce and have baby demons. Therefore, it's safe to say that the number of evil spirits working on the earth hasn't grown over the centuries and millennia. Either there was a huge number of demons per person back in Adam and Eve's day, or there's a lack of demons today. There are at least six billion people on the planet now. If everyone has a personal demon, then back in the early days, there must have been six billion of them attacking Adam, Eve, and their children. However, if there aren't that many to begin with, then today there's a shortage of demons to go around. Personally, I don't believe the devil can do everything he tries to do. He's not limitless in his ability to fight us. I think Satan just lets some people go because he's shorthanded.

So Daniel, for whatever reason, got his prayer through to God without resistance in Daniel 9, but Satan hindered his prayer in chapter 10. When most believers pray today and don't see their answers immediately manifest, they get mad at God and wonder what's going on. Instead of saying "O God, I've prayed and nothing has happened. When will You answer me?" pray, "Father, I know You are faithful. Thank You for answering me. I know it's almost manifest." Don't lose your faith just because you've been waiting three weeks for the manifestation.

THE BRIDGE

What would have happened if Daniel had moved out of faith and quit praying on the twentieth day in Daniel 10? He easily could have reasoned, *Well, God answered my prayer last time in three minutes. By this time tomorrow, it'll have been three whole weeks. I quit!* If Daniel had done that, his answer wouldn't have manifested. Even though God had already given the commandment and the messenger was on his way, the demonic opposition would have prevailed had Daniel withdrawn his faith.

God does things according to the power that is at work in us (Eph. 3:20). That's why we must believe. Faith is the bridge that God's provision uses to cross out of the spirit realm into the physical. We must provide that bridge. God is a Spirit, and He moves in the spirit world (John 4:24). Whether what's spiritually true ever manifests itself in the natural realm isn't dependent upon God answering our prayers, but upon whether we can—by faith—reach over into the spiritual realm and bring into physical manifestation what He's already done. Our faith provides the bridge for God to cross over into the physical world.

God doesn't do things without us, and we certainly can't do anything without Him. God is the one who must provide something in the first place in the spirit. But then He flows through us to get it into the natural realm. That's an awesome revelation!

AUTHORITY + POWER = RESPONSIBILITY

Daniel persevered in prayer. He may or may not have understood all of these things, but he knew God had his answer and, until it manifested, simply refused to quit. Prior to the angel's arrival and explanation, the Word doesn't indicate that Daniel knew what was happening in the spiritual world as he prayed. From his perspective, it may have seemed like God was totally silent and ignoring him. Yet Daniel persevered and continued praying in faith. However, even if God had shown him that a demonic power was hindering the messenger from bringing his answer, Daniel couldn't have done anything about it. Why? Old Testament saints didn't have any power or authority over the devil.

As a New Testament believer, God has given you authority and power. With that comes responsibility.

Submit yourselves therefore to God. Resist the devil, and he will flee from you.

JAMES 4:7

If you don't resist the devil, he won't flee. It's God's power standing behind you making it work, but nonetheless, the devil flees from *you*. You can't ask God to rebuke the devil for you; He has given that authority to you.

Many Christians today pray and then passively stand and stand and stand in "faith," patiently waiting until finally—maybe—they receive their answers. If they do receive, it's because they're like a dog with a bone. Refusing to let go, they stand there through all of the pain, circumstances, and persecution the devil throws at them. They receive their answers by default because they're still standing after Satan has hurled his worst. These believers simply fail (1) to recognize that the devil is hindering their answers from manifesting and (2) to exercise the power and authority they have been given to do something about it.

As a born-again believer, you don't have to pray the way Old Testament people did. For the sake of illustration, let's say Daniel was born again and had the privileges of a New Testament believer in Daniel 10. After praying and not seeing his answer manifest within three minutes, he could have said, "God, You're the same yesterday, today, and forever (Heb. 13:8). If You gave the commandment at the beginning of my supplication last time, I know You did the same thing this time. You've already answered. Father, I thank You that it's on its way. Since You've already given the command, would You please tell me what's the holdup?"

God would have shown Daniel, "There's demonic opposition against your prayer." Then he could have stood up and rebuked that demonic power. As a born-again believer, Daniel could have taken authority over the devil and commanded him to get out of the way. This would have dramatically shortened the period of time between "amen" (end of prayer) and "there it is" (manifestation). Daniel could have done that as a New Testament believer. As an Old Testament saint, he couldn't. All he could do was stand.

If you understand these principles, you'll have great comfort knowing that God has already done it. He has already commanded your answer, but it must come from the spiritual world into the physical world. There are a number of things that can happen to hinder that. I don't have enough space in this study guide to list everything God has shown me, but I'll be giving you several examples to help illustrate.

WHERE GOD MOVES
LESSON 10 – OUTLINE

I.   Daniel clearly exemplifies the reality of the spiritual realm.

And this whole land shall be a desolation, and an astonishment; and these nations shall serve the king of Babylon seventy years.

JEREMIAH 25:11

And I set my face unto the Lord God, to seek by prayer and supplications, with fasting, and sackcloth, and ashes: [4] And I prayed unto the Lord my God, and made my confession, and said…[19] O Lord, hear; O Lord, forgive; O Lord, hearken and do; defer not, for thine own sake, O my God: for thy city and thy people are called by thy name.

DANIEL 9:3-4 AND 19

And whiles I was speaking, and praying, and confessing my sin and the sin of my people Israel, and presenting my supplication before the Lord my God for the holy mountain of my God; [21] Yea, whiles I was speaking in prayer, even the man Gabriel [the same angel who appeared to Zacharias and Mary in Luke 1:19 and 26-28], whom I had seen in the vision at the beginning, being caused to fly swiftly, touched me about the time of the evening oblation. [22] And he informed me, and talked with me, and said, O Daniel, I am now come forth to give thee skill and understanding.

DANIEL 9:20-22, BRACKETS MINE

A.   It took Daniel about three minutes to pray this prayer (Dan. 9:4-19).

B.   God moved in the spiritual world and gave the commandment at the very beginning of Daniel's prayer, yet it took approximately three minutes for Gabriel to show up.

At the beginning of thy supplications the commandment came forth, and I am come to shew thee; for thou art greatly beloved: therefore understand the matter, and consider the vision.

DANIEL 9:23, EMPHASIS MINE

C.   That's not a long period of time, but it plainly reveals that God moved in the spiritual realm before there was any physical evidence of it.

D.   God commanded it in the spirit realm before there was physical manifestation.

II. Daniel prayed again in Daniel 10.

    A. This time, it took three weeks—not three minutes—before Daniel saw the manifestation of what he prayed for.

In those days I Daniel was mourning three full weeks. [3] I ate no pleasant bread, neither came flesh nor wine in my mouth, neither did I anoint myself at all, till three whole weeks were fulfilled.

DANIEL 10:2-3

And, behold, an hand touched me, which set me upon my knees and upon the palms of my hands. [11] And he said unto me, O Daniel, a man greatly beloved, understand the words that I speak unto thee, and stand upright: for unto thee am I now sent. And when he had spoken this word unto me, I stood trembling.

DANIEL 10:10-11

Then said he unto me, Fear not, Daniel: for from the first day that thou didst set thine heart to understand, and to chasten thyself before thy God, thy words were heard, and I am come for thy words.

DANIEL 10:12, EMPHASIS MINE

    B. God gave the command and answered on the very first day, but it didn't manifest until three weeks later because of demonic opposition.

But the prince of the kingdom of Persia [a demonic power] *withstood me one and twenty days* [three weeks]: *but, lo, Michael, one of the chief princes* [another angel, see Jude 9 and Rev. 12:7], *came to help me; and I remained there with the kings of Persia.*

DANIEL 10:13, BRACKETS MINE

    C. God answered Daniel's prayer immediately on both occasions.

III. Today, as New Testament believers, we look back to what God has already done through Christ.

    A. The provision was made before we ever had the need.

    B. It's not God moving differently for different people; it's people who receive differently.

    C. God has already done His part, but there are things that hinder what He's done in the spiritual realm from coming into the physical world.

IV. God does things according to the power that is at work in us (Eph. 3:20).

    A. Faith is the bridge that God's provision uses to cross out of the spirit realm into the physical.

    B. Whether what's spiritually true ever manifests itself in the natural realm isn't dependent upon God answering our prayers, but upon whether we can—by faith—reach over into the spiritual realm and bring into physical manifestation what He's already done.

    C. God is the one who must provide something in the first place in the spirit, but then He flows through us to get it into the natural realm.

V. As a New Testament believer, God has given you authority and power—with that comes responsibility.

    A. If you don't resist the devil, he won't flee.

Submit yourselves therefore to God. Resist the devil, and he will flee from you.

JAMES 4:7

    B. It's God's power standing behind you making it work, but nonetheless, the devil flees from *you*.

    C. You can't ask God to rebuke the devil for you—He has given that authority to you.

VI. Many Christians today pray and then passively stand and stand and stand in "faith," patiently waiting until finally—maybe—they receive their answers.

    A. These believers simply fail (1) to recognize that the devil is hindering their answers from manifesting and (2) to exercise the power and authority they've been given to do something about it.

    B. As a born-again believer, you don't have to pray the way Old Testament people did.

    C. God has already commanded your answer, but it must come from the spiritual world into the physical world.

    D. There are a number of things that can happen to hinder that.

WHERE GOD MOVES
LESSON 10 – TEACHER'S GUIDE

1.   Daniel clearly exemplifies the reality of the spiritual realm (Jer. 25:11; Dan. 9:3-4, and 19-22). It took Daniel about three minutes to pray this prayer (Dan. 9:4-19). God moved in the spiritual world and gave the commandment at the very beginning of Daniel's prayer, yet it took approximately three minutes for Gabriel to show up (Dan. 9:23). That's not a long period of time, but it plainly reveals that God moved in the spiritual realm before there was any physical evidence of it. God commanded it in the spirit realm before there was physical manifestation.

2.   Daniel prayed again in Daniel 10. This time, it took three weeks—not three minutes—before Daniel saw the manifestation of what he prayed for (Dan. 10:2-3 and 10-12). God gave the command and answered the very first day, but it didn't manifest until three weeks later because of demonic opposition (Dan. 10:13, also see Jude 9 and Rev. 12:7). God answered Daniel's prayer immediately on both occasions.

3.   Today, as New Testament believers, we look back to what God has already done through Christ. The provision was made before we ever had the need. It's not God moving differently for different people; it's people who receive differently. God has already done His part, but there are things that hinder what He's done in the spiritual realm from coming into the physical world.

1. A. Read Jeremiah 25:11 and Daniel 9:3-23. When did God move in the spiritual world and give the commandment? (At the very beginning of Daniel's prayer)
    B. God moved in the spiritual realm before there was any what? (Physical evidence of it)
2. A. Read Daniel 10:2-3 and 10-13. God gave the command and answered on the very first day, but it didn't manifest until when? (Three weeks later)
    B. Why? (Because of demonic opposition)
    C. When did God answer Daniel's prayer on both occasions? (Immediately)
3. A. As New Testament believers today, what do we look back to? (What God has already done through Christ)
    B. There are things that hinder what He's done in the spiritual realm from coming into the physical world, but God has already done what? (His part)

4. God does things according to the power that's at work in us (Eph. 3:20). Faith is the bridge that God's provision uses to cross out of the spirit realm into the physical. Whether what's spiritually true ever manifests itself in the natural realm isn't dependent upon God answering our prayers, but upon whether we can—by faith—reach over into the spiritual realm and bring into physical manifestation what He's already done. God is the one who must provide something in the first place in the spirit, but then He flows through us to get it into the natural realm.

5. As New Testament believers, God has given us authority and power—with that comes responsibility. If we don't resist the devil, he won't flee (James 4:7). It's God's power standing behind us making it work, but nonetheless, the devil flees from *us*. We can't ask God to rebuke the devil for us—He's given that authority to us.

6. Many Christians today pray and then passively stand and stand and stand in "faith," patiently waiting until finally—maybe—they receive their answers. These believers simply fail (1) to recognize that the devil is hindering their answers from manifesting and (2) to exercise the power and authority they've been given to do something about it. As born-again believers, we don't have to pray the way Old Testament people did. God has already commanded our answers, but it must come from the spiritual world into the physical world. There are a number of things that can happen to hinder that.

4. A. Read Ephesians 3:20. How does God do things? (According to the power that's at work in us)
   B. Whether what's spiritually true ever manifests itself in the natural realm isn't dependent upon God answering our prayers, but whether we can what? (By faith—reach over into the spiritual realm and bring into physical manifestation what He's already done)
5. A. Read James 4:7. As New Testament believers, what has God given us? (Authority and power)
   B. What comes with that? (Responsibility)
6. A. What is the first reason many Christians today pray and then passively stand and stand and stand in "faith," patiently waiting until finally—maybe—they receive their answers? (They simply fail to recognize that the devil is hindering their answers from manifesting)
   B. What is the second reason? (They simply fail to exercise the power and authority they've been given to do something about it)
   C. As born-again believers, do we have to pray the way Old Testament people did? (No)

WHERE GOD MOVES
LESSON 10 – DISCIPLESHIP QUESTIONS

1. According to Daniel 9:2, how did Daniel understand Jeremiah's prophecy?

2. According to Jeremiah 25:11, *"this whole land shall be a desolation, and an astonishment, and these nations shall serve the king of Babylon"* for how long?

3. According to Daniel 9:24, what are determined upon the people and the holy city?

4. What for?

   A. To finish the transgression
   B. To make an end of sins
   C. To make reconciliation for iniquity
   D. To bring in everlasting righteousness
   E. To seal up the vision and prophecy
   F. To anoint the most Holy
   G. All of the above
   H. None of the above

5. According to Daniel 9:3-4, Daniel set his face to do what?

6. According to Daniel 9:19-23, who immediately came to Daniel with God's answer?

7. When did Gabriel say that the commandment came forth?

8. What angel was sent to deliver God's messages in Luke 1:19 and 26-28?

9. According to Daniel 10:2-3, how long did Daniel fast and pray the second time?

10. According to Daniel 10:10-13, when was this angelic messenger sent?

11. What took so long?

12. Who came to help this messenger?

13. Who does Jude 9 reveal Michael as?

14. In Revelation 12:7, Michael and his angels fought against whom?

15. Ephesians 3:20 says that God is able to do exceeding abundantly above _____ according to the power that works in us.

16. John 4:24 reveals that God is a _____ and those who worship Him must worship Him in _____ and in truth.

17. James 4:7 tells us to submit to God and _____ the devil.

18. According to Hebrews 13:8, who is the same yesterday, today, and forever?

WHERE GOD MOVES
LESSON 10 – ANSWER KEY

1. By books

2. Seventy years

3. Seventy weeks

4. G. All of the above

5. To seek the Lord by prayer and fasting

6. Gabriel

7. At the beginning of Daniel's supplications

8. Gabriel

9. Three weeks

10. *"From the first day"*

11. The prince of the kingdom of Persia—a demon—withstood him twenty-one days

12. Michael, one of the chief princes

13. The archangel

14. The dragon and his angels

15. All that we ask or think

16. Spirit / spirit

17. Resist

18. Jesus Christ

WHERE GOD MOVES
LESSON 10 – SCRIPTURES

DANIEL 9:2-24

In the first year of his reign I Daniel understood by books the number of the years, whereof the word of the LORD came to Jeremiah the prophet, that he would accomplish seventy years in the desolations of Jerusalem. [3] And I set my face unto the Lord God, to seek by prayer and supplications, with fasting, and sackcloth, and ashes: [4] And I prayed unto the LORD my God, and made my confession, and said, O Lord, the great and dreadful God, keeping the covenant and mercy to them that love him, and to them that keep his commandments; [5] We have sinned, and have committed iniquity, and have done wickedly, and have rebelled, even by departing from thy precepts and from thy judgments: [6] Neither have we hearkened unto thy servants the prophets, which spake in thy name to our kings, our princes, and our fathers, and to all the people of the land. [7] O Lord, righteousness belongeth unto thee, but unto us confusion of faces, as at this day; to the men of Judah, and to the inhabitants of Jerusalem, and unto all Israel, that are near, and that are far off, through all the countries whither thou hast driven them, because of their trespass that they have trespassed against thee. [8] O Lord, to us belongeth confusion of face, to our kings, to our princes, and to our fathers, because we have sinned against thee. [9] To the Lord our God belong mercies and forgivenesses, though we have rebelled against him; [10] Neither have we obeyed the voice of the LORD our God, to walk in his laws, which he set before us by his servants the prophets. [11] Yea, all Israel have transgressed thy law, even by departing, that they might not obey thy voice; therefore the curse is poured upon us, and the oath that is written in the law of Moses the servant of God, because we have sinned against him. [12] And he hath confirmed his words, which he spake against us, and against our judges that judged us, by bringing upon us a great evil: for under the whole heaven hath not been done as hath been done upon Jerusalem. [13] As it is written in the law of Moses, all this evil is come upon us: yet made we not our prayer before the LORD our God, that we might turn from our iniquities, and understand thy truth. [14] Therefore hath the LORD watched upon the evil, and brought it upon us: for the LORD our God is righteous in all his works which he doeth: for we obeyed not his voice. [15] And now, O Lord our God, that hast brought thy people forth out of the land of Egypt with a mighty hand, and hast gotten thee renown, as at this day; we have sinned, we have done wickedly. [16] O Lord, according to all thy righteousness, I beseech thee, let thine anger and thy fury be turned away from thy city Jerusalem, thy holy mountain: because for our sins, and for the iniquities of our fathers, Jerusalem and thy people are become a reproach to all that are about us. [17] Now therefore, O our God, hear the prayer of thy servant, and his supplications, and cause thy face to shine upon thy sanctuary that is desolate, for the Lord's sake. [18] O my God, incline thine ear, and hear; open thine eyes, and behold our desolations, and the city which is called by thy name: for we do not present our supplications before thee for our righteousnesses, but for thy great mercies. [19] O Lord, hear; O Lord, forgive; O Lord, hearken and do; defer not, for thine own sake, O my God: for thy city and thy people are called by thy name. [20] And whiles I was speaking, and praying, and confessing my sin and the sin of my people Israel, and presenting my supplication before the LORD my God for the holy mountain of my God; [21] Yea, whiles I was speaking in prayer, even the man Gabriel, whom I had seen in the vision at the beginning, being caused to fly swiftly, touched me about the time of the evening oblation. [22] And he informed me, and talked with me, and said, O Daniel, I am now come forth to give thee skill and understanding. [23] At the beginning of thy supplications the commandment came forth, and I am come to shew thee; for thou art greatly beloved: therefore understand the matter, and consider the vision. [24] Seventy weeks are determined upon thy people and upon thy holy city, to finish the transgression, and to make an end of sins, and to make reconciliation for iniquity, and to bring in everlasting righteousness, and to seal up the vision and prophecy, and to anoint the most Holy.

JEREMIAH 25:11

And this whole land shall be a desolation, and an astonishment; and these nations shall serve the king of Babylon seventy years.

LUKE 1:19

And the angel answering said unto him, I am Gabriel, that stand in the presence of God; and am sent to speak unto thee, and to show thee these glad tidings.

LUKE 1:26-28

And in the sixth month the angel Gabriel was sent from God unto a city of Galilee, named Nazareth, [27] To a virgin espoused to a man whose name was Joseph, of the house of David; and the virgin's name was Mary. [28] And the angel came in unto her, and said, Hail, thou that art highly favoured, the Lord is with thee: blessed art thou among women.

DANIEL 10:2-3

In those days I Daniel was mourning three full weeks. [3] I ate no pleasant bread, neither came flesh nor wine in my mouth, neither did I anoint myself at all, till three whole weeks were fulfilled.

DANIEL 10:10-13

And, behold, an hand touched me, which set me upon my knees and upon the palms of my hands. [11] And he said unto me, O Daniel, a man greatly beloved, understand the words that I speak unto thee, and stand upright: for unto thee am I now sent. And when he had spoken this word unto me, I stood trembling. [12] Then said he unto me, Fear not, Daniel: for from the first day that thou didst set thine heart to understand, and to chasten thyself before thy God, thy words were heard, and I am come for thy words. [13] But the prince of the kingdom of Persia withstood me one and twenty days: but, lo, Michael, one of the chief princes, came to help me; and I remained there with the kings of Persia.

JUDE 9

Yet Michael the archangel, when contending with the devil he disputed about the body of Moses, durst not bring against him a railing accusation, but said, The Lord rebuke thee.

REVELATION 12:7

And there was war in heaven: Michael and his angels fought against the dragon; and the dragon fought and his angels.

EPHESIANS 3:20

Now unto him that is able to do exceeding abundantly above all that we ask or think, according to the power that worketh in us.

JOHN 4:24

God is a Spirit: and they that worship him must worship him in spirit and in truth.

JAMES 4:7

Submit yourselves therefore to God. Resist the devil, and he will flee from you.

HEBREWS 13:8

Jesus Christ the same yesterday, and to day, and for ever.

THE ANSWER IS IN THE SPIRIT
LESSON 11

Many people pray for provision and then expect God to instantly manifest their answers. If it doesn't happen, then they start doubting and say, "God, why haven't You done anything?" No, the Lord has already done His part. He's already commanded financial blessing upon all believers (Deut. 8:18). God has already given every Christian power, anointing, and the ability to prosper. Psalm 35:27 reveals His delight *"in the prosperity of his servant."* In the spirit, there's abundant supply for every born-again believer (2 Cor. 8:9).

God Himself doesn't give you the money; He gives you power to get wealth, but He doesn't drop the cash in your wallet directly. The Lord gives you an anointing—an ability—and then you must go out and set your hand to something. One of the reasons many Christians who are praying for financial blessing haven't seen it manifest yet is because they think God gives it to them directly. God will bless the work of your hands, but first you have to do something.

GOD'S PROVISION COMES THROUGH PEOPLE

You can hinder what God has already commanded and done in the spirit from manifesting in the physical realm. Many people stay on welfare because they can't make as much money working at McDonald's. So, they do nothing and continue to pray for God to dump provision into their laps. God can't bless and multiply welfare, because you aren't doing anything to get it. But if you'd go out and work at McDonald's—even if you had to take a cut in pay from welfare—God could begin to multiply that. As you work, He can prosper and bring finances to you.

God uses people to bless you.

Give, and it shall be given unto you; good measure, pressed down, and shaken together, and running over, shall men give *into your bosom.*

LUKE 6:38, EMPHASIS MINE

He sends His financial provision to you through people.

Money is an earthly institution. God Himself doesn't use it. In heaven, neither will we. Sure, there are gold, silver, and precious stones in heaven, but they're not used for exchange. Money is a human invention that we use here on earth.

God isn't going to counterfeit your country's currency and give it to you. Money is not going to just rain out of the sky. I heard a man say one time that for anyone who would send him ten dollars, he would mail them a green string. He said that if they put that green string in their wallet, God would use it to create money and they'd never be broke again. That's a trick! It can't happen. God doesn't do those kinds of things; He uses people.

So, when you pray about a financial need, God will use people to help meet that need. It won't just fall out of the sky. If you're looking for your ship to come in but you've never sent one out, you're going to be disappointed. You'll think, *God, why didn't You answer my prayer?* He did! He's blessed you with all spiritual blessings. He's commanded His favor upon you. He's given you power to get wealth. All of these things are real in the spiritual realm, but you need to cooperate in faith.

SOLD!

A friend of mine had his house up for sale "By Owner." He'd put a sign up in his yard but had been unable to sell it for two years. Only a few people had even bothered to look at it. On top of this, the market wasn't that good at the time. Since houses weren't selling, this really became a matter of concern to him.

He heard me teach this message, and the Lord spoke to him, saying, "I moved on someone to buy your house the very first day you put it up for sale, but Satan has been hindering them." It wasn't this man's fault, but demonic opposition had been hindering the manifestation of his answer.

Since my friend didn't know what the situation was, he prayed over it in tongues, believing that God was interceding through him. Two days later, his house sold. While they were going through the closing, the man buying the house told my friend, "The very first day you put that sign in your yard, I told my wife, 'That's our house.' I've been trying for two years now to get my finances together, but I haven't been able to. Then the strangest thing happened. Two days ago, the man who'd been trying to buy my house came over with cash and we closed. It has taken me a day or so to get things together so I could come over here and do this. But here I am!"

God had answered my friend's prayer two years before he saw anything happen. The holdup wasn't the Lord not moving, but Satan who had hindered through other people. If you don't understand this, you'll pray and ask God to sell your house. Then, if it doesn't sell, you'll say, "Lord, why didn't You answer my prayer?" He did. He answers every prayer. It's already done. God has already talked to the people. He has commanded this blessing upon you, but it's in the spiritual realm. By faith, you must bring it out of the spirit and into the physical realm.

BELIEVE IT IS DONE

If you can understand this, it'll make a difference in the way you receive from God. If the manifestation doesn't come right away when I pray for my healing now, I don't say,

"God, I don't know why You haven't healed me, or this other person, yet. But we're asking You to move." I don't start fasting and recruiting other people to bombard heaven with me to plead with God and make Him do it. That whole mindset is unbelief. That would mean I didn't believe I received when I prayed.

> *What things soever ye desire, when ye pray, believe that ye receive them, and ye shall have them.*

MARK 11:24

You must believe you receive the very instant you pray, not when you see it. How can you believe God answered your prayer if you don't feel healed right away? The moment you pray—BOOM—it's already done in the spirit. Your answer is a reality in the spiritual world.

If it doesn't manifest, don't doubt that God has done what His Word said He did. Believe that you received when you prayed. Then continue to pray, not asking for it again, but taking your authority and using it against any demonic powers hindering your answer from coming to pass. Ask God for revelation if there's something you're supposed to do. If you're praying for finances, you might need to get a job or sow some money. But don't doubt that God moved and already did it!

God has already provided everything you need. It's already in the spiritual world. You just need to believe it's done.

BLIND IN ONE EYE

Understanding this principle has revolutionized the way I pray. Not long after the Lord showed me these truths from Daniel 9 and 10, I held a meeting in Childress, Texas. It was 1977, and I preached a message entitled "What to Do When Your Prayers Seem Unanswered." I talked about how God had already done it—that it's not a matter of us waiting for Him to produce healing, but it's already there in the spiritual world. I discussed how faith reaches over into the spirit realm and brings those things into physical manifestation. Therefore, we can control how quickly healing manifests. Since God has already done it, we can make His healing power manifest.

After preaching this message to about a hundred people, I declared, "Let's demonstrate. Is there anyone here who's sick?" A seventeen-year-old boy came forward who was blind in one eye. I laid hands on him, prayed, rebuked everything I knew to do, and commanded him to see. Then I said, "Cover up your good eye and look through the other. How many fingers do I have up?" I held my hand up in front of his face, but he couldn't see anything— not my hand, not light, nothing! There was zero manifestation. I even had to grab his face and turn it toward my hand because he wasn't even looking in the right direction.

When many of the people saw this, they immediately thought, *Well, this doesn't work.* I could feel and hear the moans and groans of unbelief. So, I turned around and addressed the crowd, saying, "Look, I believe what I'm teaching is true. We haven't seen it manifest, but it's not because God hasn't healed him. It's not because we're waiting on God to do something. It's because we're having trouble getting it from the spiritual realm into the physical. It's our fault, not God's! You're welcome to leave if you want to. But if you believe what I taught and would like to stay and pray with me, you're welcome to." About twenty-five stayed.

So, we gathered around this boy and started praying for him. We weren't asking, "O God, You didn't do it the first time. Please heal him now!" Instead, we were saying, "Father, we believe it's true. You've already healed him. Your power has already been released. We bind whatever it is that's keeping this from coming into physical manifestation. Give us wisdom and show us what's going on." We also prayed in tongues in order to build ourselves up in faith, according to Jude 20.

This continued for about half an hour. Every five minutes or so, I'd stop, have this boy cover up his good eye and look through the other one. He still wasn't able to see my hand. I was really seeking God for wisdom!

HEALING OR MIRACLE?

All of a sudden, the Lord said, "He doesn't need a healing; he needs a miracle!" As that impression came to me, my next thought was, *What's the difference?* I'd never considered the difference between the two before. Since then, I've understood some, but it's still an area I'm learning about. However, that was the first time I'd ever thought about it. Outwardly, I was praying away in tongues. Inwardly, I was wondering, *Is this really God? What's the difference between a healing and a miracle? Would that somehow affect the way we're praying?*

Then Don Krow—my associate pastor at the time—spoke up and said, "Andrew, God told me that he doesn't need a healing; he needs a miracle!" It was word for word what the Lord had just spoken to my heart. So, we stopped and I asked this boy, "What's wrong with your eye anyway?"

"When I was a baby, I had an eye infection. They operated on me and surgically removed my lens and retina. I don't even have the necessary parts to be able to see."

As soon as he said that, I replied, "You don't need a healing; you need a miracle! You need God to give you a creative miracle and put those things in there." So, I cupped my hands over his face and declared, "Lens and retina, I command you to come into this eye in Jesus' name!"

Then I had him cover up his good eye and look through the other one. I asked, "How many fingers do I have up?" He answered "1, 2…" and he could see! The Lord had opened his eye!

God had released that power before this boy had ever been born. Through Jesus, it had already been provided and was available in the spirit realm. At the very moment we prayed, God's power was in motion to bring this miracle into physical manifestation. But there were some hindrances.

STICK WITH IT

I still don't understand everything. I'm not sure why I had to receive a revelation that it wasn't a healing but a miracle. I believe that was for me. When Don confirmed it, my faith quickened and surged. That's when I took authority and spoke to the mountain (Mark 11:23). Most people don't speak directly to their problems. Instead, they talk to God about it. The Word says to speak to the mountain.

The problem was that this boy didn't have a lens or retina to be able to see. So, I had to speak to them.

Death and life are in the power of the tongue: and they that love it shall eat the fruit thereof.

PROVERBS 18:21

When all of this happened, my faith quickened, and I commanded the lens and retina to come into his eye. Then he could see!

If we hadn't persisted in prayer, this boy's eye might have never seen. It wouldn't have been because God didn't do it; He had already made the provision, and it was available in the spirit. But most people, if they don't see the manifestation in a certain amount of time, give in to discouragement, doubt, and unbelief.

We do others a disservice when we pray for their healing but let them go before it manifests. I have some very good friends with healing ministries who pray down the line for people and never look back. They refuse to even think about it, because they don't want to slip into unbelief. This works to a degree. Some good things do happen, but that method is fraught with all kinds of problems because most people's faith—without manifestation over time—becomes weaker, not stronger.

LESSON 11 – ADDITIONAL INFORMATION

For more on how these truths apply to prayer specifically, I recommend my teaching entitled *A Better Way to Pray*.

THE ANSWER IS IN THE SPIRIT
LESSON 11 – OUTLINE

I. God has already given every Christian power, anointing, and the ability to prosper (Deut. 8:18).

Let the Lord be magnified, which hath pleasure in the prosperity of his servant.

PSALM 35:27

   A. In the spirit, there's abundant supply for every born-again believer (2 Cor. 8:9).

   B. You can hinder what God has already commanded and done in the spirit from manifesting in the physical realm.

   C. God sends His financial provision to you through people.

Give, and it shall be given unto you; good measure, pressed down, and shaken together, and running over, shall men give *into your bosom.*

LUKE 6:38, EMPHASIS MINE

   D. You need to cooperate in faith.

II. If you can understand this, it'll make a difference in the way you receive from God.

   A. You must believe you receive the very instant you pray, not when you see it.

What things soever ye desire, when ye pray, believe that ye receive them, and ye shall have them.

MARK 11:24

   B. Your answer is a reality in the spiritual world.

   C. If it doesn't manifest, don't doubt that God has done what His Word said He did.

   D. Continue to pray, not asking for it again, but taking your authority and using it against any demonic powers hindering your answer from coming to pass.

   E. Ask God for revelation if there's something you're supposed to do.

III. God has already provided everything you need.

   A. It's already in the spiritual world.

   B. You just need to believe it's done.

IV. Understanding this principle has revolutionized the way I pray.

    A. "He doesn't need a healing; he needs a miracle!"

    B. "When I was a baby, I had an eye infection. They operated on me and surgically removed my lens and retina. I don't even have the necessary parts to be able to see."

    C. So, I cupped my hands over his face and declared, "Lens and retina, I command you to come into this eye in Jesus' name!"

    D. Through Jesus, the power had already been provided and was available in the spirit realm.

    E. At the very moment we prayed, God's power was in motion to bring this miracle into physical manifestation—but there were some hindrances.

V. The Word says to speak to the mountain (Mark 11:23).

Death and life are in the power of the tongue: and they that love it shall eat the fruit thereof.

PROVERBS 18:21

    A. We do others a disservice when we pray for their healing but let them go before it manifests.

    B. Most people's faith—without manifestation over time—becomes weaker, not stronger.

LESSON 11 – ADDITIONAL INFORMATION

For more on how these truths apply to prayer specifically, I recommend my teaching entitled *A Better Way to Pray*.

THE ANSWER IS IN THE SPIRIT
LESSON 11 – TEACHER'S GUIDE

1. God has already given every Christian power, anointing, and the ability to prosper (Deut. 8:18 and Ps. 35:27). In the spirit, there's abundant supply for every born-again believer (2 Cor. 8:9). We can hinder what God has already commanded and done in the spirit from manifesting in the physical realm. God sends His financial provision to us through people (Luke 6:38). We need to cooperate in faith.

2. If we can understand this, it'll make a difference in the way we receive from God. We must believe we receive the very instant we pray, not when we see it (Mark 11:24). Our answers are a reality in the spiritual world. If our answers don't manifest, we shouldn't doubt that God has done what His Word said He did. We should continue to pray, not asking for it again, but taking our authority and using it against any demonic powers hindering our answers from coming to pass. We need to ask God for revelation if there's something we're supposed to do.

3. God has already provided everything we need. It's already in the spiritual world. We just need to believe it's done.

4. Understanding this principle will revolutionize the way we pray. Through Jesus, the power has already been provided and is available in the spirit realm. At the very moment we pray, God's power is in motion to bring the provision, healing, and/or miracle into physical manifestation—but there may be some hindrances.

1. A. Read Deuteronomy 8:18, Psalm 35:27, 2 Corinthians 8:9, and Luke 6:38. What has God already given every Christian? (Power, anointing, and the ability to prosper)
    B. Can we hinder what God has already commanded and done in the spirit from manifesting in the physical realm? (Yes)
    C. How does God send His financial provision to us? (Through people)
2. A. Read Mark 11:24. When must we believe we receive? (The very instant we pray, not when we see it)
    B. What should we do if it doesn't manifest? (We shouldn't doubt that God has done what His Word said He did, but we should continue to pray, not asking for it again, but taking our authority and using it against any demonic powers hindering our answers from coming to pass, and we need to ask God for revelation if there's something we're supposed to do)
3. A. What has God provided? (Everything we need)
    B. Where is it? (Already in the spiritual world)
    C. What do we just need to believe? (It's done)
4. A. How has the power already been provided and available in the spirit realm? (Through Jesus)
    B. At the very moment we pray, God's power is in motion to what? (Bring the provision, healing, and/or miracle into physical manifestation)

5.   The Word says to speak to the mountain (Mark 11:23 and Prov. 18:21). We do others a disservice when we pray for their healing but let them go before it's manifest. Most people's faith—without manifestation over time—becomes weaker, not stronger.

5. A. Read Mark 11:23 and Proverbs 18:21. What does the Word say we are to speak to? (The mountain)
    B. Without manifestation over time, does most people's faith become weaker or stronger? (Weaker)

THE ANSWER IS IN THE SPIRIT
LESSON 11 – DISCIPLESHIP QUESTIONS

1.   Deuteronomy 8:18 tells us to remember whom?

2.   It is the Lord our God who gives us power to get what?

3.   For what purpose?

4.   Read Psalm 35:27. We are to shout for joy and be glad that the Lord has _____.

5.   According to 2 Corinthians 8:9, though Jesus was rich, yet for our sakes, He became poor so that we, through His poverty, might be what?

6.   According to Luke 6:38, when we give, how will it be given back to us?

    A.   Good measure
    B.   Pressed down
    C.   Shaken together
    D.   Running over
    E.   All of the above
    F.   None of the above

7.   In Mark 11:23-24, who is able to say unto this mountain?

8.   In our hearts, we shall not what?

9.   But in our hearts, we shall what?

10.   What shall we believe?

11.   What shall we have?

12.   What should we believe about the things we desire when we pray?

13.   And we shall what?

14.   According to Jude 20, when we pray in the Holy Ghost, we are building ourselves up on _____.

15.   According to Proverbs 18:21, both death and life are in the power of the what?

16.   What shall they that love it eat?

THE ANSWER IS IN THE SPIRIT
LESSON 11 – ANSWER KEY

1. The Lord our God

2. Wealth

3. That He may establish His covenant

4. Pleasure in the prosperity of His servant

5. Rich

6. E.   All of the above

7. Whosoever

8. Doubt

9. Believe

10. That those things we say shall come to pass

11. Whatsoever we say

12. That we receive them

13. Have them

14. Our most holy faith

15. Tongue

16. The fruit thereof

THE ANSWER IS IN THE SPIRIT
LESSON 11 – SCRIPTURES

DEUTERONOMY 8:18
But thou shalt remember the LORD thy God: for it is he that giveth thee power to get wealth, that he may establish his covenant which he sware unto thy fathers, as it is this day.

PSALM 35:27
Let them shout for joy, and be glad, that favour my righteous cause: yea, let them say continually, Let the LORD be magnified, which hath pleasure in the prosperity of his servant.

2 CORINTHIANS 8:9
For ye know the grace of our Lord Jesus Christ, that, though he was rich, yet for your sakes he became poor, that ye through his poverty might be rich.

LUKE 6:38
Give, and it shall be given unto you; good measure, pressed down, and shaken together, and running over, shall men give into your bosom. For with the same measure that ye mete withal it shall be measured to you again.

MARK 11:23-24
For verily I say unto you, That whosoever shall say unto this mountain, Be thou removed, and be thou cast into the sea; and shall not doubt in his heart, but shall believe that those things which he saith shall come to pass; he shall have whatsoever he saith. [24] Therefore I say unto you, What things soever ye desire, when ye pray, believe that ye receive them, and ye shall have them.

JUDE 20
But ye, beloved, building up yourselves on your most holy faith, praying in the Holy Ghost.

PROVERBS 18:21
Death and life are in the power of the tongue: and they that love it shall eat the fruit thereof.

GOD HAS ALREADY PROVIDED
LESSON 12

God has already done it. He has already provided everything we will ever need. It is already a done deal. As soon as we believe and begin learning how His power works, we can make things manifest.

Many of the greatest healing evangelists understood this concept. They might not have taught it from the same scriptures or expressed it in the same terminology, but they believed it.

John G. Lake had over 100,000 confirmed, documented cases of healing. They actually closed down a hospital in Spokane, Washington, for a period of time because so few people needed their services. He and his "healing technicians" were that effective!

Since Lake had such a fruitful ministry, we ought to consider his opinion. He felt that the main reason people didn't see healing manifest in their lives was passivity in receiving. They would pray, ask, and then passively wait on God to heal them, not understanding that He'd already done it. Instead of taking their authority and commanding healing into manifestation now, they let it drag out over days, weeks, months, and years. They didn't understand how to believe God and make what He had already done in the spirit come into the physical world. In John G. Lake's estimation, that was the number one problem.

God has already done it. Believe it is already provided, and then receive it by faith. If you don't immediately see the physical manifestation of what you prayed for, then you need to get in and start battling your own unbelief. Receive wisdom if there's something you need to do. If demonic power is involved, break it. But the Scripture clearly establishes the principle that God has already done it.

ATMOSPHERE OF UNBELIEF

Jesus operated in this same understanding.

And he [Jesus] cometh to Bethsaida; and they bring a blind man unto him, and besought him to touch him. [23] And he took the blind man by the hand, and led him out of the town; and when he had spit on his eyes, and put his hands upon him, he asked him if he saw ought. [24] And he looked up, and said, I see men as trees, walking. [25] After that he put his hands again upon his eyes, and made him look up: and he was restored, and saw every man clearly. [26] And he sent him away to his house, saying, Neither go into the town, nor tell it to any in the town.

MARK 8:22-26, BRACKETS MINE

This is an unusual example of healing. It's the only time in Scripture where Jesus asked a person something like "How is it?" after He prayed for them. It's also the only time He ever prayed for a physical need a second time. So, this was a very unique situation.

Notice, first of all, that Jesus was in Bethsaida. He took the blind man by the hand and led him out of the town. Some think Jesus did weird things just to keep people off balance. They say, "You can never figure God out. He's got no rhyme or reason. He just delights in doing things in unusual ways." Not true! This was the Creator of the universe in all its meticulous detail. Everything is perfect and works together in harmony. You can predict where the stars will be a million years from now—should the Lord tarry—or ten thousand years ago because it's so ordered. It's absurd to think that the God of order Himself would do things in a completely random manner. It's simply not true.

Jesus led this man out of the town because Bethsaida was one of the worst places He had ever been!

Woe unto thee, Bethsaida! for if the mighty works had been done in Tyre and Sidon, which have been done in you, they had a great while ago repented, sitting in sackcloth and ashes.

LUKE 10:13

Jesus pronounced judgment upon Bethsaida because of all its unbelief. The Lord encountered this in His own hometown of Nazareth too.

And he could there do no mighty work, save that he laid his hands upon a few sick folk, and healed them. [6] And he marvelled because of their unbelief.

MARK 6:5-6

Jesus wanted to do more in those places, but couldn't. These people weren't in faith, so He couldn't pray for them other than for a few minor things.

Jesus operated in faith 100 percent, so we know that there was no problem with Him. But there must be some degree of faith on the part of those receiving. Now, I believe that's been blown way out of proportion. We sometimes use this as an excuse to put all the blame on the person receiving if the healing doesn't manifest. That's too simplistic. More often than not, it's the fault of the person praying as much as it is the person receiving. However, with all that being said, it's still true that there must be some degree of faith operating in the person receiving the healing.

"HOW IS IT?"

Knowing that, Jesus took this blind man by the hand and led him out of the town. The Lord was busy—infinitely more than I am. If you need healing today, I can't come pray for you. I don't have time to take you by the hand and walk you an hour out into the countryside to pray. Jesus wasn't just taking a stroll. His purpose was to get this man away from the unbelief in Bethsaida, knowing that it could hinder God's power from manifesting his healing.

However, even though Jesus got this man out of town, He perceived that He hadn't gotten all of the town out of the man. He discerned that this man was still being affected by the atmosphere of unbelief. So, after He prayed for him, He asked, "What do you see?"

Now, Jesus wasn't asking, "Did God answer My prayer? Did anything happen?" No, that would have been unbelief. The Word says you must believe you receive when you pray. For Jesus to have asked "Did it work?" would have violated His own teaching. The Lord knew that God had moved. He knew God's power was present, but it was in the spirit realm and needed to come into the physical. Jesus was aware that the unbelief of that town and the effect it had on that man was hindering an instantaneous, full manifestation of what God had already done.

So, Jesus asked, "How is it?" The man answered, *"I see men as trees, walking"* (Mark 8:24). In other words, God's power had manifested to a degree. The man had been totally blind before, but after Jesus prayed, he could see a little bit. So, Jesus did something unusual again. He laid hands on him and prayed a second time.

"But it's unbelief to pray for something twice!" It is if you *ask* twice. Then at least one of the two times, you prayed in unbelief. You must believe you receive when you pray. However, it's not unbelief to continue to pray, taking your authority and making what He's already provided manifest.

CONFRONT HINDRANCES HEAD-ON!

It's not wrong to continue to pray if you understand that God has already released His power. In the spirit realm, it's complete. But you don't want it to just stay in the spirit; you want it manifest in the physical. So, you pray again, not doubting that God has already given, but to rebuke the devil. You pray to receive wisdom and revelation in case there's something you must do. You pray to build up your faith and encourage yourself. Instead of just praying once and then trying to forget it, you are aggressively releasing your faith to deal with any hindrance and draw the provision into the physical realm.

Jesus confronted the hindrances head-on. He didn't doubt His Father's faithfulness, but He doubted this man's faithfulness—that the unbelief of this town was still hindering him from receiving. So, He asked the man this question and saw that there was still some delay in the manifestation. Instead of just letting him go, Jesus kept ministering to him until he received the full healing. It's much easier to keep something you've already got than to get something you don't yet have.

So, Jesus prayed for the man a second time. If Satan, unbelief, or whatever the hindrance is can withstand one dose of the Holy Ghost, shoot 'em again! Just hit 'em again with the same power. That time, the man received his healing and saw every man clearly.

Then Jesus told him not to go into the town or tell it to anyone there. He instructed the man to go home, but where do you think he lived? This man may have had a job, family, and friends. Yet Jesus commanded him not to tell anybody or to go back into Bethsaida. That's a pretty strict requirement! Why? Jesus knew that even though this man had received the manifestation of healing, he could still lose it if he immediately got back around all of that unbelief.

Retention of your healing isn't automatically guaranteed. Jesus warned the man who had been healed at the pool of Bethesda, *"Sin no more, lest a worse thing come unto thee"* (John 5:14). The devil comes *"to steal, and to kill, and to destroy"* (John 10:10). There's nothing he'd like better than to take away your manifestation, kill your faith, and destroy your testimony. You must maintain your healing by faith. That's why Jesus told the man not to go back into that unbelieving situation.

Jesus knew that God had healed this man completely. It was already done. But He recognized that there was a hindrance to getting it from the spiritual into the physical, so the Lord prayed with him a second time in order to get this man over that hindrance. Then He told him how to keep the healing he'd received.

I often encounter this same thing. People come to my meetings, and we help them manifest a healing. Then they go back into unbelieving churches and submit themselves to a teaching that is totally opposite what they receive from me. Their sickness or disease returns, and then they come back to me the next time I'm in town and ask, "What happened?" It's not God who took the healing away or put sickness back on them; they quit believing. They didn't have any root in themselves and so only endured for a season (Mark 4:17).

COOPERATE & COMMAND

God has already done everything. You're already blessed, healed, and prosperous. You already have joy, peace, and wisdom. Everything you could ever need is already there—in the spirit. All you need to do is believe and receive.

If you don't see the manifestation immediately, don't doubt that God has already done it; recognize that He is a Spirit and that He moves in the spirit realm (John 4:24). For what He's done—what's already true in the spirit—to manifest in the physical realm, it requires the cooperation of some physical human being. Faith is the bridge that God's provision crosses over, out of the spirit and into the physical. Sometimes it takes a period of time to build yourself up in faith to the point where you can receive, but it doesn't take God any time to be ready to give, because He's already provided.

Sometimes it's demonic opposition that hinders what God has already done from coming into manifestation. Sometimes other people are involved in our answers to prayer. Therefore, we must receive wisdom about how Satan is hindering so that we can speak to the mountain and command it to be removed.

You need to learn and cooperate with the laws of God. You resist the devil. You speak directly to the problem. You exercise the authority and power God has given you. It is important to direct your prayers properly in order to receive your desired results. God has already done it, but it's your responsibility to believe and draw His provision into the natural realm. As soon as you can get yourself into faith and learn how to do this, you can manifest what God has already done.

Instead of being a beggar, a pleader, a whiner, and a griper, you will become a commander. You'll believe what God has said He has done, and you'll take your authority and begin commanding it to manifest. Instead of just praying for healing, you will command healing. Instead of just praying for blessing, you will command blessing. That's a huge difference!

BE A BRIDGE

You need to understand that there is a real spiritual world. Through the window of God's Word, you can see and accurately perceive the spirit realm. As you discover and meditate on what other people did and what was going on behind the scenes, you can be confident that the same thing is going on around you today. Even though you can't see it or feel it with your physical senses, you can perceive it with the eyes of your heart.

Renew your mind to God's Word, and allow yourself to become a bridge that He can flow through from the spiritual realm into this physical world.

GOD HAS ALREADY PROVIDED
LESSON 12 – OUTLINE

I.   God has already done it—everything we will ever need is already a done deal.

    A.   As soon as we believe and begin learning how His power works, we can make things manifest.

    B.   If you don't immediately see the physical manifestation of what you prayed for, then you need to get in and start battling your own unbelief.

    C.   Receive wisdom if there's something you need to do.

    D.   If a demonic power is involved, break it.

    E.   But the Scripture clearly establishes the principle that God has already done it.

II. Jesus operated in this same understanding.

And he [Jesus] cometh to Bethsaida; and they bring a blind man unto him, and besought him to touch him. [23] And he took the blind man by the hand, and led him out of the town; and when he had spit on his eyes, and put his hands upon him, he asked him if he saw ought. [24] And he looked up, and said, I see men as trees, walking. [25] After that he put his hands again upon his eyes, and made him look up: and he was restored, and saw every man clearly. [26] And he sent him away to his house, saying, Neither go into the town, nor tell it to any in the town.

MARK 8:22-26, BRACKETS MINE

    A.   Jesus led this man out of the town because Bethsaida was one of the worst places He had ever been!

Woe unto thee, Bethsaida! for if the mighty works had been done in Tyre and Sidon, which have been done in you, they had a great while ago repented, sitting in sackcloth and ashes.

LUKE 10:13

And he could there [His own hometown of Nazareth] do no mighty work, save that he laid his hands upon a few sick folk, and healed them. [6] And he marvelled because of their unbelief.

MARK 6:5-6, BRACKETS MINE

B. Jesus' purpose was to get this man away from the unbelief in Bethsaida, knowing that it could hinder God's power from manifesting his healing.

C. So, after Jesus prayed for him, He asked, "What do you see?"

D. Jesus was aware that the unbelief of that town and the effect it had on that man was hindering an instantaneous, full manifestation of what God had already done.

I see men as trees, walking.

MARK 8:24

E. It's not unbelief to continue to pray, taking your authority and making what He's already provided manifest.

III. Jesus confronted hindrances head-on.

A. Jesus knew that God had healed this man completely.

B. But Jesus recognized that there was a hindrance to getting it from the spiritual into the physical, so the Lord prayed with him a second time in order to get this man over that hindrance.

C. Then Jesus told him how to keep the healing he'd received.

IV. Everything you could ever need is already there—in the spirit.

A. For what God's done—what's already true in the spirit—to manifest in the physical realm, it requires the cooperation of some physical human being.

B. Sometimes it takes a period of time to build yourself up in faith to the point where you can receive, but it doesn't take God any time to be ready to give, because He's already provided.

C. You must receive wisdom about how Satan is hindering so that you can speak to the mountain and command it to be removed.

D. You need to learn and cooperate with the laws of God.

E. As soon as you can get yourself into faith and learn how to do this, you can manifest what God has already done.

F. Renew your mind to God's Word, and allow yourself to become a bridge that He can flow through from the spiritual realm into this physical world.

GOD HAS ALREADY PROVIDED
LESSON 12 – TEACHER'S GUIDE

1.   God has already done it—everything we will ever need is already a done deal. As soon as we believe and begin learning how His power works, we can make things manifest. If we don't immediately see the physical manifestation of what we prayed for, then we need to get in and start battling our own unbelief. We need to receive wisdom if there's something we need to do. If a demonic power is involved, we need to break it. But the Scripture clearly establishes the principle that God has already done it.

2.   Jesus operated in this same understanding (Mark 8:22-26). He led this man out of the town because Bethsaida was one of the worst places He had ever been (Luke 10:13 and Mark 6:5-6)! His purpose was to get this man away from the unbelief in Bethsaida, knowing that it could hinder God's power from manifesting his healing. So, after He prayed for him, He asked, "What do you see?" Jesus was aware that the unbelief of that town and the effect it had on the man was hindering an instantaneous, full manifestation of what God had already done (Mark 8:24). It's not unbelief to continue to pray, taking our authority and making what He's already provided manifest.

3.   Jesus confronted hindrances head-on. He knew that God had healed this man completely. But He recognized that there was a hindrance to getting it from the spiritual into the physical, so the Lord prayed with him a second time in order to get this man over that hindrance. Then He told him how to keep the healing he'd received.

1. A.   When can we make things manifest? (As soon as we believe and begin learning how God's power works)
   B.   What should we do if we don't immediately see the physical manifestation of what we prayed for? (Start battling our own unbelief, receive wisdom if there's something we need to do, and if a demonic power is involved—break it)
2. A.   Read Mark 8:22-26, Luke 10:13, and Mark 6:5-6. What was Jesus aware of that was hindering an instantaneous, full manifestation of what God had already done? (The unbelief of that town and the effect it had on the man)
   B.   Is it unbelief to continue to pray, taking our authority and making what He's already provided manifest? (No)
3. A.   What did Jesus do with hindrances? (He confronted them head-on)
   B.   Why did the Lord pray with this man a second time? (In order to get the man over that hindrance)

4.   Everything we could ever need is already there—in the spirit. For what God's done—what's already true in the spirit—to manifest in the physical realm, it requires the cooperation of some physical human being. Sometimes it takes us a period of time to build ourselves up in faith to the point where we can receive, but it doesn't take God any time to be ready to give, because He's already provided. We must receive wisdom about how Satan is hindering so that we can speak to the mountain and command it to be removed. We need to learn and cooperate with the laws of God. As soon as we can get ourselves into faith and learn how to do this, we can manifest what God has already done. Let's renew our minds to God's Word and allow ourselves to become bridges that He can flow through from the spiritual realm into this physical world.

4. A.   Sometimes it takes us a period of time to build ourselves up in faith to the point where we can receive, but does it take God any time to be ready to give? (No, because He's already provided)

   B.   What must we receive wisdom about so we can speak to the mountain and command it to be removed? (How Satan is hindering)

   C.   What do we need to learn and cooperate with? (The laws of God)

GOD HAS ALREADY PROVIDED
LESSON 12 – DISCIPLESHIP QUESTIONS

1. When Jesus came to Bethsaida in Mark 8:22-26, what kind of man did they bring unto Him?

2. Jesus took him by the hand and led him where?

3. When Jesus had spit on his eyes and put His hands upon him, what did He ask him?

4. What was the man's reply?

5. Then Jesus put His hands again upon his eyes and made him do what?

6. He was restored and saw every man how?

7. Jesus sent him away where?

8. With what instructions?

9. According to Luke 10:13, how would Tyre and Sidon have responded if those same things had been done in them?

10. In Mark 6:5-6, Jesus could there do no what?

11. Jesus laid His hands upon whom and healed them?

12. Why did Jesus marvel?

13. In John 5:14, what did Jesus tell the man?

14. According to John 10:10, who comes only to steal, kill, and destroy?

15. Who came to give us abundant life?

16. How long does Mark 4:17 reveal that those who have no root in themselves endure?

17. What will arise for the Word's sake?

18. When are they offended?

19. According to John 4:24, who is a Spirit?

GOD HAS ALREADY PROVIDED
LESSON 12 – ANSWER KEY

1. A blind man

2. Out of the town

3. If he saw anything

4. *"I see men as trees, walking"*

5. Look up

6. Clearly

7. To his house

8. *"Neither go into the town, nor tell it to any in the town"*

9. *"They had a great while ago repented"*

10. Mighty work

11. A few sick folk

12. Because of their unbelief

13. *"Behold, thou art made whole: sin no more, lest a worse thing come unto thee"*

14. The thief

15. Jesus

16. For a time

17. Affliction and persecution

18. Immediately

19. God

GOD HAS ALREADY PROVIDED
LESSON 12 – SCRIPTURES

MARK 8:22-26

And he cometh to Bethsaida; and they bring a blind man unto him, and besought him to touch him. [23] And he took the blind man by the hand, and led him out of the town; and when he had spit on his eyes, and put his hands upon him, he asked him if he saw ought. [24] And he looked up, and said, I see men as trees, walking. [25] After that he put his hands again upon his eyes, and made him look up: and he was restored, and saw every man clearly. [26] And he sent him away to his house, saying, Neither go into the town nor tell it to any in the town.

LUKE 10:13

Woe unto thee, Chorazin! woe unto thee, Bethsaida! for if the mighty works had been done in Tyre and Sidon, which have been done in you, they had a great while ago repented, sitting in sackcloth and ashes.

MARK 6:5-6

And he could there do no mighty work, save that he laid his hands upon a few sick folk, and healed them. [6] And he marvelled because of their unbelief. And he went round about the villages, teaching.

JOHN 5:14

Afterward Jesus findeth him in the temple, and said unto him, Behold, thou art made whole: sin no more, lest a worse thing come unto thee.

JOHN 10:10

The thief cometh not, but for to steal, and to kill, and to destroy: I am come that they might have life, and that they might have it more abundantly.

MARK 4:17

And have no root in themselves, and so endure but for a time: afterward, when affliction or persecution ariseth for the word's sake, immediately they are offended.

JOHN 4:24

God is a Spirit: and they that worship him must worship him in spirit and in truth.

THE BATTLEFIELD
LESSON 13

God is a Spirit, and He moves in the spiritual world (John 4:24). Everything God has provided—by grace—is already a reality in the spiritual realm. But whether or not it ever manifests in the physical realm depends on our ability to receive—not on God's giving.

There are things we can do to shorten the manifestation time. There are also things we can do to lengthen it. Dealing with the devil and overcoming his hindrances to the manifestation of what God has already provided is popularly called "spiritual warfare." Since there has been such a large emphasis on this in recent times, these next few lessons may possibly be the most controversial of this entire study.

SPIRITUAL WARFARE

Satan does exist. There is evil in this world. Demonic forces are fighting against God and His kingdom. Prior to the last couple of decades, most of the body of Christ had been ignorant of Satan's devices. Many believed that all the devils were over in Africa or some other undeveloped part of the world. But they didn't believe that any of the Western, developed, "civilized" countries had any such thing as demonic activity. In the past twenty-plus years, that notion has been thoroughly shattered, especially among charismatic Christians. There still may be some evangelicals and mainline denominational folks who are unaware, but not very many.

Anyone who truly believes the Word of God has to acknowledge that Satan is a real foe. The devil tempted Jesus and opposed Him during His entire ministry. The Bible records many instances where the Lord healed people by casting out demons.

God anointed Jesus of Nazareth with the Holy Ghost and with power: who went about doing good, and healing all that were oppressed of the devil; for God was with him.

ACTS 10:38

God's Word is very clear that sickness and disease are oppressions from the devil.

Overall, it has been good for Christians to recognize the fact that Satan exists and that his demonic powers are active today. However, in the process, much of the body of Christ has swung from ignorance to a very weird extreme. That's why many "spiritual warfare" teachings and practices today actually credit the devil with abilities and powers he doesn't really have.

Satan is a factor. He does hinder what God has already done in the spiritual realm from manifesting in the physical realm. It is important to learn how to resist the devil and take authority over him. But I want to make it crystal clear that Satan is a defeated foe. The only reason he is able to do anything is because of our own ignorance, unbelief, and fear. Although the body of Christ today has come to an awareness of the devil's existence, it has remained, for the most part, functionally ignorant of Satan's true devices (2 Cor. 2:11).

BETWEEN YOUR EARS

Again, the book of Ephesians was written from the standpoint that everything has already been done. It's just a matter now of possessing what God has already provided, not trying to get Him to give us something new. With this in mind, let's look at how Paul wound this letter down in the last chapter:

Finally, my brethren, be strong in the Lord, and in the power of his might. [11] Put on the whole armour of God, that ye may be able to stand against the wiles of the devil. [12] For we wrestle not against flesh and blood, but against principalities, against powers, against the rulers of the darkness of this world, against spiritual wickedness in high places.

EPHESIANS 6:10-12

These verses make it very clear that we are in a battle—and those who don't believe it are destined to lose.

However, the battle is between your ears. It's not out there somewhere in the "heavenly places"; it's in your mind.

Now, before you take offense, I encourage you to go ahead and fully consider what I'm saying. See the scriptures for yourself, and then draw your conclusions from the Word, not just current teaching and popular examples being promoted in the body of Christ today.

We are in a battle, but it's not out there in the heavenly places. We are fighting demonic powers—and they do exist in heavenly places—but the battlefield (place of engagement) is our minds.

DECEPTION & LIES

Notice Ephesians 6:11:

Put on the whole armour of God, that ye may be able to stand against the wiles of the devil.

Wiles are lies, cunningness, and craftiness. All of these words imply that Satan's only power is deception. He doesn't have actual power of his own to force anyone to do anything.

We must surrender ourselves to him first. Therefore, the devil is really a non-factor to those who know and understand the truth.

I'll be establishing this with many other scriptures, but allow me to make some additional statements first. Again, I challenge you to follow through until I get to the verses that verify these things. Don't just tune this out because it's contrary to "popular theology" today. As a believer in Christ, you need to understand the truth.

Satan is an absolutely defeated foe. He has zero power to do anything. All he can do is try to deceive you through wiles, cunningness, craftiness, and lies and then use against you the very power you surrender to him. That's why ignorance is so expensive. The devil's goal is to keep you ignorant of the truth and believing his lies.

After soundly rebuking the Corinthians for falling into all kinds of weird things, Paul confided,

I fear, lest by any means, as the serpent beguiled *Eve through his* subtilty, *so your minds should be* corrupted *from the simplicity that is in Christ.*

2 CORINTHIANS 11:3, EMPHASIS MINE

Notice all the words denoting deceptive practices: *"beguiled," "subtilty,"* and *"corrupted."* Satan comes against us by trying to corrupt our minds from the simplicity that's in Christ. In other words, he tries to make us think that the Gospel is harder than it really is.

TEMPTED

In Genesis, why didn't the devil choose a tiger instead of a serpent? He could have intimidated Eve with a roar or two. Why didn't he have a woolly mammoth just stick its foot on top of her head and demand, "Eat this fruit or I'll crush your skull"? Why did Satan choose the serpent—the craftiest animal on the face of the earth—to come against Eve? Because the devil knew he had absolutely no power to force or intimidate Adam or Eve into anything. He had to deceive them instead (Gen. 3:1).

Satan started the deception by asking, "Has God really said...?" (Gen. 3:1). He challenged the Word of God. It's the truth of God's Word that enables us to seek God, yield to Him, and resist the devil. If Satan hadn't challenged the Word and gotten them to question and second-guess it, his temptation would've gone nowhere. The serpent didn't come to force or intimidate, but to deceive.

Satan tempted Adam and Eve with something they already had. He asked, "Don't you want to be like God?" The truth was, they were already like Him. In fact, they were more like God before they ate of the fruit of the Tree of the Knowledge of Good and Evil than they were afterward.

The devil says, "Oh, sure, God loves the world. But what makes you think He loves *you*?" Then he gets you into emotions and trying to discern in some physical, natural way whether or not God loves you. There you are on the devil's turf in the physical realm, not understanding from God's Word that in the spiritual realm, it's already done. Because you don't feel loved and you don't have any goose bumps, you pray "O God, please pour out Your love in my life," which is actually a prayer of unbelief.

Satan loves to hinder people from coming to the Lord, but his only "power" is deception and lies. The devil can't keep you from doing anything. If he could, he would have kept you from being born again. You were at your worst and your weakest. You hadn't been going to church, fasting, praying, studying the Word, tithing, or living right. You might even have been an adulterer, a dope addict, mean, selfish, etc. Yet in that dismal state, you called out and received the greatest miracle of all—the new birth. If Satan were really as powerful as he claims to be, then he would have kept you from receiving salvation. Instead, all he can do is taunt you immediately afterward, saying, "You didn't get it, you didn't get it!" But he can't stop you from doing anything. Satan can't do anything to you without your consent and cooperation.

The devil would rather you not be born again, but now that you're saved, the next best thing is to persuade you to say, "Oh, sure, God can do these things, but He hasn't done them yet." Satan loves that!

DON'T FALL ON YOUR CAN

I remember playing tug-of-war as a kid. There would be two teams pulling on opposite ends of a long rope over a large mud hole. As a boy, my team and I tried our best to pull the other side into the mud. However, if we saw them winning—and that mud pit drawing nearer—we'd just let go of the rope. We might not have won, but at least the other team fell on their cans doing it!

Satan does the same thing today. If he can't prevent you from winning, he'll shift gears to catch you off-guard and make you fall down on your can. Basically, he comes to believers and says, "If you're really such a great Christian, why don't you have this and do that?" The devil will condemn you over what you don't have and try to keep you focused on just the physical realm.

But the truth is, in the spirit, you already have everything. The key to seeing what you have in the spirit manifest in your life is believing and acknowledging it.

That the communication of thy faith may become effectual by the acknowledging of every good thing which is in you in Christ Jesus.

PHILEMON 6

The way you get your faith to work is by starting to acknowledge the good things in you in Christ.

However, most Christians say, "There isn't any good thing in me!" and point to Romans 7.

For I know that in me (that is, in my flesh,) *dwelleth no good thing.*

ROMANS 7:18, EMPHASIS MINE

You need to understand the parentheses to properly interpret this verse. This wouldn't have been a true statement had Paul left out *"that is, in my flesh,"* because in him dwelt God Himself—and everything God is and had given him—which is good. But Paul specified his flesh—his physical, carnal, natural, not-born-again self. It's fine for Christians to understand that in their flesh—apart from Christ—they are nothing. But in Christ, they can do all things and much good dwells within them. To live in victory, you need to be focused on who you are in Christ. Satan aims his warfare here. He specifically targets your understanding and acknowledging of who you are and what you have in Christ. All he has are lies and deception. The devil doesn't have any more power to make you fail in any area of your life than he had to make Adam and Eve fail. He has to deceive you.

COMPLETE IN CHRIST

If you were the devil trying to deceive Adam and Eve, how would you do it? They had never sinned, never had any kind of problems, and lived in paradise with plenty of food. Basically, they were perfect people living perfect lives in a perfect place. How do you tempt someone like that?

He couldn't tempt them with money; there was no such thing. Every need was abundantly supplied. He couldn't tempt them with adultery; there wasn't anyone else to commit adultery with. He couldn't tempt them with hurt, pain, and bitterness over past experiences; there was nothing in them that depression or discouragement could latch on to. Perfect people living in a perfect place couldn't be tempted by money, sex, power, glory, etc. What could they be tempted with?

Satan lied to them by saying, "You don't have it all. As good as this is, there's more!" The truth is, they did have it all. But the devil enticed them to speculate about what might be, what could be. Through that, he caused perfect people living perfect lives in a perfect place to fall.

Adam and Eve threw it all away because a talking snake convinced them that they didn't have enough. Most people today would give anything to live in such a perfect situation. If you could convince perfect people living in paradise with no physical problems whatsoever to think they didn't have it all, to doubt God's Word, and to question His goodness, then I guarantee that you can convince people living in a fallen world that they don't have it all, who can look in any direction and see pain, tragedy, lack, and need.

However, the truth is, if you have been born again, you do have everything. You are complete in Christ (Col. 2:10). Everything you will ever need has already been given to you. You are not standing and fighting against some demonic entity with superior power and authority. Instead, all you're doing is combating his lies and deceptions—the same ones he used on Adam and Eve.

PROCESSES OF YOUR MIND

The battle against the devil is waged in your thoughts. That's why God's Word is so essential. Satan's only power is deception. He lies and represents himself as more powerful than he is. But truth is the antidote to deception.

And ye shall know the truth, and the truth shall make you free.

JOHN 8:32

If you know the truth, the truth will make you free.

For though we walk in the flesh, we do not war after the flesh: [4] (For the weapons of our warfare are not carnal, but mighty through God to the pulling down of strong holds;) [5] Casting down imaginations, and every high thing that exalteth itself against the knowledge of God, and bringing into captivity every thought to the obedience of Christ.

2 CORINTHIANS 10:3-5, EMPHASIS MINE

Notice how our warfare is against thoughts, imaginations, strongholds, and knowledge that come against the Word of God. These are all processes of our minds.

Satan is powerless unless you believe his lies and fall into his deception. Most Christians believe the devil has tremendous power and authority, much more than they do as physical human beings. That's simply not true. Satan is a defeated foe. Although he has been beaten, he walks about *"as a roaring lion…seeking whom he may devour"* (1 Pet. 5:8). The devil isn't a true lion; he just walks around roaring like one, trying to intimidate the body of Christ. But the truth is, he's had his teeth pulled, and all he can do now is gum you. Apart from the power you give him through believing his lies, Satan can't steal anything from you. He uses your ignorance, your fear, and your unbelief to try to oppress and destroy you.

LESSON 13 – ADDITIONAL INFORMATION

My teachings entitled *Christian Philosophy* and *The Believer's Authority* both amplify and expand on the concepts presented in this Lesson.

THE BATTLEFIELD
LESSON 13 – OUTLINE

I. Dealing with the devil and overcoming his hindrances to the manifestation of what God has already provided is popularly called "spiritual warfare."

God anointed Jesus of Nazareth with the Holy Ghost and with power: who went about doing good, and healing all that were oppressed of the devil; for God was with him.

ACTS 10:38

    A. Overall, it has been good for Christians to recognize the fact that Satan exists and that his demonic powers are active today.

    B. However, Satan is a defeated foe.

    C. The only reason he is able to do anything is because of our own ignorance, unbelief, and fear.

    D. Although the body of Christ today has come to an awareness of the devil's existence, it has remained, for the most part, functionally ignorant of Satan's true devices (2 Cor. 2:11).

II. The battle is between our ears.

Finally, my brethren, be strong in the Lord, and in the power of his might. [11] Put on the whole armour of God, that ye may be able to stand against the wiles of the devil. [12] For we wrestle not against flesh and blood, but against principalities, against powers, against the rulers of the darkness of this world, against spiritual wickedness in high places.

EPHESIANS 6:10-12, EMPHASIS MINE

    A. We are in a battle, but it's not out there in heavenly places.

    B. We are fighting demonic powers—and they do exist in heavenly places—but the battlefield (place of engagement) is our minds.

    C. All Satan can do is try to deceive us through wiles, cunningness, craftiness, and lies and then use against us the very power we surrender to him.

    D. The devil's goal is to keep us ignorant of the truth and believing his lies.

I fear, lest by any means, as the serpent beguiled *Eve through his* subtilty, *so your minds should be* corrupted *from the simplicity that is in Christ.*

2 CORINTHIANS 11:3, EMPHASIS MINE

   E.   Satan comes against us by trying to corrupt our minds from the simplicity that's in Christ.

III.   Satan chose the serpent—the craftiest animal on the face of the earth—to come against Eve because he knew he had absolutely no power to force or intimidate Adam or Eve into anything.

   A.   He had to deceive them instead (Gen. 3:1).

   B.   If Satan hadn't challenged the Word and gotten them to question and second-guess it, his temptation would've gone nowhere.

   C.   Satan tempted Adam and Eve with something they already had.

IV.   Satan loves to hinder people from coming to the Lord, but his only "power" is deception and lies.

   A.   If Satan were really as powerful as he claims to be, then he would have kept you from receiving salvation.

   B.   Satan can't stop you from doing anything.

   C.   Satan can't do anything to you without your consent and cooperation.

   D.   The devil will condemn you over what you don't have and try to keep you focused on just the physical realm.

   E.   But the truth is, in the spirit, you already have everything.

V.   The key to seeing what you have in the spirit manifest in your life is believing and acknowledging it.

That the communication of thy faith may become effectual by the acknowledging of every good thing which is in you in Christ Jesus.

PHILEMON 6

   A.   The way you get your faith to work is by starting to acknowledge the good things in you in Christ.

For I know that in me (that is, in my flesh,) *dwelleth no good thing.*

ROMANS 7:18, EMPHASIS MINE

B. To live in victory, you need to be focused on who you are in Christ.

C. Satan specifically targets your understanding and acknowledging of who you are and what you have in Christ.

D. Adam and Eve threw it all away because a talking snake convinced them that they didn't have enough.

E. If you have been born again, you do have everything—you are complete in Christ (Col. 2:10).

VI. The battle against the devil is waged in your thoughts.

A. That's why God's Word is so essential.

B. Satan's only power is deception—but the truth is the antidote to deception.

And ye shall know the truth, and the truth shall make you free.

JOHN 8:32

For though we walk in the flesh, we do not war after the flesh: [4] (For the weapons of our warfare are not carnal, but mighty through God to the pulling down of strong holds;*) [5] Casting down* imaginations, *and every high thing that exalteth itself against the* knowledge *of God, and bringing into captivity every* thought *to the obedience of Christ.*

2 CORINTHIANS 10:3-5, EMPHASIS MINE

C. Notice how your warfare is against thoughts, imaginations, strongholds, and knowledge that come against the Word of God—these are all processes of your mind.

D. Although he has been beaten, the devil walks about *"as a roaring lion...seeking whom he may devour"* (1 Pet. 5:8).

E. Apart from the power you give him through believing his lies, Satan can't steal anything from you.

F. He uses your ignorance, your fear, and your unbelief to try to oppress and destroy you.

LESSON 13 – ADDITIONAL INFORMATION

My teachings entitled *Christian Philosophy* and *The Believer's Authority* both amplify and expand on the concepts presented in this Lesson.

THE BATTLEFIELD
LESSON 13 – TEACHER'S GUIDE

1.   Dealing with the devil and overcoming his hindrances to the manifestation of what God has already provided is popularly called "spiritual warfare" (Acts 10:38). Overall, it has been good for Christians to recognize the fact that Satan exists and that his demonic powers are active today. However, Satan is a defeated foe. The only reason he is able to do anything is because of our own ignorance, unbelief, and fear. Although the body of Christ today has come to an awareness of the devil's existence, it has remained, for the most part, functionally ignorant of Satan's true devices (2 Cor. 2:11).

2.   The battle is between our ears (Eph. 6:10-12). We are in a battle, but it's not out there in heavenly places. We are fighting demonic powers—and they do exist in heavenly places—but the battlefield (place of engagement) is our minds. All Satan can do is try to deceive us through wiles, cunningness, craftiness, and lies and then use against us the very power we surrender to him. The devil's goal is to keep us ignorant of the truth and believing his lies (2 Cor. 11:3). Satan comes against us by trying to corrupt our minds from the simplicity that's in Christ.

3.   Satan chose the serpent—the craftiest animal on the face of the earth—to come against Eve because he knew he had absolutely no power to force or intimidate Adam or Eve into anything. He had to deceive them instead (Gen. 3:1). If Satan hadn't challenged the Word and gotten them to question and second-guess it, his temptation would've gone nowhere. Satan tempted Adam and Eve with something they already had.

1.   A.   Read Acts 10:38 and 2 Corinthians 2:11. Dealing with the devil and overcoming his hindrances to the manifestation of what God has already provided is popularly called what? (Spiritual warfare)

     B.   What is the only reason Satan—a defeated foe—is able to do anything? (Because of our own ignorance, unbelief, and fear)

2.   A.   Read Ephesians 6:10-12 and 2 Corinthians 11:3. Where is the battlefield— place of engagement? (Between our ears—in our minds)

     B.   All Satan can do is what? (Try to deceive us through wiles, cunningness, craftiness, and lies, and then use against us the very power we surrender to him)

     C.   What is the devil's goal? (To keep us ignorant of the truth and believing his lies)

3.   A.   Read Genesis 3:1. Why did Satan choose the serpent—the craftiest animal on the face of the earth—to come against Eve? (Because he knew he had absolutely no power to force or intimidate Adam or Eve into anything—he had to deceive them instead)

     B.   Satan's temptation would have gone nowhere if he hadn't what? (Challenged the Word and gotten them to question and second-guess it)

     C.   What did Satan tempt Adam and Eve with? (Something they already had)

4.   Satan loves to hinder people from coming to the Lord, but his only "power" is deception and lies. If Satan were really as powerful as he claims to be, then he would have kept us from receiving salvation. He can't stop us from doing anything. Satan can't do anything to us without our consent and cooperation. The devil will condemn us over what we don't have and try to keep us focused on just the physical realm. But the truth is, in the spirit, we already have everything.

5.   The key to seeing what we have in the spirit manifest in our lives is believing and acknowledging it (Philem. 6). The way we get our faith to work is by starting to acknowledge the good things in us in Christ (Rom. 7:18). To live in victory, we need to be focused on who we are in Christ! Satan specifically targets our understanding and acknowledging of who we are and what we have in Christ. Adam and Eve threw it all away because a talking snake convinced them that they didn't have enough. If we have been born again, we do have everything—we are complete in Christ (Col. 2:10).

6.   The battle against the devil is waged in our thoughts. That's why God's Word is so essential. Satan's only power is deception—but the truth is the antidote to deception (John 8:32). Notice how our warfare is against thoughts, imaginations, strongholds, and knowledge that come against the Word of God (2 Cor. 10:3-5)—these are all processes of our minds. Although he has been beaten, the devil walks about *as a roaring lion…seeking whom he may devour* (1 Pet. 5:8). Apart from the power we give him through believing his lies, Satan can't steal anything from us. He uses our ignorance, our fear, and our unbelief to try to oppress and destroy us.

4.   A.   Satan can't do anything to us without what? (Our consent and cooperation)
     B.   What will the devil condemn us over and try to keep us focused on? (He'll condemn us over what we don't have and try to keep us focused on just the physical realm)
     C.   What is the truth? (In the spirit, we already have everything)
5.   A.   Read Philemon 6, Romans 7:18, and Colossians 2:10. What is the key to seeing what we have in the spirit manifest in our lives? (Believing and acknowledging it)
     B.   How do we get our faith to work? (By starting to acknowledge the good things in us in Christ)
6.   A.   Read John 8:32, 2 Corinthians 10:3-5, and 1 Peter 5:8. Why is God's Word so essential? (Because the battle against the devil is waged in our thoughts)
     B.   What is the antidote to deception? (The truth)
     C.   Satan uses our ignorance, our fear, and our unbelief to do what? (To try to oppress and destroy us)

THE BATTLEFIELD
LESSON 13 – DISCIPLESHIP QUESTIONS

1. According to John 4:24, how must we worship God?

2. According to Acts 10:38, God anointed Jesus who went about doing what?

3. According to 2 Corinthians 2:11, who do we not want to get an advantage over us?

4. According to Ephesians 6:10-12, what are we to put on?

5. That we may stand against what?

6. Who do we wrestle against?

    A. Principalities
    B. Powers
    C. Rulers of the darkness of this world
    D. Spiritual wickedness in high places
    E. All of the above
    F. None of the above

7. According to 2 Corinthians 11:3, what does the serpent try to corrupt from the simplicity in Christ?

8. According to Genesis 3:1, what was more subtle than any other beast of the field?

9. According to Philemon 6, where is every good thing?

10. According to Romans 7:18, to will is present with us, but what do we not find?

11. According to Colossians 2:10, we are what in Christ?

12. According to John 8:32, knowing the truth shall what?

13. According to 2 Corinthians 10:3-5, are the weapons of our warfare carnal?

14. What are they?

15. Casting down what?

16. Bringing into captivity what?

17. According to 1 Peter 5:8, our adversary, the devil, walks about like a roaring lion seeking _____.

THE BATTLEFIELD
LESSON 13 – ANSWER KEY

1. In spirit and truth

2. Doing good and healing all who were oppressed of the devil

3. Satan

4. The whole armor of God

5. The wiles of the devil

6. E. All of the above

7. Our minds

8. The serpent

9. In us in Christ Jesus—in our born-again spirits

10. *"How to perform that which is good"*

11. Complete

12. Make us free

13. No

14. *"Mighty through God to the pulling down of strong holds"*

15. Imaginations and every high thing that exalts itself against the knowledge of God

16. Every thought to the obedience of Christ

17. Whom he may devour

THE BATTLEFIELD
LESSON 13 – SCRIPTURES

JOHN 4:24
God is a Spirit: and they that worship him must worship him in spirit and in truth.

ACTS 10:38
How God anointed Jesus of Nazareth with the Holy Ghost and with power: who went about doing good, and healing all that were oppressed of the devil; for God was with him.

2 CORINTHIANS 2:11
Lest Satan should get an advantage of us: for we are not ignorant of his devices.

EPHESIANS 6:10-12
Finally, my brethren, be strong in the Lord, and in the power of his might. [11] Put on the whole armour of God, that ye may be able to stand against the wiles of the devil. [12] For we wrestle not against flesh and blood, but against principalities, against powers, against the rulers of the darkness of this world, against spiritual wickedness in high places.

2 CORINTHIANS 11:3
But I fear, lest by any means, as the serpent beguiled Eve through his subtilty, so your minds should be corrupted from the simplicity that is in Christ.

GENESIS 3:1
Now the serpent was more subtil than any beast of the field which the LORD God had made. And he said unto the woman, Yea, hath God said, Ye shall not eat of every tree of the garden?

PHILEMON 6
That the communication of thy faith may become effectual by the acknowledging of every good thing which is in you in Christ Jesus.

ROMANS 7:18
For I know that in me (that is, in my flesh,) dwelleth no good thing: for to will is present with me; but how to perform that which is good I find not.

COLOSSIANS 2:10
And ye are complete in him, which is the head of all principality and power.

JOHN 8:32

And ye shall know the truth, and the truth shall make you free.

2 CORINTHIANS 10:3-5

For though we walk in the flesh, we do not war after the flesh: [4] (For the weapons of our warfare are not carnal, but mighty through God to the pulling down of strong holds;) [5] Casting down imaginations, and every high thing that exalteth itself against the knowledge of God, and bringing into captivity every thought to the obedience of Christ.

1 PETER 5:8

Be sober, be vigilant; because your adversary the devil, as a roaring lion, walketh about, seeking whom he may devour.

DELIVERED!
LESSON 14

The devil is a factor, but not because he is superior in power and authority. He deceives people, and they yield to him through fear. This is what actually empowers him. Satan takes a person's own fear and uses it against them to "eat their lunch and pop the bag!"

My awareness of the spiritual realm increased dramatically in 1968 when I first became really turned on to the Lord. I not only realized that God was alive and well but also that many things happening in this world were caused by demons. The denomination I was raised in believed that all the devils were over in Africa. They didn't think there were such things as "demons" here in America. It was a nonissue. It wasn't even practical to talk about it. But as I started reading the Word, this truth just jumped out at me. The Holy Spirit showed me that many problems—especially sickness, disease, and emotional problems—were demonic in origin. So, I started praying for people and seeing them delivered.

We didn't know very much, but God did some awesome things. We saw addicts come off drugs instantly without withdrawal. We also saw homosexuals completely set free. Although we experienced some great successes, we were still quite ignorant of Satan's devices. We knew there was warfare, but we didn't know exactly how it worked. It was as if we were fighting the devil with our eyes closed, just flailing in the air—every once in a while, we'd actually hit him and see some awesome victories.

MISTAKES

However, some bad things came out of this too. I read a book on deliverance by a fellow who focused almost exclusively on this aspect of ministry. I mentioned his name once in a meeting, and a lady came up to me afterward who had been a member of his church for several years. She told me that while she attended there, the devil just destroyed both her and her family. Based on her personal knowledge of how this man and his ministry were plagued by demonic powers, she encouraged me that what I was sharing from the Word about Satan is true.

We read this man's book out of sheer desperation, trying to figure out deliverance. He taught that you had to see some physical manifestation—like vomiting—whenever someone got delivered. You also had to talk to the demons and ask them their names. Then, once you found out the "strongman," you had to cast them into a certain place. You couldn't just cast them out; you had to tell them where to go. He also said that you couldn't do it by yourself; there always had to be at least two people present to minister because the demons could overcome just one. There were all of these other things that really had no scriptural precedent. They were just this man's personal example. I'm not saying he's of the devil, just that he made some mistakes.

I've made some mistakes ministering deliverance too. Many of them were based on the information we received from reading this book. I used to counsel people for three weeks in order to "prep" them for deliverance. Some people still require that today! I know someone in Colorado Springs who went for deliverance and had to fill out a five-page form. They had to make an appointment and wait forty-five days in order to finally see someone and be set free of demons. That's absolutely foolish! Jesus never made people fill out any forms. Neither did He require them to wait for ministry a whole month and a half. I'm not condemning anyone, because I used to do it that way too. However, since then, I've found better ways to cast out demons.

SPACED OUT

My friends and I were fringe Baptists when I saw my first demonic manifestation, and we knew for sure what it was. As Baptists, we were pretty radical due to our belief in supernatural things like demonization and speaking in tongues. A certain woman had come to our little Baptist church and received the Lord. Although soundly converted, she still had some problems she was working through as a former lesbian.

One day at work, she just completely flipped out. She didn't know her name, where she'd come from, or even what she was doing in that building. Literally losing her mind, she didn't know anything. Someone walked up to her, called her by name, and said, "I'll meet you after work, and you can ride home with me." From that person, she figured out her name. After following the woman home, she looked in her purse, found some keys, and one of them opened the door. That's where we found her—at home and totally spaced out!

We believed this was demonic. If we'd have taken her to some government agency, they would have put her in a mental ward somewhere and doped her up, and she probably never would have been the same again. Therefore, we knew the answer was spiritual, not physical.

We just took her and locked her in a room. We didn't know anything, other than that this was obviously the devil. So, we just started praying and singing songs. That's when this woman became violent. One time, when we were holding her down, she—with one arm—took two of us and threw us over her head and against a wall. Now, that's supernatural strength, just like Legion in the Bible (Luke 8:29-30)!

So, we began seeing demonic manifestations. We just locked her in that room and took shifts with her, refusing to give up. Even though we didn't know exactly how to minister deliverance to her, over seven days, we saw all kinds of demons come out of her through our persistence and faith. Because of that, fame spread and people came. We saw many set free, but we also fell into some of this weirdness (i.e., empowering the devil and giving him much more credit than was due).

"NOT TONIGHT"

One Wednesday evening, a homosexual man we'd been dealing with for several weeks in preparation for deliverance came to the mid-week service. He'd brought with him another homosexual who needed to be delivered too. He told me, "I'm ready to be delivered tonight."

I answered, "Not tonight."

"Why not?"

"Because it's just me by myself. The associate pastor has gone to a conference." We were the ones casting demons out of people.

He answered, "I'm not leaving this place with these demons!"

"And I'm not casting them out!"

He looked right at me and declared, "You'd better do something because I'm not leaving with them."

I had no idea what to do, so I got Jamie. She wasn't my wife yet, but we were prayer partners. She'd never seen a demon cast out of someone before. In fact, she wasn't even baptized in the Holy Spirit yet! But Jamie went with me into the back room of that church.

This room had windows on two sides and chairs stacked on top of each other all along the wall. I started talking to this guy and saying, "I'm not doing this."

He answered, "You'd better plead the blood!" That's another weird concept we were taught. We had to "plead the blood" to keep the demons from coming out of them and entering us. It's totally inaccurate!

I started praying, "Father, I don't know what to do!" Immediately, this guy fell to the ground, started barking like a dog, writhing like a snake, and throwing chairs up against the windows. The other demonized fellow climbed up on top of a stack of ten chairs. Jamie stood there praying as fast and furious as she could!

SUPER SIMPLE

I didn't know what to do, so I started asking the demons their names. "What's your name? In the name of Jesus, tell me your name!" Without going into all of the details, we had elaborate systems for naming and talking to them. All kinds of demonic manifestations happened.

These demons were making a fool of me. They would manifest, name themselves, and leave before another started manifesting. In desperation, I prayed, "O God, help me!" The Lord simply reminded me of when He had commanded the evil spirits to shut up and come out (Mark 1:25). I thought *Well, that'd be good,* so I declared "In the name of Jesus, I command all of you to shut up and come out of this man!" and—BOOM—he instantly stopped.

This guy fell to the floor and appeared to be dead. But when I rolled him over, he was worshiping God, saying, "Thank You, Jesus! I'm free! They're gone. Thank You!" He'd been totally set free. We suspect that at least ten demons left this man.

I thought to myself, *That was super simple compared to what we normally do!* We had grown accustomed to talking to them, asking their names, and doing all this other stuff. I just resolved right then, "I've been giving the devil too much place." I'd been thinking I had to plead the blood, have at least two people present, etc., etc., etc. But it wasn't any of that stuff; I just spoke in faith and—BOOM—they were gone. I studied the Word, and my boldness grew as I discovered that this was how Jesus did it.

PHYSICALLY ATTACKED

During that period of time, I inadvertently put too much of my focus on the devil. Since there were so many people coming to us for deliverance and so much demonic stuff happening, we were constantly talking about Satan. I found myself spending more time speaking to the devil in "prayer" than God (back then, I would pray two to four hours a day). I knew something had to be wrong with that.

Many people today are into this weird type of "spiritual warfare." Their whole "prayer life" is wrapped up in binding and rebuking the devil. In the process, they are constantly addressing and talking to Satan during their prayer time more than they talk to God. Something's wrong with that!

During this same time, I was trying to open Arlington Christian Center in Arlington, Texas. We rented a building that had previously been a fraternity house. We were going to turn this facility into a place where we could house and minister to people with demonic problems. We painted it and were in the process of cleaning it out.

One evening, I led an all-night prayer meeting there with my church. Everyone else had already come, prayed, and gone, so I was left in the building by myself. As I continued to pray, something in that room began to choke me. I didn't see anything, but I was physically being choked and beaten. Demons physically attacked me!

"WHAT DO YOU MEAN?"

I ran out of that building, locked the door behind me, and jumped in my car. After backing out of the driveway, I was just about to peel rubber and hightail it out of there when the Lord spoke to me. He asked, "Where are you going?"

I responded, "God, I'm getting out of here. There are demons in that building!"

He calmly continued, "In Ephesians 6, all of the armor you use against the devil is for the front. There's no armor for the back."

Although I asked Him "What do You mean?" I already knew in my heart. He meant that I couldn't turn my back on the devil. I had to face him. But I went ahead and asked Him again anyway, saying, "Lord, what do You mean? You wouldn't want me to go back in that house, would You?" There was silence.

The Lord won't argue with you. He'll just make a statement and let you decide what you're going to do with it. This was about two or three o'clock in the morning. After sitting in that car for a while, I finally pulled back into the driveway, turned the engine off, and went back in. I locked myself in that house and fought those demonic powers until six in the morning. Afterward, the house was clear, and the demons were gone.

During that time, I also had a number of dreams where Satan would physically attack me. After waking up and thinking *It's only a dream*, I would go to the bathroom and find myself bleeding. I definitely experienced some demonic manifestations!

TOO MUCH CREDIT

Some people would say, "That's because the devil is powerful, and you were messing with his territory." No, I was giving Satan too much importance in my life, with all the time I spent binding and rebuking, learning about, and focusing my attention on him. The Lord showed me that I had glorified the devil and given him more power than he actually had. I immediately repented and decided that the best defense is a good offense. So, I started being constant and bold in praising and worshiping God. I believed that if I kept my focus on the Lord, it would totally destroy Satan's inroad into my life.

It's now forty years later, and I've never had another demonic manifestation like that. I've had devils manifest around me in people, like when I'm casting them out of someone (I even have some taped. You can hear the non-human voices and screams coming out of folks). But I've never had to physically fight a demon since. The only reason it happened then was because I had empowered the devil through my own fear and because of the undue emphasis I was placing upon him in my life.

This happens over and over again in the body of Christ today. We've given Satan too much credit. He is a factor, going around seeking whom he may devour, but the only reason the devil can actually do something to someone is because they empower him through their fear. Much of what is being taught as "spiritual warfare" today is ascribing to the devil more power and authority than he really has.

"Spiritual warfare" conferences that ascribe great power to the devil and talk about having to bind ruling principalities over places before anything positive can happen are presenting ideas that are contrary to God's Word. Satan has zero power and zero authority. All he has is deception. But these false concepts are actually causing many Christians to yield to and empower the devil.

DELIVERED!
LESSON 14 – OUTLINE

I. The devil is a factor, but not because he is superior in power and authority.

    A. He deceives people, and they yield to him through fear.

    B. Satan takes a person's own fear and uses it against them to "eat their lunch and pop the bag!"

II. My awareness of the spiritual realm increased dramatically in 1968 when I first became really turned on to the Lord.

    A. The Holy Spirit showed me that many problems—especially sickness, disease, and emotional problems—were demonic in origin.

    B. Although we experienced some great successes, we were still quite ignorant of Satan's devices.

    C. We knew there was warfare, but we didn't know exactly how it worked.

III. A certain woman had come to Andrew's little Baptist church and received the Lord.

    A. Although soundly converted, she still had some problems she was working through as a former lesbian.

    B. They found her at home and totally spaced out.

    C. They just locked her in a room and took shifts with her, refusing to give up (Luke 8:29-30).

    D. Even though they didn't know exactly how to minister deliverance to her, over seven days, they saw all kinds of demons come out through their persistence and faith.

    E. Because of that, fame spread and people came.

IV. One Wednesday evening, a homosexual man they had been dealing with for several weeks in preparation for deliverance came to the mid-week service.

    A. He told Andrew, "I'm ready to be delivered tonight!"

    B. Andrew didn't know what to do, so he started asking the demons their names.

    C. The Lord simply reminded Andrew of when He had commanded the evil spirits to shut up and come out (Mark 1:25).

D. So Andrew declared "In the name of Jesus, I command all of you to shut up and come out of this man!" and—BOOM—the man instantly stopped.

E. Andrew studied the Word, and his boldness grew as he discovered that this was how Jesus did it.

V. During that period of time, Andrew inadvertently put too much of his focus on the devil.

A. Since there were so many people coming to them for deliverance and so much demonic stuff happening, they were constantly talking about Satan.

B. Demons physically attacked him.

C. He was giving Satan too much importance in his life with all the time he spent binding and rebuking, learning about, and focusing his attention on him.

D. The Lord showed him that he had glorified the devil and given him more power than he actually had.

E. So he started being constant and bold in praising and worshiping God, believing that if he kept his focus on the Lord, it would totally destroy Satan's inroad into his life.

VI. We've given Satan too much credit.

A. He is a factor, going around seeking whom he may devour, but the only reason the devil can actually do something to someone is because they empower him through their fear.

B. Much of what is being taught as "spiritual warfare" today is ascribing to the devil more power and authority than he really has.

C. Satan has zero power and zero authority—all he has is deception.

D. But these false concepts are actually causing many Christians to yield to and empower the devil.

DELIVERED!
LESSON 14 – TEACHER'S GUIDE

1. The devil is a factor, but not because he is superior in power and authority. He deceives people, and they yield to him through fear. Satan takes a person's own fear and uses it against them to "eat their lunch and pop the bag!"

2. Andrew's awareness of the spiritual realm increased dramatically in 1968 when he first became really turned on to the Lord. The Holy Spirit showed him that many problems—especially sickness, disease, and emotional problems—were demonic in origin. Although he and his friends experienced some great successes, they were still quite ignorant of Satan's devices. They knew there was warfare, but they didn't know exactly how it worked.

3. A certain woman had come to Andrew's little Baptist church and received the Lord. Although soundly converted, she still had some problems she was working through as a former lesbian. They found her at home and totally spaced out. They just locked her in a room and took shifts with her, refusing to give up (Luke 8:29-30). Even though they didn't know exactly how to minister deliverance to her, over seven days they saw all kinds of demons come out through their persistence and faith. Because of that, fame spread and people came.

1. A. What does the devil do? (He deceives people)
    B. Satan takes a person's own fear and does what? (Uses it against them)
2. A. What often happens when we first become really turned on to the Lord? (Our awareness of the spiritual realm increases dramatically)
    B. Many problems—especially sickness, disease, and emotional problems—are what in origin? (Demonic)
3. A. Read Luke 8:29-30. Even though they didn't know exactly how to minister deliverance to this woman, how did they see all kinds of demons come out of her? (Through persistence and faith)
    B. What happened because of that? (Fame spread and people came)

4.   One Wednesday evening, a homosexual man Andrew and his friends had been dealing with for several weeks in preparation for deliverance came to the mid-week service. He told him, "I'm ready to be delivered tonight!" Andrew didn't know what to do, so he started asking the demons their names. The Lord simply reminded Andrew of when He had commanded the evil spirits to shut up and come out (Mark 1:25). So he declared "In the name of Jesus, I command all of you to shut up and come out of this man!" and—BOOM—the man instantly stopped.

5.   Andrew studied the Word, and his boldness grew as he discovered that this was how Jesus did it. During that period of time, Andrew inadvertently put too much of his focus on the devil. Since there were so many people coming to them for deliverance and so much demonic stuff happening, he and his friends were constantly talking about Satan. Demons physically attacked him. Andrew was giving Satan too much importance in his life with all the time he spent binding and rebuking, learning about, and focusing his attention on him. The Lord showed Andrew that he had glorified the devil and given him more power than he actually had. So Andrew started being constant and bold in praising and worshiping God, believing that if he kept his focus on the Lord, it would totally destroy Satan's inroad into his life.

6.   We've given Satan too much credit. He is a factor, going around seeking whom he may devour, but the only reason the devil can actually do something to someone is because people empower him through their fear. Much of what is being taught as "spiritual warfare" today is ascribing to the devil more power and authority than he really has. Satan has zero power and zero authority—all he has is deception. But these false concepts are actually causing many Christians to yield to and empower the devil.

4.   A.   Read Mark 1:25. What did the Lord remind Andrew of? (When He had commanded the evil spirits to shut up and come out)

     B.   As Andrew studied the Word, why did his boldness grow? (Because he discovered that this was how Jesus did it)

5.   A.   How was Andrew giving Satan too much importance in his life? (With all the time he spent binding and rebuking, learning about, and focusing his attention on him)

     B.   What did Andrew do when the Lord showed him he had glorified the devil and given him more power than he actually had? (Andrew started being constant and bold in praising and worshiping God, believing that if he kept his focus on the Lord, it would totally destroy Satan's inroad into his life)

6.   A.   What does much of what is being taught as "spiritual warfare" today ascribe to the devil? (More power and authority than he really has)

     B.   How much power and authority does Satan have? (Zero—all he has is deception)

     C.   What are these false concepts causing many Christians to do? (Yield to and empower the devil)

DELIVERED!
LESSON 14 – DISCIPLESHIP QUESTIONS

1. Who was speaking in Luke 8:29-30?

2. What did Jesus command to come out of the man?

3. When had it caught the man?

4. With and in what was this man kept bound?

5. What did he do with these bands?

6. Who drove him into the wilderness?

7. What did Jesus ask him?

8. What did he answer?

9. Because many devils were what?

10. In Mark 1:25, who rebuked the unclean spirit?

11. What did Jesus say?

12. What did He tell the devil to do?

DELIVERED!
LESSON 14 – ANSWER KEY

1. Jesus

2. The unclean spirit

3. Oftentimes

4. Chains and fetters

5. He broke them

6. The devil

7. What is your name

8. Legion

9. Entered into him

10. Jesus

11. Hold your peace

12. Come out of him

DELIVERED!
LESSON 14 – SCRIPTURES

LUKE 8:29-30

(For he had commanded the unclean spirit to come out of the man. For oftentimes it had caught him: and he was kept bound with chains and in fetters; and he brake the bands, and was driven of the devil into the wilderness.) **[30]** And Jesus asked him, saying, What is thy name? And he said, Legion: because many devils were entered into him.

MARK 1:25

And Jesus rebuked him, saying, Hold thy peace, and come out of him.

THE TRIUMPHANT PROCESSION
LESSON 15

And you, being dead in your sins and the uncircumcision of your flesh, hath he quickened together with him, having forgiven you all trespasses; [14] Blotting out the handwriting of ordinances that was against us, which was contrary to us, and took it out of the way, nailing it to his cross; [15] And having spoiled principalities and powers, he made a show of them openly, triumphing over them in it.

COLOSSIANS 2:13-15, EMPHASIS MINE

Spoil means to take everything of value from a conquered foe. It's not talking about fruit and meat that spoils and turns rotten. This kind of "spoil" is from the venue of conquest. It's talking about conquering an enemy and taking everything from them.

Satan, principalities, and all other demonic powers have been spoiled. Through the cross and resurrection, Jesus Christ stripped the devil of all power and authority. The first Adam may have surrendered it at the Fall, but the last Adam took it back at the resurrection. Now Satan has no power or authority. His only weapon is deception. If you yield to the devil's lies, he'll use your power and authority against you.

Show is the same Greek word we get "exhibition" and "exhibit" from. In other words, God exhibited—made an exhibition out of—Satan.

In high school biology, you probably had to catch insects and other things. You would kill them, mount them, and then write what they were underneath. There they were, impaled by a pin that held them to a piece of poster board. You called it an "exhibit."

That's how I see the devil: impaled, nailed to the cross with the very same spikes that once held Jesus. He's an exhibit—completely stripped of anything of value. Jesus Christ has made a show—an exhibition—of Satan.

THE VICTORY PARADE

The phrase translated *"triumphing over them"* literally refers to the triumphant procession (Col. 2:15). The Romans had a custom of parading the spoils of war and the conquered foe in front of the people after coming home from a conquest. When they went out to fight an enemy, if they conquered, they would return and have this glorious victory parade. If they didn't win, they wouldn't have this "triumphant procession."

The Roman citizens knew that if they didn't have this parade, the enemy who had been terrorizing them wasn't defeated yet. They would still be anxious and worry about his return. Their side might have won a great battle, but if they hadn't completely conquered the opposing general or king and had this parade, then the

Roman populace would live under constant fear that he might once again marshal his forces against them.

However, when they conquered the enemy, the Romans would take this opposing general or king and parade him—dead or alive—in front of the people. If he was dead, they would show his severed head and lifeless body. However, they usually preferred to capture him alive. They would totally strip him of all armor, kingly garments, and jewelry that made him appear strong and important. Completely naked and humiliated, he would be tied to a horse or chariot. He would either walk or be dragged through the streets. They'd also cut off both thumbs and big toes so he would never again be able to hold a sword or stand in battle. In this manner, the Romans paraded their conquered foes.

This triumphant procession showed all the Roman citizens that their enemy had been vanquished. It totally defused all fear that this guy might ever be able to mount another campaign against them. The parade displayed him in such a way that the common people would mock him, beat him, and spit on him. The purpose of the parade was to completely remove their fear.

The Scripture plainly declares that this is what Jesus did to the devil. He absolutely defeated him at every turn. Christ destroyed *"him that had the power of death, that is, the devil"* so that He could *"deliver them who through fear of death were all their lifetime subject to bondage"* (Heb. 2:14-15). Notice that it's the fear of death that opens the door to bondage. Satan has no power of his own now. He can only come against you with deception. But Jesus has delivered us.

HAVE YOU MISSED IT?

There's been a victory parade—a triumphant procession. The devil has been paraded, according to the Scriptures, and shown to be an absolute zero with the rim knocked off. He's a nothing!

The problem is that most of the body of Christ has missed the parade—especially among the "spiritual warfare" people. Satan is alive and there is a battle being waged, but it's not in the heavenlies with demonic beings who have awesome power and great authority. All the devil has is his tremendous ability to lie and deceive. Don't glorify Satan! Don't ascribe to him power he doesn't really have. Stand against his lies and believe the truth. Focus your attention on God, not demons. The true battle is in your head. Therefore, remember the parade!

Many "spiritual warfare" people think that you must do a whole list of things before you can go into an area and effectively preach the Gospel. You have to do "spiritual mapping" and discover what ungodly things have happened in the past to create "spiritual strongholds." Then you must send in "intercessors" that spend months, years, and decades praying, rebuking, and binding demonic powers so that the Word of God can finally have an impact. Wrong, wrong, wrong!

There is zero precedent for this in the Word of God. You can't find it anywhere in the New Testament. It's absolutely wrong.

Yes, there are demonic powers. Yes, there is a hierarchy of demons. Yes, they are assigned to specific places. But, **NO**, that's not how you deal with them. It's a wrong application to preach that the reason more people aren't being born again and set free is because we haven't prayed and done enough "spiritual warfare."

Jesus never sent anyone in advance to pray, bind the devil, and prepare a place so that the Word of God could go forth. He did send His disciples ahead to let people know He was coming. They also did miracles and drew folks to hear Him. But neither Jesus, Peter, nor Paul ever sent believers ahead of them just to pray and do these other things. It's absolutely wrong.

OLD TESTAMENT VS. THE NEW

In the Old Testament, you will find different examples of individuals praying for certain cities and specific people. Abraham interceded for the cities of Sodom and Gomorrah (Gen. 18:31-32). Moses interceded for his siblings and the children of Israel (Num. 12:1, 9-10, 13-14; 14:2, 5, and 19). They pleaded for mercy with an angry God who wanted to execute judgment for sin. However, that's very different from today.

There's a huge difference between what happened in the Old Testament and what happens now in the New. In the Old Covenant, Jesus had not yet made atonement for our sins. He hadn't yet gone to hell for us and become our eternal intercessor (Heb. 7:25). Therefore, it was appropriate for these Old Testament saints to ask for mercy, because mercy wasn't yet totally given. It was being shown in measure, but it was like it was on credit and not the actual transaction. The Atonement had not yet been made.

But on this side of the cross, there's a huge difference in the way we relate to God. God is pouring out mercy and grace today, not wrath (2 Cor. 5:19). He's not imputing men's sins unto them. It is absolutely wrong to think that God is angry at us because of sin and that He's ready to judge this nation. It is incorrect to believe that God is about to unleash judgment unless we repent and the intercessors unite to beg and plead with Him to stay His wrath. Jesus Christ already atoned for all sin. He is the intercessor to end all of that kind of intercession.

There is a godly type of intercession today. It's simply saying, "Father, I know that You are a good God. You love us. You would have spared Sodom and Gomorrah if there would have only been ten righteous people. There are more than ten righteous people in this country. I know that all of these so-called 'prophecies' saying that unless we repent, You are going to send doom, gloom, and destruction aren't from You. Thank You, Father, that You don't want to judge us."

Don't misunderstand me—there are consequences for sin. When people hate God and quit seeking Him, they become mean and selfish. Crime and problems escalate, tragedies and terrorist attacks happen, but that's just sowing and reaping. Sowing bad seeds and reaping a negative harvest is different from God sending His wrath. God is not bringing judgment on people in this day and age. A time is coming when He will, and He'll be just in doing so. But during the church age, He is releasing mercy and grace.

NEW TESTAMENT INTERCESSION

A New Testament intercessor recognizes that God has turned from His wrath because of the atoning work of Jesus Christ. There is now no need to beg Him for mercy the way Moses did (Ex. 32:12). Jesus atoned not only for our sins but for the sins of the entire world. God has turned from His wrath and is now extending mercy and grace to all people everywhere.

It's wrong for a born-again believer to stand there and tell God to repent like Moses did. Moses wasn't wrong, because at the time, God was pouring out His wrath. However, we are living in a New Covenant.

God was in Christ, reconciling the world unto himself, not imputing their trespasses unto them.

2 CORINTHIANS 5:19

To pray "O God, turn from Your fierce wrath. O God, pour out Your power. Please move" is to deny the atonement and intercession of the Lord Jesus Christ.

There's a huge difference between the way intercession was done in the Old Testament and the way it's done in the New. Much of what's being taught as "intercession" and "spiritual warfare" today is absolutely an Old Testament mentality. It's anti-Christ. It's denying the truth that Jesus spoiled the devil of all power and authority. It's glorifying Satan. Basically, it's just people who missed the parade.

THE ANTIDOTE FOR DECEPTION

True spiritual warfare is fought on a personal level. You resist the lies and deception of the devil. This is primarily done through knowing the truth.

And ye shall know the truth, and the truth shall make you free.

JOHN 8:32

Understanding the truth is the antidote for deception.

Deception's power and strength come from the fact that you don't know you are deceived. But once you realize the proper standard—the truth—deception immediately loses its power.

If someone was terrorizing and threatening to kill you, you would be afraid. However, if I showed you that person's corpse, your fear would immediately leave. Once you knew the truth of their demise, their threats would no longer intimidate you.

God's Word is truth (John 17:17). I take God's Word and meditate on it. Through the Word, I love God and commune with Him. I also fellowship with the Lord's people and stay positive by constantly seeking Him. These are just some practical ways I personally wage spiritual warfare. The best defense is a good offense!

Praise is a very powerful weapon against the devil. It literally drives him out. He can't stand to be around the praise and worship of God. Once every couple of months, I'll rebuke and bind the devil over something, but it's not because he has this awesome power coming against me; it's just that the battle in my mind—in my thoughts—has become so intense that I verbalize my resistance, saying, "I rebuke these thoughts in Jesus' name. Satan, you have zero right and zero power over me!" But most of the time, I don't ever have to say anything out loud. I just counter the lies that come my way with truth and continue in constant praise.

If you've been dominated by the devil for a long time, this might not be aggressive enough at first. If you are demonized and are trying to come out of it, you might need to emphasize, rebuke, and speak things aloud more. However, once you're free, it's fairly easy to keep that freedom just by staying in the truth.

SEND IN THE TRUTH

I used to just rebuke demons in other people when they came to me. But I've come to realize that if I cast a demon out of someone on my faith alone, I'm actually doing them a disservice (Matt. 12:43-45). Those evil spirits will just come back on them again if they don't know, understand, and apply the truth against the lies they once believed.

The best way to deliver people is to tell them the truth, to instruct them in the Word of God, to teach them about the triumphant procession and their victory in Jesus. Help them understand God's promises concerning their problem, and encourage them to diligently apply this truth to their thoughts. I could give you hundreds of testimonies of people who heard me preach the truth of God's Word and were set free from demons without me even so much as rebuking a devil. I'm talking about severe demonizations—people who were non-functional or even doped up and in a mental ward—being completely delivered because they simply listened to the truth and received it in their hearts. They were set free without me even praying for them.

There are other times when I do cast demons out of people. Sometimes Satan has ingrained certain lies so deeply into someone's thinking that they still need another person to pray and rebuke it even though they've seen and embraced the truth. That's why I often cast demons out of people when praying over sickness, depression, and the like. The demons leave and the people get free. But I always impart some truth to them to use for their protection and to keep the devil from coming back in again.

I wage spiritual warfare over a city or a country by sending in the truth. I do that by sharing God's Word through television, radio, CDs, books, videos, and the internet. As people hear the truth, their hearts open and become more receptive to the Gospel. Then I also go in—or send others who have been trained—to preach and teach the Word in person. True spiritual warfare is bringing the truth of God's Word to people.

LESSON 15 – ADDITIONAL INFORMATION

Again, these truths are developed more in depth in *A Better Way to Pray, Spiritual Authority,* and *The Believer's Authority*.

THE TRIUMPHANT PROCESSION
LESSON 15 – OUTLINE

I. Through the cross and resurrection, Jesus Christ stripped the devil of all power and authority.

And you, being dead in your sins and the uncircumcision of your flesh, hath he quickened together with him, having forgiven you all trespasses; [14] Blotting out the handwriting of ordinances that was against us, which was contrary to us, and took it out of the way, nailing it to his cross; [15] And having spoiled principalities and powers, he made a show of them openly, triumphing over them in it.

COLOSSIANS 2:13-15, EMPHASIS MINE

   A. *Spoil* means to take everything of value from a conquered foe.

   B. Satan, principalities, and all other demonic powers have been spoiled.

   C. Jesus Christ has made a show—an exhibition—of Satan.

II. The phrase translated *"triumphing over them"* literally refers to the triumphant procession (Col. 2:15).

   A. The Romans had a custom of parading the spoils of war and the conquered foe in front of the people after coming home from a conquest.

   B. The Roman citizens knew that if they didn't have this parade, the enemy who had been terrorizing them wasn't defeated yet.

   C. This triumphant procession showed all the Roman citizens that their enemy had been vanquished.

   D. The purpose of the parade was to completely remove their fear.

III. The Scripture plainly declares that this is what Jesus did to the devil.

   A. Christ destroyed *"him that had the power of death, that is, the devil"* so that He could *"deliver them who through fear of death were all their lifetime subject to bondage"* (Heb. 2:14-15).

   B. Notice that it's the fear of death that opens the door to bondage.

   C. The devil has been paraded, according to the Scriptures, and shown to be an absolute zero with the rim knocked off—he's a nothing!

D. The problem is that most of the body of Christ has missed the parade—especially among the "spiritual warfare" people.

IV. Many "spiritual warfare" people think that you must do spiritual warfare before you can go into an area and effectively preach the Gospel.

A. Neither Jesus, Peter, nor Paul ever sent believers ahead of them just to pray and do these other things.

God was in Christ, reconciling the world unto himself, not imputing their trespasses unto them.

2 CORINTHIANS 5:19

B. To pray "O God, turn from Your fierce wrath. O God, pour out Your power. Please move" is to deny the atonement and intercession of the Lord Jesus Christ.

C. There's a huge difference between the way intercession was done in the Old Testament and the way it's done in the New.

D. Much of what is being taught as "intercession" and "spiritual warfare" today is absolutely an Old Testament mentality.

V. True spiritual warfare is fought on a personal level.

A. You resist the lies and deception of the devil.

B. This is primarily done through knowing the truth.

And ye shall know the truth, and the truth shall make you free.

JOHN 8:32

C. Understanding the truth is the antidote for deception.

D. Deception's power and strength come from the fact that you don't know you are deceived.

E. But once you realize the proper standard—the truth—deception immediately loses its power.

F. God's Word is truth (John 17:17).

VI. I wage spiritual warfare over a city or a country by sending in the truth.

A. I do that by sharing God's Word through television, radio, CDs, books, videos, and the internet.

B. As people hear the truth, their hearts open and become more receptive to the Gospel.

C. Then I also go in—or send others who have been trained—to preach and teach the Word in person.

D. True spiritual warfare is bringing the truth of God's Word to people!

LESSON 15 – ADDITIONAL INFORMATION

Again, these truths are developed more in depth in *A Better Way to Pray, Spiritual Authority,* and *The Believer's Authority.*

THE TRIUMPHANT PROCESSION
LESSON 15 – TEACHER'S GUIDE

1.   Through the cross and resurrection, Jesus Christ stripped the devil of all power and authority (Col. 2:13-15). *Spoil* means to take everything of value from a conquered foe. Satan, principalities, and all other demonic powers have been spoiled. Jesus Christ has made a show—an exhibition—of Satan.

2.   The phrase translated *"triumphing over them"* literally refers to the triumphant procession (Col. 2:15). The Romans had a custom of parading the spoils of war and the conquered foe in front of the people after coming home from a conquest. The Roman citizens knew that if they didn't have this parade, the enemy who had been terrorizing them wasn't defeated yet. This triumphant procession showed all the Roman citizens that their enemy had been vanquished. The purpose of the parade was to completely remove their fear.

3.   The Scripture plainly declares that this is what Jesus did to the devil. Christ destroyed *"him that had the power of death, that is, the devil"* so that He could *"deliver them who through fear of death were all their lifetime subject to bondage"* (Heb. 2:14-15). Notice that it's the fear of death that opens the door to bondage. The devil has been paraded, according to the Scriptures, and shown to be an absolute zero with the rim knocked off—he's a nothing! The problem is that most of the body of Christ has missed the parade—especially among the "spiritual warfare" people.

1. A. Read Colossians 2:13-15. When and how did Jesus Christ strip the devil of all power and authority? (Through the cross and resurrection)
    B. What does *spoil* mean? (To take everything of value from a conquered foe)
2. A. What does the phrase in Colossians 2:15 *"triumphing over them"* literally refer to? (The triumphant procession)
    B. What was the purpose of the parade? (To completely remove fear)
3. A. Read Hebrews 2:14-15. What does the Scripture plainly declare? (This is what Jesus did to the devil)
    B. What opens the door to bondage? (The fear of death)

4.   Many "spiritual warfare" people think that we must do spiritual warfare before we can go into an area and effectively preach the Gospel. Neither Jesus, Peter, nor Paul ever sent believers ahead of them just to pray and do these other things (2 Cor. 5:19). To pray, "O God, turn from Your fierce wrath. O God, pour out Your power. Please move" is to deny the atonement and intercession of the Lord Jesus Christ. There's a huge difference between the way intercession was done in the Old Testament and the way it's done in the New. Much of what is being taught as "intercession" and "spiritual warfare" today is absolutely an Old Testament mentality.

5.   True spiritual warfare is fought on a personal level. We resist the lies and deception of the devil. This is primarily done through knowing the truth (John 8:32). Understanding the truth is the antidote for deception. Deception's power and strength come from the fact that we don't know we are deceived. But once we realize the proper standard—the truth—deception immediately loses its power. God's Word is truth (John 17:17).

6.   We wage spiritual warfare over a city or a country by sending in the truth. Andrew does that by sharing God's Word through television, radio, CDs, books, videos, and the internet. As people hear the truth, their hearts open and become more receptive to the Gospel. Then he also goes in—or sends others who have been trained—to preach and teach the Word in person. True spiritual warfare is bringing the truth of God's Word to people!

4. A.   Read 2 Corinthians 5:19. To pray "O God, turn from Your fierce wrath. O God, pour out Your power. Please move" is to deny the aonement and intercession of whom? (The Lord Jesus Christ)
    B.   There's a huge difference between the way intercession was done in the Old Testament and the way it's done when? (In the New)
5. A.   Read John 8:32 and 17:17. On what level is true spiritual warfare fought? (A personal level)
    B.   When does deception immediately lose its power? (Once we realize the proper standard—the truth)
6. A.   How do we wage spiritual warfare over a city or a country? (By sending in the truth)
    B.   What is true spiritual warfare? (Bringing the truth of God's Word to people)

THE TRIUMPHANT PROCESSION
LESSON 15 – DISCIPLESHIP QUESTIONS

1. According to Colossians 2:13-15, who has been quickened—made alive—who were dead in sins?

2. This that was contrary to us was taken out of the way and nailed to what?

3. According to Hebrews 2:14-15, through death, who destroyed the devil?

4. How were they subject to bondage?

5. According to Genesis 18:31-32, if there were twenty righteous inside the city, would the Lord destroy it?

6. If there were ten righteous inside the city, would the Lord destroy it?

7. According to Numbers 12:1, why did Miriam and Aaron speak against Moses?

8. According to Numbers 12:9-10, what was kindled against Miriam and Aaron?

9. According to Numbers 12:13-14, who cried unto the Lord for Miriam's healing?

10. According to Numbers 14:2, who murmured against whom?

11. According to Numbers 14:5 and 19, what did Moses and Aaron do?

12. According to Hebrews 7:25, why does Jesus ever live?

13. According to 2 Corinthians 5:19, God was _____ the world unto Himself.

14. What has God committed unto us?

15. According to Exodus 32:12, what did Moses ask the Lord to do?

16. According to John 8:32, what makes us free?

17. According to John 17:17, how are we sanctified?

18. What is truth?

19. According to Matthew 12:43-45, if the unclean spirit finds his previous home empty, swept, and garnished, whom does he get to enter in and dwell there?

20. Even so shall it be unto whom?

THE TRIUMPHANT PROCESSION
LESSON 15 – ANSWER KEY

1. Us

2. His cross

3. Jesus

4. Through fear of death

5. No

6. No

7. Because of the Ethiopian woman whom he had married

8. The anger of the Lord

9. Moses

10. All the children of Israel against Moses and Aaron

11. They fell on their faces before all the assembly, beseeching God to have mercy and forgive the people

12. To make intercession for those who come to God by Him

13. Reconciling

14. The word of reconciliation

15. To turn from His fierce wrath and repent of this evil against His people

16. The truth we know

17. Through the Father's truth

18. His Word

19. Seven other spirits more wicked than himself

20. This wicked generation

THE TRIUMPHANT PROCESSION
LESSON 15 – SCRIPTURES

COLOSSIANS 2:13-15

And you, being dead in your sins and the uncircumcision of your flesh, hath he quickened together with him, having forgiven you all trespasses; [14] Blotting out the handwriting of ordinances that was against us, which was contrary to us, and took it out of the way, nailing it to his cross; [15] And having spoiled principalities and powers, he made a show of them openly, triumphing over them in it.

HEBREWS 2:14-15

Forasmuch then as the children are partakers of flesh and blood, he also himself likewise took part of the same; that through death he might destroy him that had the power of death, that is, the devil; [15] And deliver them who through fear of death were all their lifetime subject to bondage.

GENESIS 18:31-32

And he said, Behold now, I have taken upon me to speak unto the Lord: Peradventure there shall be twenty found there. And he said, I will not destroy it for twenty's sake. [32] And he said, Oh let not the Lord be angry, and I will speak yet but this once: Peradventure ten shall be found there. And he said, I will not destroy it for ten's sake.

NUMBERS 12:1

And Miriam and Aaron spake against Moses because of the Ethiopian woman whom he had married: for he had married an Ethiopian woman.

NUMBERS 12:9-10

And the anger of the LORD was kindled against them; and he departed. [10] And the cloud departed from off the tabernacle; and, behold, Miriam became leprous, white as snow: and Aaron looked upon Miriam, and, behold, she was leprous.

NUMBERS 12:13-14

And Moses cried unto the LORD, saying, Heal her now, O God, I beseech thee. [14] And the LORD said unto Moses, If her father had but spit in her face, should she not be ashamed seven days? let her be shut out from the camp seven days, and after that let her be received in again.

NUMBERS 14:2

And all the children of Israel murmured against Moses and against Aaron: and the whole congregation said unto them, Would God that we had died in the land of Egypt! or would God we had died in this wilderness.

NUMBERS 14:5

Then Moses and Aaron fell on their faces before all the assembly of the congregation of the children of Israel.

NUMBERS 14:19

Pardon, I beseech thee, the iniquity of this people according unto the greatness of thy mercy, and as thou hast forgiven this people, from Egypt even until now.

HEBREWS 7:25

Wherefore he is able also to save them to the uttermost that come unto God by him, seeing he ever liveth to make intercession for them.

2 CORINTHIANS 5:19

To wit, that God was in Christ, reconciling the world unto himself, not imputing their trespasses unto them; and hath committed unto us the word of reconciliation.

EXODUS 32:12

Wherefore should the Egyptians speak, and say, For mischief did he bring them out, to slay them in the mountains, and to consume them from the face of the earth? Turn from thy fierce wrath, and repent of this evil against thy people.

JOHN 8:32

And ye shall know the truth, and the truth shall make you free.

JOHN 17:17

Sanctify them through thy truth: thy word is truth.

MATTHEW 12:43-45

When the unclean spirit is gone out of a man, he walketh through dry places, seeking rest, and findeth none. [44] Then he saith, I will return into my house from whence I came out; and when he is come, he findeth it empty, swept, and garnished. [45] Then goeth he, and taketh with himself seven other spirits more wicked than himself, and they enter in and dwell there: and the last state of that man is worse than the first. Even so shall it be also unto this wicked generation.

PROCLAIM THE WORD!
LESSON 16

Paul is a great example of true spiritual warfare. In Acts 19, the apostle ministered in the city of Ephesus. While there, he experienced much opposition. In fact, Paul considered leaving town, but the Lord told him to stay and build up the believers. Later in church history, Ephesus became one of the most active and important centers of Christianity. However, despite fierce opposition, Scripture never records Paul ever leading the believers to gather together to intercede, do spiritual warfare, and rebuke the demonic principalities over the city.

At the time, Ephesus was known for the pagan goddess "Diana of the Ephesians." Her majestic and ornate temple was considered one of the wonders of the world. Legend said that her image fell directly from heaven into this temple. That's why devotees from throughout all of Asia came to Ephesus to worship.

Yet Paul never organized the believers to rebuke Diana of the Ephesians. He never invoked them to do "spiritual warfare" against her. What did he do instead? Paul preached the truth. He countered their wrong conceptions and taught the people God's Word. Through boldly preaching the Gospel, Paul broke the power of Diana and saw multitudes in the city receive the Lord Jesus Christ.

That's the scriptural method: Preach God's Word! This is exactly what Paul advised Timothy to do as the young man pastored the growing Ephesian church that his beloved mentor had planted.

All scripture is given by inspiration of God, and is profitable for doctrine, for reproof, for correction, for instruction in righteousness: [17] That the man of God may be perfect, throughly furnished unto all good works. [4:1] I charge thee therefore before God, and the Lord Jesus Christ, who shall judge the quick and the dead at his appearing and his kingdom; [2] Preach the word; be instant in season, out of season; reprove, rebuke, exhort with all longsuffering and doctrine.

2 TIMOTHY 3:16-4:2, EMPHASIS MINE

DEALING WITH DIANA TODAY?

There was a demonic power reigning in Ephesus, but Paul didn't gather "intercessors" and "prayer warriors" to do battle. He told people the truth, got them saved and set free, and discipled them to go out and do the same. God's Word is what set people free. The truth is what broke Diana of the Ephesians' power.

Several years ago, the leaders of the intercession and spiritual warfare movements went over to Ephesus (in modern-day Turkey). They believed God told them that the biggest demonic power in our day and age was Diana of the Ephesians. They thought she was the principality actually controlling the many Muslim people living in the most unreached parts of the world called "The 10/40 Window." At the amphitheater in Ephesus (ruins from Paul's time), they gathered about 20,000 "intercessors" and "prayer warriors" from all around the world. All they did was pray and do "spiritual warfare" in order to "destroy" Diana of the Ephesians.

They didn't preach the Gospel. They didn't go over there to share the truth of God's Word and win people to the Lord. Instead, they all assembled and simply held a prayer and praise service in which they supposedly "dealt with" Diana of the Ephesians. That's exactly the opposite of what Paul did.

Personally, I don't believe that "Diana of the Ephesians" is even a factor today. She was defeated 2,000 years ago by Paul and the fast-spreading truth of the Gospel. Nobody worships Diana today. Of course, "spiritual warfare" people would say that she's the demonic entity behind the Islamic faith. However, that's a completely subjective argument. It's what their impressions are, but there's no way to biblically clarify and verify it. Therefore, I don't believe it is true.

Yes, there are demonic entities operating in the world today. They are there because people have empowered them through yielding to their lies. The way to change the situation isn't by dealing directly with the demons in prayer. Their power is cut off when people believe the truth. As individuals, families, and communities come out of deception, demonic powers are weakened and broken.

WHO CAME FIRST?

Many Christians think that San Francisco has demonic powers of homosexuality and lesbianism hovering over the city and keeping those people in bondage. There probably is a greater concentration of those particular spirits dwelling there than in other places, but how do you deal with them?

The spiritual warfare people try to deal with it through intercessory prayer, spiritual mapping, prayer walks, binding the devil, and other similar kinds of things. That's not the scriptural New Testament model. These demonic powers are really a non-factor, other than the fact that people have yielded to and empowered them. You can't just bind those principalities and command them to depart.

Some Christians think that if you just got rid of the demonic powers, then the people would be set free to respond to the Gospel. That's completely backward! When the people respond positively to the truth, the demons will lose their power and leave.

Who came to San Francisco first—the demons or the homosexuals? Some people who were homosexuals, or favored them, were elected to places of power in the government.

They passed laws giving special welfare benefits, legal benefits, and other things that made San Francisco attractive to homosexuals. Therefore, homosexuals from all around the country and the world flocked to San Francisco. There weren't demonic powers already there who drew these people. The homosexuals came and brought their demons with them.

You don't get rid of the homosexual demonic powers by going into the heavenlies and doing battle directly with them. Preach the truth instead. As these people understand and believe that God loves them and made them Adam and Eve, not Adam and Steve, they will be set free. Then they will resist those devils with the truth, and the entire climate over San Francisco will change.

THE SOUL THAT SINS SHALL DIE

I have friends who believe that the United States won't see revival until the atrocities done in the past to the Native Americans are repented of and forgiven. They think we must do "spiritual warfare" to dislodge the demons that came to power over our country through broken covenants and innocent bloodshed centuries ago. Again, this contradicts New Testament Scripture. You might be able to quote some Old Testament verses, but these concepts don't square with God's Word this side of the cross.

Ezekiel prophesied that every individual would answer for their own sin—and no one else's—under the New Covenant.

> *What mean ye, that ye use this proverb concerning the land of Israel, saying, The fathers have eaten sour grapes, and the children's teeth are set on edge?* [i.e., "generational curse"] *[3] As I live, saith the Lord GOD, ye shall not have occasion any more to use this proverb in Israel. [4] Behold, all souls are mine; as the soul of the father, so also the soul of the son is mine:* the soul that sinneth, it shall die.

EZEKIEL 18:2-4, BRACKETS AND EMPHASIS MINE

God doesn't judge children for the sins of their parents today (Ezek. 18:20).

Many terrible atrocities were committed against the Native Americans. My wife is a Native American, but she's not carrying around bitterness and harboring hurt from what happened centuries ago. However, if I met a Native American who was upset at me because of what my great-great-great-grandfather did to his people, I would apologize. It was wrong and shouldn't have happened, but it's not what's holding this man, or anyone else, in bondage today.

A man stands before God on his own. He is not a product of what happened 300 years ago. Those things might have influenced him, but it is absolutely his choice to choose life or death. If he can understand and believe the truth that Jesus Christ dealt with all sin once and for all at the cross, forgiveness would set him free. Deception is what keeps us in bondage, and the truth is what sets us free.

I simply refuse to empower the devil! Saying that revival can't happen until we do all of these things is giving Satan power that he doesn't really have.

EUROPE

Christians have actually retraced the route of the Crusades (back in the eleventh, twelfth, and thirteenth centuries) through Europe. They have done penance and apologized to descendants of people they believed their ancestors hurt centuries ago. They've done all of this believing that Europe will stay in spiritual darkness until this "reconciliation" takes place. Wrong!

What's keeping Europe in spiritual darkness? People there haven't heard and believed God's Word. European television channels strictly censor my programs. They often edit my teaching so much that it takes a lot of the power out of it. One time, they bleeped out something I said about spanking one's kids as if it were profanity! I can't say, "Jesus is the way, the truth, and the life." Instead, I have to state, "The Bible says that Jesus is the way, the truth, and the life." I have to present it as an opinion, not a fact. God's Word has been very much hindered in the European airways. It's this lack of the truth of God's Word that keeps Europe in Satan's grasp.

All across Europe, laws have been passed against preaching the Gospel. In France, they've made it illegal to evangelize. If you lay hands on someone and pray for their healing, you could be put in jail for practicing medicine without a license. All of these things are against the Gospel. The reason that Europe is staying in the state it's in is because it is not open to the Good News, not because of demonic powers.

Demonic powers are a part of it; they are inspiring people to take those steps. But you can't solve the problem just by doing "spiritual warfare" and binding demons; you must get God's Word into the people.

PREACHING & TEACHING

Christians have spent millions of dollars traveling to some of these least evangelized nations. They go over there and "prayer walk"; that is, they just walk around "binding" spiritual powers. They are specifically told not to witness to anyone—just to pray. If the same amount of money had been spent preaching the Gospel to these unreached people, there would be revival! This is the wrong approach and it's not working.

This meeting in Ephesus with the 20,000 people who just prayed and did "spiritual warfare" occurred before the September 11, 2001, terrorist attacks. It didn't break the demonic powers operating through Muslim extremists. It never will. This is not the scriptural method of dealing with demonic influence in people's lives.

I am doing everything I can to get the Word out! I am teaching God's Word on television and radio in America, Europe, and around the world. My ministry distributes thousands of teaching materials (i.e., audio messages, articles, and Bible commentary) each year. Many are available free online. I also support many international Christian workers who are boldly preaching the Gospel. This should be the approach of the entire church.

PROCLAIM THE WORD!
LESSON 16 – OUTLINE

I. Paul is a great example of true spiritual warfare.

  A. In Acts 19, the apostle ministered in the city of Ephesus.

  B. Scripture never records Paul ever leading the believers to gather together to intercede, do spiritual warfare, and rebuke the demonic principalities over the city.

  C. Through boldly preaching the Gospel, Paul broke the power of Diana and saw multitudes in the city receive the Lord Jesus Christ.

  D. That's the scriptural method: Preach God's Word.

All scripture is given by inspiration of God, and is profitable for doctrine, for reproof, for correction, for instruction in righteousness: [17] That the man of God may be perfect, throughly furnished unto all good works. [4:1] I charge thee *therefore before God, and the Lord Jesus Christ, who shall judge the quick and the dead at his appearing and his kingdom; [2]* Preach the word; *be instant in season, out of season; reprove, rebuke, exhort with all longsuffering and doctrine.*

2 TIMOTHY 3:16-4:2, EMPHASIS MINE

  E. Paul told people the truth, got them saved and set free, and discipled them to go out and do the same.

II. As individuals, families, and communities come out of deception, demonic powers are weakened and broken.

  A. You don't get rid of demonic powers by going into the heavenlies and doing battle directly with them.

  B. Preach the truth instead.

  C. As these people understand and believe that God loves them, they will be set free.

  D. Then they will resist those devils with the truth, and the entire climate over the city or country will change.

III. Ezekiel prophesied that every individual would answer for their own sin—and no one else's—under the New Covenant.

What mean ye, that ye use this proverb concerning the land of Israel, saying, The fathers have eaten sour grapes, and the children's teeth are set on edge? [i.e., "generational curse"] [3] As I live, saith the Lord God, *ye shall not have occasion any more to use this* proverb in Israel. *[4] Behold, all souls are mine; as the soul of the father, so also the soul of the son is mine:* the soul that sinneth, it shall die.

EZEKIEL 18:2-4, BRACKETS AND EMPHASIS MINE

    A. God doesn't judge children for the sins of their parents today (Ezek. 18:20).

    B. A man stands before God on his own.

    C. If he can understand and believe the truth that Jesus Christ dealt with all sin once and for all at the cross, forgiveness would set him free.

    D. Deception is what keeps us in bondage, and the truth is what sets us free.

    E. You can't solve the problem just by doing "spiritual warfare" and binding demons; you must get God's Word into the people.

IV. Andrew is doing everything he can to get the Word out.

    A. He is am teaching God's Word on television and radio in America, Europe, and around the world.

    B. His ministry distributes thousands of teaching materials (i.e., audio messages, articles, and Bible commentary) each year.

    C. Many are available free online.

    D. He also supports many international Christian workers who are boldly preaching the Gospel.

    E. This should be the approach of the entire church.

PROCLAIM THE WORD!
LESSON 16 – TEACHER'S GUIDE

1. Paul is a great example of true spiritual warfare. In Acts 19, the apostle ministered in the city of Ephesus. Scripture never records Paul ever leading the believers to gather together to intercede, do spiritual warfare, and rebuke the demonic principalities over the city. Through boldly preaching the Gospel, Paul broke the power of Diana and saw multitudes in the city receive the Lord Jesus Christ. That's the scriptural method: Preach God's Word (2 Tim. 3:16-4:2). Paul told people the truth, got them saved and set free, and discipled them to go out and do the same.

2. As individuals, families, and communities come out of deception, demonic powers are weakened and broken. We don't get rid of demonic powers by going into the heavenlies and doing battle directly with them; we preach the truth instead. As these people understand and believe that God loves them, they will be set free. Then they will resist those devils with the truth, and the entire climate over the city or country will change.

3. Ezekiel prophesied that every individual would answer for their own sin—and no one else's—under the New Covenant (Ezek. 18:2-4). God doesn't judge children for the sins of their parents today (Ezek. 18:20); each person stands before God on their own. If they can understand and believe the truth that Jesus Christ dealt with all sin once and for all at the Cross, forgiveness would set them free. Deception is what keeps them in bondage, and the truth is what sets them free. We can't solve the problem just by doing "spiritual warfare" and binding demons. We must get God's Word into the people.

4. Let's do everything we can to get the Word out. This should be the approach of the entire church.

1. A. Read Acts 19 (Notice especially verses 2-6, 8-12, 17-20, and 26) and 2 Timothy 3:16-4:2. How did Paul break the power of Diana and see multitudes in the city receive the Lord Jesus Christ? (Through boldly preaching the Gospel)
   B. What is the scriptural method? (Preach God's Word)
   C. Paul told people the truth, got them saved and set free, and then what? (Discipled them to go out and do the same)
2. A. How are demonic powers weakened and broken? (As individuals, families, and communities come out of deception)
   B. When will the entire climate change over a city or country? (As the people understand and believe that God loves them, they will resist those devils with the truth)
3. A. Read Ezekiel 18:2-4 and 20. Under the New Covenant, how does each person stand before God? (On their own)
   B. What must we get into the people? (God's Word)
4. A. What should be the approach of the entire church? (The church do everything it can to get the Word out)

PROCLAIM THE WORD!
LESSON 16 – DISCIPLESHIP QUESTIONS

1. According to 2 Timothy 3:16–4:2, what is given by inspiration of God?

2. What is it profitable for?

   A. Doctrine
   B. Reproof
   C. Correction
   D. Instruction in righteousness
   E. All of the above
   F. None of the above

3. That who may be perfect?

4. *"Throughly furnished"* unto what?

5. Who shall judge the quick—i.e., the living—and the dead?

6. When shall Jesus do this?

7. What should we preach?

8. When should we be ready to do this?

9. What should we do with all long-suffering and doctrine?

   A. Reprove
   B. Condemn
   C. Exhort
   D. Both A. and B.
   E. Both A. and C.

10. According to Ezekiel 18:2-4, who was this proverb used concerning?

11. What have the fathers eaten?

12. Whose teeth are set on edge?

13. Who said they would not have occasion to use this proverb any more in Israel?

14. All souls are whose?

15. What shall happen to the soul that sins?

16. According to Ezekiel 18:20, who shall die?

17. What shall the son not bear?

18. What shall the father not bear?

19. What shall be upon the righteous?

20. What shall be upon the wicked?

PROCLAIM THE WORD!
LESSON 16 – ANSWER KEY

1. All scripture

2. E. All of the above

3. The man of God

4. All good works

5. The Lord Jesus Christ

6. At His appearing and His kingdom

7. The Word

8. In season and out of season

9. E. Both A. and C.

10. The land of Israel

11. Sour grapes

12. The children's

13. The Lord God

14. The Lord God

15. It shall die

16. The soul that sins

17. The iniquity of the father

18. The iniquity of the son

19. His righteousness

20. His wickedness

PROCLAIM THE WORD!
LESSON 16 – SCRIPTURES

2 TIMOTHY 3:16 – 4:2

All scripture is given by inspiration of God, and is profitable for doctrine, for reproof, for correction, for instruction in righteousness: [17] That the man of God may be perfect, thoroughly furnished unto all good works. [4:1] I charge thee therefore before God, and the Lord Jesus Christ, who shall judge the quick and the dead at his appearing and his kingdom; [2] Preach the word; be instant in season, out of season; reprove, rebuke, exhort with all longsuffering and doctrine.

EZEKIEL 18:2-4

What mean ye, that ye use this proverb concerning the land of Israel, saying, The fathers have eaten sour grapes, and the children's teeth are set on edge? [3] As I live, saith the Lord God, ye shall not have occasion any more to use this proverb in Israel. [4] Behold, all souls are mine; as the soul of the father, so also the soul of the son is mine: the soul that sinneth, it shall die.

EZEKIEL 18:20

The soul that sinneth, it shall die. The son shall not bear the iniquity of the father, neither shall the father bear the iniquity of the son: the righteousness of the righteous shall be upon him, and the wickedness of the wicked shall be upon him.

A PLOY OF THE DEVIL
LESSON 17

"Spiritual warfare," as it's popularly presented today, is actually a ploy of the devil. Consider the fruit: Christians are encouraging Christians not to preach the Gospel but just to pray instead. You might wonder, *Why would Satan want believers to pray more?* Simple! The devil delights when we give ourselves to praying fruitless, religious prayers.

Who do you think "inspired" the so-called "prayers" of the scribes, Pharisees, and hypocrites that Jesus so emphatically denounced? They sounded trumpets, stood on street corners, and did all of these other religious things when they prayed. If you think the devil would never encourage people just to pray, you are sadly mistaken. Church history abounds with example after example of the Enemy luring Christians into doing all kinds of impressive-looking—but powerless—spiritual calisthenics.

As believers, our focus should be on preaching the Gospel and proclaiming the truth of God's Word to all people everywhere. However, there are groups today spending big bucks to send hundreds, even thousands, of Christians around the world on so-called "mission trips" with instructions not to preach the Gospel. "Don't witness to anyone! Your job is just to walk, pray, and do spiritual warfare." Although their hearts might be in the right place and some participants' lives are positively impacted for missions, overall, it's wrong, wrong, wrong! If they took the same amount of money and effort and invested them into preaching the Gospel, distributing tracts, and sharing the Truth in those nations, they would see infinitely greater results.

PREACH & PRAY

It's not a matter of either preaching or praying; they should be done together. Prayer is like water to a seed. If the seed has been planted, then it needs to be watered. But you can water and water and water barren ground, and nothing will come of it. People are born again by the incorruptible seed of God's Word (1 Pet. 1:23). Therefore, before you water, you must plant the seed!

When Paul went forth to preach, he asked his friends to pray for him: *"That utterance may be given unto me, that I may open my mouth boldly, to make known the mystery of the gospel"* (Eph. 6:19). He didn't say, "Pray that people's ears may be opened to hear. Pray that demonic powers (like Diana of the Ephesians) would leave." No! Paul asked people to pray that he would speak with revelation, authority, and power and that miracles would be done in Jesus' mighty name.

Prayer is an important part of the Gospel, but it can never be substituted for the preaching of God's Word. Paul's boldness to share the truth literally destroyed Diana of the

Ephesians' power. Finally, Demetrius and the other silversmiths came together because they were just about out of work. People had quit buying their pagan idol images. They said,

Not only this our craft is in danger to be set at nought; but also that the temple of the great goddess Diana should be despised, and her magnificence should be destroyed, whom all Asia and the world worshippeth.

ACTS 19:27

Until the spiritual warfare intercessors recently dug her up and gave her power she didn't previously have, Diana of the Ephesians hadn't been a factor in almost 2,000 years. Such is the power of God's Word.

God has already accomplished everything. He has already given it to us in the spiritual realm. The only war we're fighting is to receive that provision in physical manifestation.

THE TRUTH SETS PEOPLE FREE

How is that war fought? Is it in the heavenlies? Do we have to climb tall buildings and rent airplanes to do battle with spiritual wickedness in high places? Must we send people to foreign countries around the world to rebuke the devil over there?

If demonic powers were really the force people claim, you wouldn't have to climb a building or rent a plane to get up close to them. You wouldn't have to send people over to foreign countries to pray either. It's not like your prayers only work within a hundred-yard radius. Even if these ideas were true, you could just bind the demons from right where you are. Prayer is that powerful! You don't have to do spiritual warfare in close proximity; preach the Gospel instead. Tell people the truth.

Broadcast God's Word by radio, television, and internet. Distribute tracts, books, and other quality literature. Train disciples and send them out. Start Bible colleges and churches everywhere. At the very least, become a ministry partner and support the work of someone who is doing these things. The New Testament emphasizes the proclaiming of God's Word.

However, popular emphasis hasn't been on preaching the Word. Instead, most spiritual warfare people are into all kinds of weirdness. I've even heard accounts of public meetings where women laid on top of men and went through the motions of giving birth. They call it "travailing" and doing "spiritual warfare." Really, it's just lewd and totally ungodly. The Lord never led anyone to do that type of thing.

Am I against true spiritual warfare? No! Am I against true intercession? No! I'm just against the weirdness being called "spiritual warfare" and "intercession" today. The body of Christ needs to reexamine these teachings in the light of God's Word and the New Covenant.

The only reason Satan is a factor is because there are so many deceived people empowering him and promoting his doctrines. If we preached only the truth, the devil would be reduced to nothing. But since there's so much error—not only in the world but also in the body of Christ—we'll constantly be battling lies with the truth until Jesus comes back. No one has it all figured out, so we're continually renewing our minds to the truth. There are things we are fighting, and spiritual warfare is real, but it's not because Satan has all this power; it's because he has deceived so many people. The antidote isn't intercession—binding demonic powers and enlisting millions of Christians to "pray"; it is telling people the truth and seeing them set free.

REVIVAL

The same holds true for revival. I'm for revival. I want to see the positive effects of revival sweep through America and all around the world. We need a revival, but how do we go about receiving one?

The "intercessors" say that we must pray harder, longer, and recruit more and more people—a hundred, a thousand, a million, ten million—to pray and fast with them. They view God as the one responsible for sending revival, and that He's holding it back from us for some unknown reason. Since He's "not pleased," they are repenting, doing restitution, and all of these other things to appease Him so that He'll send revival.

God has already been appeased! Jesus Christ made atonement for all sin 2,000 years ago. God's not angry anymore. Through His death, burial, and resurrection, Jesus released all the power it takes for massive worldwide revival. We just haven't been receiving it.

You need to believe what God has already done, not beg and plead with Him for revival. You start being a vessel of God's miracles to others! You begin healing the sick and raising people from the dead! I guarantee that you'll see the effects of revival. In fact, you'll have all the revival you can handle! I'm definitely for revival. But it's going to come as people yield themselves to God, not as they twist His arm more through "intercession" and "spiritual warfare."

I know that many people will reject these truths I'm sharing because they are so contrary to the mainstream theology in the body of Christ today. Although there are only a few of us preaching this right now, I challenge you to take another look at God's Word for yourself. Study the atonement of Jesus. Follow the example of the book of Acts. You won't find "intercession" or "spiritual warfare" being done as it is promoted today. Satan is a factor, but he's not the powerful menace he's been made out to be by people who've missed the parade.

JESUS: OUR MIGHTY DELIVERER

Visualize the triumphant procession. See Satan defeated, stripped of all power and authority, and nailed to the cross. Allow this vision of the devil—impaled and on exhibition—to sink deep into your heart. Once you've been to the victory parade, you will never fear him again. Satan won't be able to intimidate you the way he did in the past. You will be set free and able to boldly minister God's freedom to others.

A PLOY OF THE DEVIL
LESSON 17 – OUTLINE

I.   "Spiritual warfare," as it's popularly presented today, is actually a ploy of the devil.

    A. Consider the fruit: Christians are encouraging Christians not to preach the Gospel but just to pray instead.

    B. The devil delights when we give ourselves to praying fruitless, religious prayers.

    C. Church history abounds with example after example of the Enemy luring Christians into doing all kinds of impressive-looking—but powerless—spiritual calisthenics.

    D. As believers, our focus should be on preaching the Gospel and proclaiming the truth of God's Word to all people everywhere.

II.   It's not a matter of either preaching or praying; they should be done together.

    A. People are born again by the incorruptible seed of God's Word (1 Pet. 1:23).

    B. Therefore, before you water, you must plant the seed!

That utterance may be given unto me, that I may open my mouth boldly, to make known the mystery of the gospel.

EPHESIANS 6:19

    C. Paul asked people to pray that he would speak with revelation, authority, and power and that miracles would be done in Jesus' mighty name.

    D. Prayer is an important part of the Gospel, but it can never be substituted for the preaching of God's Word.

Not only this our craft is in danger to be set at nought; but also that the temple of the great goddess Diana should be despised, and her magnificence should be destroyed, whom all Asia and the world worshippeth.

ACTS 19:27

    E. The New Testament emphasizes the proclaiming of God's Word!

III. Through His death, burial, and resurrection, Jesus released all the power it takes for massive worldwide revival.

    A. We just haven't been receiving it.

    B. Revival is going to come as people yield themselves to God, not as they twist His arm more through "intercession" and "spiritual warfare."

    C. Study the atonement of Jesus, and follow the example of the book of Acts.

    D. Once you've been to the victory parade, you will never fear Satan again.

    E. You will be set free and able to boldly minister God's freedom to others!

A PLOY OF THE DEVIL
LESSON 17 – TEACHER'S GUIDE

1. "Spiritual warfare," as it's popularly presented today, is actually a ploy of the devil. Consider the fruit: Christians are encouraging Christians not to preach the Gospel but just to "pray" instead. The devil delights when we give ourselves to praying fruitless, religious prayers. Church history abounds with example after example of the Enemy luring Christians into doing all kinds of impressive-looking—but powerless—spiritual calisthenics. As believers, our focus should be on preaching the Gospel and proclaiming the truth of God's Word to all people everywhere.

2. It's not a matter of either preaching or praying; they should be done together. People are born again by the incorruptible seed of God's Word (1 Pet. 1:23). Therefore, before we water, we must plant the seed (Eph. 6:19). Paul asked people to pray that he would speak with revelation, authority, and power and that miracles would be done in Jesus' mighty name. Prayer is an important part of the Gospel, but it can never be substituted for the preaching of God's Word (Acts 19:27). The New Testament emphasizes the proclaiming of God's Word.

3. Through His death, burial, and resurrection, Jesus released all the power it takes for massive worldwide revival. We just haven't been receiving it. Revival is going to come as people yield themselves to God, not as they twist His arm more through "intercession" and "spiritual warfare." Let's study the atonement of Jesus and follow the example of the book of Acts. Once we've been to the victory parade, we will never fear Satan again. We will be set free and able to boldly minister God's freedom to others.

1. A. What does the devil delight in? (When we give ourselves to praying fruitless, religious prayers)
   B. Church history abounds with example after example of the Enemy luring Christians into what? (Doing all kinds of impressive-looking—but powerless—spiritual calisthenics)
   C. As believers, what should our focus be on? (Preaching the Gospel and proclaiming the truth of God's Word to all people everywhere)
2. A. Read 1 Peter 1:23, Ephesians 6:19, and Acts 19:26-27. What should be done together? (Preaching and praying)
   B. What did Paul ask people to pray? (That he would speak with revelation, authority, and power and that miracles would be done in Jesus' mighty name)
   C. Although prayer is an important part of the Gospel, it can never be substituted for what? (The preaching and proclaiming of God's Word)
3. A. How did Jesus release all the power it takes for massive worldwide revival? (Through His death, burial, and resurrection)
   B. How does revival come? (We receive it—as we yield ourselves to God)
   C. We should study the Atonement of Jesus and follow what example? (The example of the book of Acts)

A PLOY OF THE DEVIL
LESSON 17 – DISCIPLESHIP QUESTIONS

1. According to 1 Peter 1:23, are we born again of a corruptible seed?

2. What is the incorruptible seed?

3. What lives and abides forever?

4. Who was speaking in Ephesians 6:19?

5. Paul asked that utterance be what?

6. That he may open his mouth how?

7. To make what known?

8. Who was speaking in Acts 19:27?

9. What did Demetrius say about his craft?

10. What was in danger of being despised?

11. Diana's magnificence was about to be what?

12. Who worshiped her?

A PLOY OF THE DEVIL
LESSON 17 – ANSWER KEY

1. No

2. The Word of God

3. The incorruptible seed of God's Word

4. Paul

5. Given to him

6. Boldly

7. The mystery of the Gospel

8. Demetrius, a silversmith

9. It was in danger to be set at nought

10. The temple of Diana

11. Destroyed

12. All Asia and the world

A PLOY OF THE DEVIL
LESSON 17 – SCRIPTURES

1 PETER 1:23

Being born again, not of corruptible seed, but of incorruptible, by the word of God, which liveth and abideth for ever.

EPHESIANS 6:19

And for me, that utterance may be given unto me, that I may open my mouth boldly, to make known the mystery of the gospel.

ACTS 19:27

So that not only this our craft is in danger to be set at nought; but also that the temple of the great goddess Diana should be despised, and her magnificence should be destroyed, whom all Asia and the world worshippeth.

PUT YOUR FAITH TO WORK
LESSON 18

You don't need more faith—so quit trying to get it! If you're born again, you've already been given all the faith you will ever need. Right now, you have more than enough faith. You're just ignorant of what you've got and how to use it.

The disciples had the same problem. Notice their response to Jesus' teaching:

Take heed to yourselves: If thy brother trespass against thee, rebuke him; and if he repent, forgive him. [4] And if he trespass against thee seven times in a day, and seven times in a day turn again to thee, saying, I repent; thou shalt forgive him. [5] And the apostles said unto the Lord, Increase our faith.

LUKE 17:3-5

Jesus had raised people from the dead, opened blind eyes and deaf ears, healed lepers, cast out devils, and done many other miraculous things no one else had ever done. However, it was His command to continually forgive—not these other things—that provoked the disciples to say, "Lord, increase our faith!"

Faith is for everyday life! It's not only to effect miraculous healing and financial deliverance. Although these things are important, it's your daily interpersonal relationships that will place the greatest demand on your faith. You've missed it if you think faith is primarily for impossible situations, like when the doctor says you're going to die or you're facing bankruptcy. Faith certainly applies to your crises, but you need faith for the people you live and work with day in and day out all week long. How else can you turn the other cheek when someone hurts you?

It takes faith to always unconditionally love and forgive your coworkers, your spouse, your children, your parents, and your neighbors. The disciples were so overwhelmed by Jesus' command to forgive—even up to seven times in one day—that they exclaimed, "Lord, increase our faith!"

MORE THAN ENOUGH FAITH

Jesus answered,

If ye had faith as a grain of mustard seed, ye might say unto this sycamine tree, Be thou plucked up by the root, and be thou planted in the sea; and it should obey you.

LUKE 17:6

In a sense, it appears as if Jesus didn't really answer their question. They had said "Increase our faith," and He answered, "If you had faith the size of a mustard seed, you could do this." What the Lord was telling them was, "Guys, you don't need more faith. You don't have a faith problem. You just aren't using the faith you've already got."

A mustard seed is one of the smallest seeds there is. It's so tiny that when you hold one between your thumb and index finger, it's hard to tell that you even have anything there. Jesus said, "If your faith is only this much—the size of a mustard seed—you could tell this tree to be planted in the sea, and it would obey you." In other words, you don't need "big" faith, or even "more" faith. You just need to learn how to use the faith you already have.

Most Christians today don't understand this concept. They believe faith works but think theirs is deficient. That's a deception from the devil! Satan has blinded us to what we already have.

You already possess the same amount and quality of faith Jesus had when He physically walked on the earth. It's inside every born-again believer. Satan lies to Christians to keep them from understanding this. They believe faith works, but they don't believe that they have enough of it. They think it comes and goes—sometimes strong, sometimes weak. It's like they can't get a handle on it, can't hold it, and can't control it, because it's intangible. That's a totally wrong attitude about faith. You have—right now—more than enough faith. You just need to use it.

A SERVANT CALLED "FAITH"

In verses 7-10, Jesus immediately launched into a parable to illustrate His meaning. If you understand that you already have faith and you need to use what you've got, then this parable makes sense. If you try to apply it any other way, this parable doesn't make sense. The context dictates its meaning.

But which of you, having a servant plowing or feeding cattle, will say unto him by and by, when he is come from the field, Go and sit down to meat? [8] And will not rather say unto him, Make ready wherewith I may sup, and gird thyself, and serve me, till I have eaten and drunken; and afterward thou shalt eat and drink? [9] Doth he thank that servant because he did the things that were commanded him? I trow not [old English for "I don't think so!" or "That's not how it works!"]. [10] So likewise ye, when ye shall have done all those things which are commanded you, say, We are unprofitable servants: we have done that which was our duty to do.

LUKE 17:7-10, BRACKETS MINE

Jesus was saying, "You need to use the faith you've already got! Even if it's only as big as a mustard seed, it's enough to cast a tree into the sea. You would put your servant to work if you owned one, wouldn't you? You already have faith. Now, put it to work!"

Servanthood and slavery were an everyday part of life in Jesus' time. If you owned a slave, you expected them to serve you. It didn't matter that they were tired and had just come in from working all day in the fields. If it was suppertime, you expected them to serve you your food. Their time to eat was after you were finished and satisfied. They didn't eat with you, and they definitely didn't eat before you. You were the master.

In today's touchy, feely, politically correct mindset, most people would say, "Well, you shouldn't treat a servant that way!" But in the time that Jesus spoke this parable, servants and slaves weren't pampered; they were used. You didn't just allow them to lie around and do nothing all day because you didn't want to impose on them. Neither were you kind and gentle with them. You commanded them to take care of your needs before they took care of their own. You didn't have to be mean and nasty about it, but as their master, you definitely gave them orders. If you had a slave, you put them to work.

Faith should be put to work, not pampered. Not using your faith is like allowing your slave to sit on the couch and do nothing but watch television all day. Instead of growing stronger and more efficient through use, their muscles atrophy and their abilities become dull. Then you wonder why your faith isn't producing anything. You haven't put it to work! You're not using it! Start putting your faith to work the way a master uses a slave. It's not a matter of not having the servant; it's a matter of not using what you've got.

THE GIFT OF GOD

Most believers are ignorant of the faith they already have. If I started giving you some testimonies of what faith has accomplished—the dead raised, blind eyes and deaf ears opened, miraculous provisions—you would say, "Praise God, I believe those things happen."

If we were in a service where someone died and I asked "How many here believe the Lord can raise this person from the dead?" you would agree with me that it can be done. If I asked "How many of you believe that if I pray, this person will come back from the dead?" you would continue agreeing with me totally. In fact, you'd probably work your way up to the front so you could see this miracle happen. But I'd probably lose you and the majority of people when I said, "All right, if you believe this, you pray for them." All of a sudden, your anticipation would turn to dread. Why? Because if you're like most people, you don't believe your faith is adequate. You don't doubt that faith works; you just don't believe you have the quantity or quality of faith you need.

I could talk most Christians into saying "I just need more faith" and get them to pray, "O God, please give me more faith!" But that would violate everything we've seen in the Word thus far. You already have faith. You already have the same power that raised Jesus Christ from the dead living on the inside of you. You don't have a faith problem; you have a knowledge problem. You don't know what you've got, nor the laws that govern how it works.

For by grace are ye saved through faith; and that not of yourselves: it is the gift of God: *[9]* not of works, lest any man should boast.

EPHESIANS 2:8-9, EMPHASIS MINE

This verse can be interpreted in at least two different ways. *"That"* speaks of your salvation, which is a gift of God and not of yourself (your own works). However, *"that"* can also mean the faith you actually used to receive salvation. *That faith* is also not of yourself, but it is *"the gift of God."* Can you see it?

GOD'S WORDS CARRY FAITH

The faith it takes to receive salvation comes by hearing God's Word.

How then shall they call on him in whom they have not believed? and how shall they believe in him of whom they have not heard? and how shall they hear without a preacher? [15] And how shall they preach, except they be sent? as it is written, How beautiful are the feet of them that preach the gospel of peace, and bring glad tidings of good things! [16] But they have not all obeyed the gospel. For Esaias saith, Lord, who hath believed our report? [17] So then faith cometh by hearing, and hearing by the word of God.

ROMANS 10:14-17

You simply cannot believe unless you hear the Word of God. God's words carry faith!

Every word that comes out of your mouth is a container. I can say things that build you up and encourage you. I could even bring you to tears of joy through complimenting and praising you. However, I can also say things to tear you down and dishearten you. I could bring you to tears of sorrow, hurt, grief, pain, and anger. Words are powerful!

Words contain either faith or unbelief. God's words are full of faith. God Himself is faith-full, and the words He has spoken are faith-filled. They are containers full of God's own faith. You can't believe God for salvation without first having God's Word bring you His faith. It truly takes a supernatural faith in order to be born again.

Therefore, we do have God's supernatural faith in us, and it doesn't come and go. The gifts and callings of God are without repentance (Rom. 11:29). We just aren't using what we have, primarily because we don't know we have it.

PUT YOUR FAITH TO WORK
LESSON 18 – OUTLINE

I. If you're born again, you've already been given all the faith you'll ever need.

Take heed to yourselves: If thy brother trespass against thee, rebuke him; and if he repent, forgive him. [4] And if he trespass against thee seven times in a day, and seven times in a day turn again to thee, saying, I repent; thou shalt forgive him. [5] And the apostles said unto the Lord, Increase our faith.

LUKE 17:3-5

A. Faith certainly applies to your crises, but you need faith for the people you live and work with day in and day out all week long.

B. It takes faith to always unconditionally love and forgive your coworkers, your spouse, your children, your parents, and your neighbors.

If ye had faith as a grain of mustard seed, ye might say unto this sycamine tree, Be thou plucked up by the root, and be thou planted in the sea; and it should obey you.

LUKE 17:6

C. What the Lord was telling them was, "Guys, you don't need more faith. You don't have a faith problem. You just aren't using the faith you've already got!"

D. You already possess the same amount and quality of faith Jesus had when He physically walked on the earth.

E. You just need to use it!

II. Then in verses 7-10, Jesus immediately launched into a parable to illustrate His meaning.

But which of you, having a servant plowing or feeding cattle, will say unto him by and by, when he is come from the field, Go and sit down to meat? [8] And will not rather say unto him, Make ready wherewith I may sup, and gird thyself, and serve me, till I have eaten and drunken; and afterward thou shalt eat and drink? [9] Doth he thank that servant because he did the things that were commanded him? I trow not [old English for "I don't think so!" or "That's not how it works!"]. [10] So likewise ye, when ye shall have done all those things which are commanded you, say, We are unprofitable servants: we have done that which was our duty to do.

LUKE 17:7-10, BRACKETS MINE

A. Jesus was saying, "You need to use the faith you've already got. Even if it's only as big as a mustard seed, it's enough to cast a tree into the sea. You would put your servant to work if you owned one, wouldn't you? You already have faith. Now, put it to work!"

B. Faith should be put to work, not pampered.

C. Start putting your faith to work the way a master uses a slave.

D. It's not a matter of not having the servant; it's a matter of not using what you've got.

III. Most believers are ignorant of the faith they already have.

A. You don't doubt that faith works; you just don't believe you have the quantity or quality of faith you need.

B. You don't have a faith problem; you have a knowledge problem.

C. You don't know what you've got, nor the laws that govern how it works.

IV. The faith it takes to receive salvation comes by hearing God's Word.

For by grace are ye saved through faith; and that not of yourselves: it is the gift of God: *[9]* not of works, lest any man should boast.

EPHESIANS 2:8-9, EMPHASIS MINE

A. *That faith* is also not of yourself, but it is *"the gift of God."*

How then shall they call on him in whom they have not believed? and how shall they believe in him of whom they have not heard? and how shall they hear without a preacher? [15] And how shall they preach, except they be sent? as it is written, How beautiful are the feet of them that preach the gospel of peace, and bring glad tidings of good things! [16] But they have not all obeyed the gospel. For Esaias saith, Lord, who hath believed our report? [17] So then faith cometh by hearing, and hearing by the word of God.

ROMANS 10:14-17

B. God Himself is faith-full, and the words He has spoken are faith-filled.

C. You can't believe God for salvation without first having God's Word bring you His faith.

D. Therefore, you do have God's supernatural faith in you, and it doesn't come and go (Rom. 11:29).

E. We just aren't using what we have, primarily because we don't know we have it.

PUT YOUR FAITH TO WORK
LESSON 18 – TEACHER'S GUIDE

1.   If we're born again, we've already been given all the faith we will ever need (Luke 17:3-5). Faith certainly applies to our crises, but we need faith for the people we live and work with day in and day out all week long. It takes faith to always unconditionally love and forgive our coworkers, our spouses, our children, our parents, and our neighbors (Luke 17:6). What the Lord was telling the disciples was, "Guys, you don't need more faith. You don't have a faith problem. You just aren't using the faith you've already got." We already possess the same amount and quality of faith Jesus had when He physically walked on the earth. We just need to use it.

2.   Then in verses 7-10, Jesus immediately launched into a parable to illustrate His meaning. Jesus was saying, "You need to use the faith you've already got! Even if it's only as big as a mustard seed, it's enough to cast a tree into the sea. You would put your servant to work if you owned one, wouldn't you? You already have faith. Now, put it to work!" Faith should be put to work, not pampered. Let's start putting our faith to work the way a master uses a slave. It's not a matter of not having the servant; it's a matter of not using what we've got.

3.   Most of us as believers are ignorant of the faith we already have. We don't doubt that faith works; we just don't believe we have the quantity or quality of faith we need. We don't have a faith problem; we have a knowledge problem. We don't know what we've got, nor the laws that govern how it works.

1. A. Read Luke 17:3-6. If we're born again, what have we already been given? (All the faith we will ever need)
    B. Although faith certainly applies to our crises, we need faith for whom? (The people we live and work with day in and day out all week long)
    C. What amount and quality of faith do we already possess? (The same amount and quality of faith as Jesus had when He physically walked on the earth)
2. A. Read Luke 17:7-10. Should faith be put to work or pampered? (Put to work)
    B. How should we start putting our faith to work? (The way a master uses a slave)
3. A. What are most of us as believers ignorant of? (The faith we already have)
    B. What don't we know? (What we've got, nor the laws that govern how it works)

4.   The faith it takes to receive salvation comes by hearing God's Word (Eph. 2:8-9). *That faith* is also not of ourselves, but it is *"the gift of God."* God Himself is faith-full, and the words He has spoken are faith-filled (Rom. 10:14-17). We can't believe God for salvation without first having God's Word bring us His faith. Therefore, we do have God's supernatural faith in us, and it doesn't come and go (Rom. 11:29); we just aren't using what we have, primarily because we don't know we have it.

4. A. Read Ephesians 2:8-9; Romans 10:14-17, and 11:29. We can't believe God for salvation without first having God's Word bring us what? (His faith)
    B. Does God's supernatural faith in us come and go? (No)
    C. Why aren't we using what we have? (Primarily because we don't know we have it)

PUT YOUR FAITH TO WORK
LESSON 18 – DISCIPLESHIP QUESTIONS

1. Luke 17:3-6 advises us to take heed unto whom?

2. What should we do if a brother trespasses against us?

3. What should we do if he repents?

4. What if he trespasses and repents seven times in a day?

5. To what kind of seed is faith likened?

6. What kind of tree is referred to?

7. Read Luke 17:7-10. Even though the servant just came in from working hard out in the field, what will the master tell them to do?

    A. Go and sit down to meat
    B. Come and sit down with me to meat
    C. Serve me my food, then—afterward—you can eat
    D. All of the above
    E. None of the above

8. Will the master thank that servant for doing what was commanded?

9. When we've done all we have been commanded, what should we say?

10. According to Ephesians 2:8-9, for by _____ are we saved.

11. Through what?

12. According to Romans 10:14-17, is it possible to call on someone in whom we have not believed?

13. In order to believe in God, what must we do first?

14. How shall they hear without a what?

15. How shall they preach, except they be what?

16. What are beautiful?

17. Have they all obeyed the Gospel?

18. Who has believed our what?

19. How does faith come?

20. According to Romans 11:29, the gifts and calling of God are without what?

PUT YOUR FAITH TO WORK
LESSON 18 – ANSWER KEY

1. Ourselves

2. Rebuke him

3. Forgive him

4. Forgive him

5. A mustard seed

6. A sycamine tree

7. C. Serve me my food, then—afterward—you can eat

8. No

9. *"We are unprofitable servants: we have done that which was our duty to do"* (Luke 17:10)

10. Grace

11. Faith

12. No

13. Hear

14. Preacher

15. Sent

16. The feet of them who preach the Gospel of peace

17. No

18. Report

19. By hearing the Word of God

20. Repentance

PUT YOUR FAITH TO WORK
LESSON 18 – SCRIPTURES

LUKE 17:3-10

Take heed to yourselves: If thy brother trespass against thee, rebuke him; and if he repent, forgive him. [4] And if he trespass against thee seven times in a day, and seven times in a day turn again to thee, saying, I repent; thou shalt forgive him. [5] And the apostles said unto the Lord, Increase our faith. [6] And the Lord said, If ye had faith as a grain of mustard seed, ye might say unto this sycamine tree, Be thou plucked up by the root, and be thou planted in the sea; and it should obey you. [7] But which of you, having a servant plowing or feeding cattle, will say unto him by and by, when he is come from the field, Go and sit down to meat? [8] And will not rather say unto him, Make ready wherewith I may sup, and gird thyself, and serve me, till I have eaten and drunken; and afterward thou shalt eat and drink? [9] Doth he thank that servant because he did the things that were commanded him? I trow not. [10] So likewise ye, when ye shall have done all those things which are commanded you, say, We are unprofitable servants: we have done that which was our duty to do.

EPHESIANS 2:8-9

For by grace are ye saved through faith; and that not of yourselves: it is the gift of God: [9] not of works, lest any man should boast.

ROMANS 10:14-17

How then shall they call on him in whom they have not believed? [15] and how shall they believe in him of whom they have not heard? and how shall they hear without a preacher? And how shall they preach, except they be sent? as it is written, How beautiful are the feet of them that preach the gospel of peace, and bring glad tidings of good things! [16] But they have not all obeyed the gospel. For Esaias saith, Lord, who hath believed our report? [17] So then faith cometh by hearing, and hearing by the word of God.

ROMANS 11:29

For the gifts and calling of God are without repentance.

SUPERNATURAL FAITH
LESSON 19

The church I grew up in used several examples to illustrate how everyone had faith. They put a chair in front of me and said, "It's faith to sit in this chair. How do you know it will hold you up?" They would say, "It's faith to go through an intersection when the stoplight is green. You're using faith that the people on the other side will stop on red." They'd also say, "It's faith to take a flight on an airplane. You don't know what makes it work. You don't know the pilot. These are things you regularly do that involve faith." All of this, to a degree, is faith—but it's a human faith.

God is a faith being, and human beings were created in His image. Therefore, every person—saved or not—has faith within them because it was a part of God and is now a part of us. However, this type of faith—to sit in a chair, drive through an intersection, or fly on an airplane—is human faith. It's based completely on what you can see, taste, hear, smell, and feel. If you saw that the chair was missing a leg or two and tottered, you wouldn't sit on it. If you heard a loud metallic squeal and smelled smoke coming from the direction of the wing, you wouldn't fly on that plane. Neither would you go through the green light if you spotted someone from the other direction barreling toward the intersection at a high speed. Sense knowledge—what you can see, taste, hear, smell, and feel—affects human faith.

However, in order to receive salvation, you had to believe in things your natural senses couldn't perceive. You've never seen God or the devil. You've never seen heaven or hell, and you've never seen a sin. You've seen people commit sin, but what does a "sin" actually look like? You can't see sin, and you can't see when it's forgiven. Yet you had to believe in all of these invisible, intangible things. The only way you can do this is with a supernatural, God kind of faith.

GOD'S FAITH

God's type of faith isn't limited to some kind of physical proof. He speaks forth and acknowledges things before there's any visible manifestation.

(As it is written, I have made thee a father of many nations,) before him whom he believed, even God, who quickeneth the dead, and calleth those things which be not as though they were.

ROMANS 4:17

God makes alive the dead and calls things that be not (physically manifest) as though they were. In this instance, God called Abram (prince) "Abraham" (father of many nations) even before he had his first child. That's God's kind of faith.

God created the heavens and the earth. He said *"Let there be light,"* and there was (Gen. 1:3). Then, days later, He created the sun, moon, and stars. Now, I'm not sure how all of this worked, but the Word clearly records that God created light before there was even a source for it to come from. God's faith isn't limited the way human faith is.

Receiving salvation is like sitting down in a chair you can't see. Human faith can't do that. You wouldn't put yourself in a position to fall and get hurt if you couldn't see or feel something. Yet you believed God—whom you can't physically see or feel—for forgiveness of sin—which you can't physically see or feel. How did you do that? By using God's supernatural faith.

Both salvation and the faith to receive it are gifts from God (Eph. 2:8-9). God's Word contains His faith. That's why you must hear it in order to be born again.

Being born again, not of corruptible seed, but of incorruptible, by the word of God, which liveth and abideth for ever.

1 PETER 1:23

God's Word contains the faith it takes to believe that God became flesh, lived a perfect life, and suffered your punishment in His death. It takes God's supernatural faith to believe that Jesus was resurrected and your sins are now forgiven. You can't believe these things with mere human faith; it's God's Word that brought you this faith.

You used God's supernatural faith—not just human faith—to receive salvation. It was a gift that came when you received His Word. You didn't just put your faith *in* God—you were born again by *the* faith *of* God. As sinners, we were so destitute that we couldn't save ourselves or even just believe that our sins had been forgiven. God's good news (the Gospel) had to come to us so we could receive His supernatural faith contained in it and use it for salvation.

THE FAITH OF CHRIST

You used *the* faith *of* Jesus Christ to be justified.

Knowing that a man is not justified by the works of the law, but by the faith of Jesus Christ, even we have believed in Jesus Christ, that we might be justified by the faith of Christ, and not by the works of the law: for by the works of the law shall no flesh be justified.

GALATIANS 2:16, EMPHASIS MINE

You put faith in what Jesus did, but you used *the* faith *of* Christ to be justified.

Once you are born again, you also live by *the* faith *of* the Son of God:

I am crucified with Christ: nevertheless I live; yet not I, but Christ liveth in me: and the life which I now live in the flesh I live by the faith of the Son of God, who loved me, and gave himself for me.

GALATIANS 2:20, EMPHASIS MINE

I'm aware that other translations say "I live by faith *in* the Son of God," but my conclusion after a lot of study is that the actual accurate rendering is, *"I live by the faith* of *the Son of God"* (emphasis mine).

So you were *"justified* [made righteous, born again] *by the faith of Christ"* and now *"live by the faith of the Son of God"* (Gal. 2:16 and 20, brackets mine). This is very important.

You were both born again and now live by the supernatural faith of God Himself. That's why Jesus said, "You don't need more faith; you just need to learn how to put what you've already got to work. The faith you have is enough to see a sycamine tree plucked up and planted into the sea. Use what you've got!" (Luke 17:6-10, paraphrase mine).

DOING WHAT JESUS DID

Since the faith we were born again by and now live by is the supernatural faith of God's own Son, it has the potential to do anything Jesus did.

Verily, verily, I say unto you, He that believeth on me, the works that I do shall he do also; and greater works than these shall he do.

JOHN 14:12

How can we do the works that Jesus did? Let's not even talk about doing greater works yet. How can we work miracles, receive words of wisdom and knowledge, turn the other cheek, go the extra mile, cast out demons, and walk in unconditional love? It's because you and I have the same faith Jesus used to accomplish these things. Since it's His supernatural faith—not our human faith—it is capable of doing anything He did!

However, most Christians say, "Well, I'm only human, you know. I'm just a man." That's stinkin' thinkin'! I *was* only human, but then I became born again. There's part of me now that's wall-to-wall Holy Ghost. There's a part of me now that has the faith of the Son of God. Yes, the flesh part is still capable of failure and everything else. But the born-again part of me is powerful.

If you stayed conscious of and focused on the fact that you have the faith of the Son of God, you'd see a difference in what you're hoping, expecting, and believing for.

When you truly believe that you have this potential inside, you won't put up with defeat, discouragement, and a mundane life anymore. You have and now live by the faith of Jesus Christ Himself.

THE MEASURE OF FAITH

God gave every born-again believer *the* measure of faith.

For I say, through the grace given unto me, to every man that is among you, not to think of himself more highly than he ought to think; but to think soberly, according as God hath dealt to every man the measure of faith.

ROMANS 12:3, EMPHASIS MINE

It's not *a* measure, but *the* measure of faith.

Most Christians think that God dishes out faith using many different measures. They believe He gives this person a ladle full and that person a tablespoon. This one gets a teaspoon and that one an eyedropper. That's totally inaccurate. God gives every believer the same measure of faith—a ladle full—because it's *the* measure of faith.

Reinhard Bonnke—the powerful German, world-traveling, healing evangelist who has preached to crowds of well over a million at a time in Africa—was being interviewed once on television. Someone in the audience asked the question, "Why do you see so many more miracles happen overseas than here in the United States? Is it because they have more faith?" My ears immediately perked up to hear his answer.

"You Americans are the only people I've ever encountered who have this concept of 'more faith,'" he responded. "Either a person believes or they don't. You don't have to have 'big faith.'" Then he gave some examples of people who had just heard God's Word for the first time and received. "This whole concept of 'big faith' and 'little faith' is erroneous. It's wrong!"

FAITH IS A FRUIT

You may be wondering, *But what about the centurion in Matthew 8? When the Lord heard what he said,* "he [Jesus] marvelled, and said to them that followed, Verily I say unto you, I have not found so great faith, no, not in Israel" (Matt. 8:10, brackets mine). Some people point to that and say, "Right there is a scriptural precedent. Jesus said he had 'great faith.'"

A couple of things are involved here. This was prior to the New Covenant and the new birth (the New Covenant didn't technically take effect until Christ's work of the Atonement was complete). Under the Old Covenant (before the cross), people put their human faith in the promises of God. I'm not saying they didn't have faith, but it was different than the way a New Testament (post-resurrection) believer has faith. It's through the new birth that you receive a born-again spirit. That is where your new nature and the faith of Christ reside. Old Testament people didn't have access to this.

Also, faith is a fruit of the Spirit.

But the fruit of the Spirit is love, joy, peace, longsuffering, gentleness, goodness, faith.

GALATIANS 5:22

Old Testament saints didn't have the indwelling presence of the Holy Spirit. He came upon them at times, but He didn't live in them the way He does now with New Testament believers. So it was a different way for them (the centurion and others like him) to believe God prior to Jesus dying for our sins, resurrecting from the dead, and people being born again.

Even after the new birth, some believers manifest great faith and others manifest very little, if any. But it's inaccurate to say that some Christians have "big" faith and others have "little" faith. Many people only use a small portion of the faith God has given them. But the truth is, every born-again believer has the measure of faith—the faith of the Son of God (Rom. 12:3 and Gal. 2:20).

ACKNOWLEDGE WHAT YOU HAVE

You don't have a faith problem; you have a knowledge problem. In order to see your faith work, you need to understand and acknowledge what you have.

Paul prayed, *"That the communication of thy faith may become effectual by the acknowledging of every good thing which is in you in Christ Jesus"* (Philem. 6).

Don't ask God for more, praying, "Lord, increase my faith!" Instead, believe God's Word and begin to acknowledge that when you were born again, you were given the supernatural faith of God.

SUPERNATURAL FAITH
LESSON 19 – OUTLINE

I. God is a faith being, and human beings were created in His image.

    A. Therefore, every person—saved or not—has faith within them because it was a part of God and is now a part of us.

    B. However, this type of faith—to sit in a chair, drive through an intersection, or fly on an airplane—is human faith.

    C. It's based completely on what you can see, taste, hear, smell, and feel.

    D. However, in order to receive salvation, you had to believe in things your natural senses couldn't perceive.

    E. The only way you can do this is with a supernatural, God kind of faith.

II. God's type of faith isn't limited to some kind of physical proof.

(As it is written, I have made thee a father of many nations,) before him whom he believed, even God, who quickeneth the dead, and calleth those things which be not as though they were.

ROMANS 4:17

    A. You believed God—whom you can't physically see or feel—for forgiveness of sin—which you can't physically see or feel.

    B. Both salvation and the faith to receive it are gifts from God (Eph. 2:8-9).

    C. God's Word contains His faith.

Being born again, not of corruptible seed, but of incorruptible, by the word of God, which liveth and abideth for ever.

1 PETER 1:23

    D. You used God's supernatural faith—not just human faith—to receive salvation.

    E. It was a gift that came when you received His Word.

III. You didn't just put your faith *in* God—you were born again by *the* faith *of* God!

    A. You put faith in what Jesus did, but you used *the* faith *of* Christ to be justified.

Knowing that a man is not justified *by the works of the law, but* by the faith of Jesus Christ, *even* we have believed in Jesus Christ, *that we might be* justified by the faith of Christ, *and not by the works of the law: for by the works of the law shall no flesh be justified.*

GALATIANS 2:16, EMPHASIS MINE

B. Once you are born again, you also live by *the* faith *of* the Son of God.

I am crucified with Christ: nevertheless I live; yet not I, but Christ liveth in me: and the life which I now live in the flesh I live by the faith of the Son of God, *who loved me, and gave himself for me.*

GALATIANS 2:20, EMPHASIS MINE

C. You were both born again and now live by the supernatural faith of God Himself.

D. Since the faith we were born again by and now live by is the supernatural faith of God's own Son, it has the potential to do anything Jesus did.

Verily, verily, I say unto you, He that believeth on me, the works that I do shall he do also; and greater works than these shall he do.

JOHN 14:12

IV. God gave every born-again believer *the* measure of faith.

For I say, through the grace given unto me, to every man that is among you, not to think of himself more highly than he ought to think; but to think soberly, according as God hath dealt to every man the measure of faith.

ROMANS 12:3, EMPHASIS MINE

A. God gives every believer the same measure of faith—a ladle full—because it's *the* measure of faith.

B. Faith is a fruit of the Spirit.

But the fruit of the Spirit is love, joy, peace, longsuffering, gentleness, goodness, faith.

GALATIANS 5:22

C. Many people only use a small portion of the faith God has given them.

D. In order to see your faith work, you need to understand and acknowledge what you have.

That the communication of thy faith may become effectual by the acknowledging of every good thing which is in you in Christ Jesus.

PHILEMON 6

E. Believe God's Word and begin to acknowledge that when you were born again, you were given the supernatural faith of God.

SUPERNATURAL FAITH
LESSON 19 – TEACHER'S GUIDE

1.   God is a faith being, and human beings were created in His image. Therefore, every person—saved or not—has faith within them because it was a part of God and is now a part of us. However, this type of faith—to sit in a chair, drive through an intersection, or fly on an airplane—is human faith. It's based completely on what we can see, taste, hear, smell, and feel. However, in order to receive salvation, we had to believe in things our natural senses couldn't perceive. The only way we can do this is with a supernatural, God kind of faith.

2.   God's type of faith isn't limited to some kind of physical proof (Rom. 4:17). We believed God—whom we can't physically see or feel—for forgiveness of sin—which we can't physically see or feel. Both salvation and the faith to receive it are gifts from God (Eph. 2:8-9). God's Word contains His faith (1 Pet. 1:23). We used God's supernatural faith—not just human faith—to receive salvation. It was a gift that came when we received His Word.

3.   We didn't just put our faith *in* God—we were born again by *the* faith *of* God. We put faith in what Jesus did, but we used *the* faith *of* Christ to be justified (Gal. 2:16). Once we are born again, we also live by *the* faith *of* the Son of God (Gal. 2:20). We were both born again and now live by the supernatural faith of God Himself. Since the faith we were born again by and now live by is the supernatural faith of God's own Son, it has the potential to do anything Jesus did (John 14:12).

1. A. What is human faith completely based on? (What we can see, taste, hear, smell, and feel)
    B. How can we believe in things our natural senses can't perceive? (With a supernatural, God kind of faith)
2. A. Read Romans 4:17, Ephesians 2:8-9, and 1 Peter 1:23. Is God's type of faith limited to some kind of physical proof? (No)
    B. What are both salvation and the faith to receive it? (Gifts from God)
    C. What does God's Word contain? (His faith)
3. A. Read Galatians 2:16, 20; and John 14:12. What were we born again by and now live by? (The supernatural faith of God Himself)
    B. Why does this faith have the potential to do anything Jesus did? (Because it's the supernatural faith of God's own Son)

4.   God gave every born-again believer *the* measure of faith (Rom. 12:3). God gives every believer the same measure of faith—a ladle full—because it's *the* measure of faith. Faith is a fruit of the Spirit (Gal. 5:22). Many people only use a small portion of the faith God has given them. In order to see our faith work, we need to understand and acknowledge what we have (Philem. 6). Let's believe God's Word and begin to acknowledge that when we were born again, we were given the supernatural faith of God.

4. A. Read Romans 12:3, Galatians 5:22, and Philemon 6. What has God given every born-again believer? (*The* measure of faith)
    B. What is a fruit of the Spirit? (Faith)
    C. In order to see our faith work, what do we need to understand and acknowledge? (What we have)

SUPERNATURAL FAITH
LESSON 19 – DISCIPLESHIP QUESTIONS

1. According to Romans 4:17, how does God call those things which be not?

2. In Genesis 1:3, God said, *"Let there be _____."*

3. According to Ephesians 2:8-9, how are we saved?

4. Did we work for it?

5. According to 1 Peter 1:23, what is the incorruptible seed?

6. Read Galatians 2:16. Is a man justified by the works of the Law?

7. According to Galatians 2:20, we as believers are crucified with whom?

8. Who lives in us?

9. Read Luke 17:6-10. What kind of seed is faith likened to?

    A. A peach seed
    B. A sycamine tree
    C. A mustard seed
    D. All of the above
    E. None of the above

10. According to John 14:12, what shall believers do?

11. Read Romans 12:3. We are not to think of ourselves _____ than we ought.

12. Why did Jesus marvel in Matthew 8:10?

13. What kind of fruit is listed in Galatians 5:22?

14. Philemon 6 admonishes us to acknowledge what?

SUPERNATURAL FAITH
LESSON 19 – ANSWER KEY

1. As though they were

2. *"Light"*

3. By grace through faith

4. No

5. The Word of God which lives and abides forever

6. No

7. Christ

8. Christ

9. C. A mustard seed

10. The works that Jesus did and greater works

11. More highly

12. Because of the centurion's faith

13. The fruit of the Spirit

14. Every good thing in us in Christ Jesus

SUPERNATURAL FAITH
LESSON 19 – SCRIPTURES

ROMANS 4:17

(As it is written, I have made thee a father of many nations,) before him whom he believed, even God, who quickeneth the dead, and calleth those things which be not as though they were.

GENESIS 1:3

And God said, Let there be light: and there was light.

EPHESIANS 2:8-9

For by grace are ye saved through faith; and that not of yourselves: it is the gift of God: [9] Not of works, lest any man should boast.

1 PETER 1:23

Being born again, not of corruptible seed, but of incorruptible, by the word of God, which liveth and abideth for ever.

GALATIANS 2:16

Knowing that a man is not justified by the works of the law, but by the faith of Jesus Christ, even we have believed in Jesus Christ, that we might be justified by the faith of Christ, and not by the works of the law: for by the works of the law shall no flesh be justified.

GALATIANS 2:20

I am crucified with Christ: nevertheless I live; yet not I, but Christ liveth in me: and the life which I now live in the flesh I live by the faith of the Son of God, who loved me, and gave himself for me.

LUKE 17:6-10

And the Lord said, If ye had faith as a grain of mustard seed, ye might say unto this sycamine tree, Be thou plucked up by the root, and be thou planted in the sea; and it should obey you. [7] But which of you, having a servant plowing or feeding cattle, will say unto him by and by, when he is come from the field, Go and sit down to meat? [8] And will not rather say unto him, Make ready wherewith I may sup, and gird thyself, and serve me, till I have eaten and drunken; and afterward thou shalt eat and drink? [9] Doth he thank that servant because he did the things that were commanded him? I trow not. [10] So likewise ye, when ye shall have done all those things which are commanded you, say, We are unprofitable servants: we have done that which was our duty to do.

JOHN 14:12

Verily, verily, I say unto you, He that believeth on me, the works that I do shall he do also; and greater works than these shall he do; because I go unto my Father.

ROMANS 12:3

For I say, through the grace given unto me, to every man that is among you, not to think of himself more highly than he ought to think; but to think soberly, according as God hath dealt to every man the measure of faith.

MATTHEW 8:10

When Jesus heard it, he marvelled, and said to them that followed, Verily I say unto you, I have not found so great faith, no, not in Israel.

GALATIANS 5:22

But the fruit of the Spirit is love, joy, peace, longsuffering, gentleness, goodness, faith.

PHILEMON 6

That the communication of thy faith may become effectual by the acknowledging of every good thing which is in you in Christ Jesus.

THE LAW OF FAITH
LESSON 20

Peter had this measure of God's supernatural faith. He healed a lame man at the entrance of the temple (Acts 3:6-8). People were healed as his shadow touched them (Acts 5:15). He even raised Dorcas from the dead (Acts 9:39-40). These are the kinds of things Peter's faith produced. Notice to whom he addressed his second letter:

Simon Peter, a servant and an apostle of Jesus Christ, to them that have obtained like precious faith with us through the righteousness of God and our Saviour Jesus Christ.

2 PETER 1:1, EMPHASIS MINE

Peter didn't earn this faith through good works, but received it when he was born again *"through the righteousness of God and our Saviour Jesus Christ."*

Along with Peter, you obtained this *"like precious faith"* when you were born again. It is *the* measure of faith (Rom. 12:3). If you don't believe this, you might as well rip 2 Peter out of your Bible and throw it away! Why? Because he wrote it to those of like precious faith.

You don't have a faith problem; you already have the faith of the Son of God. However, in order to see the supernatural results Peter did, you need to learn how to exercise it!

DISCOVERING HOW TO USE IT

I was baptized in the Holy Spirit during a miraculous encounter with the Lord on March 23, 1968. Immediately, I experienced a quickening inside and just began to understand things. Passion and a new motivation rose up from within, and I started seeing some people healed (cancer, sickness, deafness). Although I still saw only a small percentage of the large amount of folks I prayed for healed, that was a lot better than before. My faith had begun to work, and I started to realize that it was a powerful force. But I didn't yet know that I had the measure of faith—the faith of the Son of God.

So, I sought the Lord and asked Him for more faith and more faith and more faith. In the process, I became frustrated. Then God revealed to me this truth I've been sharing with you. It made a huge difference in my life! Instead of begging the Lord to give me more faith, I started praising and thanking Him for what He'd already given. I began diving into God's Word—not to get faith—but to better understand what I already had and how it operated. Through studying "faith" in the Word, I started understanding the laws that govern faith and how to cooperate with them.

Faith for salvation comes by hearing the Word of God (Rom. 10:17). Then, after you're born again, you have God's supernatural faith in you (Rom. 12:3; Gal. 2:16, and 20). Therefore, when you study the Bible and hear God's Word preached as a Christian, faith is already present. You are just discovering what you've been given and how to use it!

That's why you are encouraged when you read 2 Peter 1:1. You can honestly say, "I have the same precious faith that Peter had. He had the measure of faith; I have the measure of faith. Paul had the faith of the Son of God, and so do I. Anything Peter did, I can do. Anything Paul did, I can do. Anything Jesus did, I can do. Glory to God!"

FAITH FOLLOWS GOD'S RULES

Grace and peace be multiplied unto you through the knowledge of God, and of Jesus our Lord, [3] According as his divine power hath given unto us all things [faith is certainly one of these] *that pertain unto life and godliness, through the knowledge of him that hath called us to glory and virtue: [4] Whereby are given unto us exceeding great and precious promises: that by these ye might be partakers of the divine nature.*

2 PETER 1:2-4, BRACKETS MINE

Before salvation, hearing God's Word brings faith to you. If you'll accept it, you can be born again using the faith that came to you through the Word. Then, once you are born again, you already have faith on the inside. It's a fruit of the Spirit. But reading and understanding the Word gives you knowledge of what you already have. The Word teaches you how faith works so you can cooperate and receive the manifestation of your salvation benefits more completely.

You do have the supernatural faith of the Son of God, but since it's His faith, it has to follow His rules. You can't use God's faith just to do your own thing. It's not yours; it's His! In a sense, you are borrowing it. The only way this supernatural faith will produce results is if you use it in the manner God wants you to.

Technically speaking, it's not your faith. Some people say they're of the Baptist faith, and others respond that they're Episcopal, Methodist, or Presbyterian faith, as if there are different Christian "faiths." However, Ephesians 4:5 reveals that there's just *"one Lord"* and *"one faith"*—God's faith. You can't just choose to believe any old way, because if you believe wrong, it won't work. You must use that faith the way God wants you to because it's His supernatural faith, not your human faith.

God's Word speaks of *"the law of faith."*

Where is boasting then? It is excluded. By what law? of works? Nay: but by the law of faith.

ROMANS 3:27

Although this isn't the main point of Romans 3, it's still a true statement. God's faith in you operates according to *"the law of faith."*

CONSTANT AND UNIVERSAL

Faith works according to the laws God created to govern its use. The word *law*, in this sense, means "constant, without fluctuation or variation" and "universal." That means faith works for everyone, everywhere, in the same way, much like the law of gravity.

Gravity is constant—without fluctuation or variation—and universal (applying to everyone on earth). That's why we call it a "law." For instance, if I am in Colorado using the law of gravity to sit in a chair, and if for some reason, you couldn't do the same over in China, gravity would be a "phenomenon" and not a law. In order for something to be classified as a "law," it has to apply the same way to everyone everywhere.

Most people don't look at faith as being governed by law. They think God could do anything He wants to if they just ask Him and "believe." They don't understand that there are certain restrictions the Lord has placed upon Himself, and therefore His faith always abides by these laws.

Again, this truth is evident in the natural realm with the law of gravity. What happens if a person jumps off the Empire State Building? Does God want to see them die? Is the Lord punishing that person? No. But He won't suspend the law of gravity in order to save their life either. God doesn't want people hurt and killed by gravity, but that's exactly what will happen if they violate this law.

THAT'S THE WAY IT IS!

Faith is governed by law. God did that for your benefit. He doesn't want you to die of sickness, fail financially, or suffer mental and emotional problems. However, if you don't learn how faith works and begin to cooperate, these same laws (which were meant to bless you)—when violated—will kill you. That's an awesome truth!

God cannot—because He will not—violate His own laws. It's against His righteous and holy nature. When God says something, that's the way it is. He doesn't change things He has established just because of people's whims, needs, or ignorance. Some people— whom God loves with all of His heart—die, not because it's His will, but because they violate His laws of faith.

THE LAW OF FAITH
LESSON 20 – OUTLINE

I.   Peter had this measure of God's supernatural faith (Acts 3:6-8, 5:15, and 9:39-40).

Simon Peter, a servant and an apostle of Jesus Christ, to them that have obtained like precious faith with us *through the righteousness of God and our Saviour Jesus Christ.*

2 PETER 1:1, EMPHASIS MINE

   A.   Peter didn't earn this faith through good works, but received it when he was born again *"through the righteousness of God and our Saviour Jesus Christ."*

   B.   Along with Peter, you obtained this *"like precious faith"* when you were born again.

   C.   It is *the* measure of faith (Rom. 12:3).

   D.   However, in order to see the supernatural results Peter did, you need to learn how to exercise it.

II. Faith for salvation comes by hearing the Word of God (Rom. 10:17).

   A.   Then, after you are born again, you have God's supernatural faith in you (Rom. 12:3; Gal. 2:16, and 20).

   B.   Therefore, when you study the Bible and hear God's Word preached as a Christian, faith is already present.

   C.   You are just discovering what you've been given and how to use it!

   D.   You can honestly say, "I have the same precious faith that Peter had. He had the measure of faith; I have the measure of faith. Paul had the faith of the Son of God, and so do I. Anything Peter did, I can do. Anything Paul did, I can do. Anything Jesus did, I can do. Glory to God!"

Grace and peace be multiplied unto you through the knowledge of God, and of Jesus Christ our Lord, [3] According as his divine power hath given unto us all things [faith is certainly one of these] *that pertain unto life and godliness, through the knowledge of him that hath called us to glory and virtue: [4] Whereby are given unto us exceeding great and precious promises: that by these ye might be partakers of the divine nature.*

2 PETER 1:2-4, BRACKETS MINE

E. The Word teaches you how faith works so you can cooperate and receive the manifestation of your salvation benefits more completely.

III. The only way this supernatural faith will produce results is if you use it in the manner God wants you to.

Where is boasting then? It is excluded. By what law? of works? Nay: but by the law of faith.

ROMANS 3:27

A. Faith works according to the laws God created to govern its use.

B. Faith works for everyone, everywhere, in the same way, much like the law of gravity.

C. God cannot—because He will not—violate His own laws.

D. When God says something, that's the way it is.

E. Some people—whom God loves with all of His heart—die, not because it's His will, but because they violate His laws of faith.

THE LAW OF FAITH
LESSON 20 – TEACHER'S GUIDE

1.   Peter had this measure of God's supernatural faith (Acts 3:6-8, 5:15, and 9:39-40). He didn't earn this faith through good works, but received it when he was born again *"through the righteousness of God and our Saviour Jesus Christ"* (2 Pet. 1:1). Along with Peter, we obtained this *"like precious faith"* when we were born again. It is *the* measure of faith (Rom. 12:3). However, in order to see the supernatural results Peter did, we need to learn how to exercise it!

2.   Faith for salvation comes by hearing the Word of God (Rom. 10:17). Then, after we're born again, we have God's supernatural faith in us (Rom. 12:3; Gal. 2:16, and 20). Therefore, when we study the Bible and hear God's Word preached as a Christian, faith is already present. We are just discovering what we've been given and how to use it! We can honestly say, "We have the same precious faith that Peter had. He had the measure of faith; we have the measure of faith. Paul had the faith of the Son of God, and so do we. Anything Peter did, we can do. Anything Paul did, we can do. Anything Jesus did, we can do. Glory to God!" The Word teaches us how faith works so we can cooperate and receive the manifestation of our salvation benefits more completely (2 Pet. 1:2-4).

3.   The only way this supernatural faith will produce results is if we use it in the manner God wants us to. Faith works according to the laws God created to govern its use (Rom. 3:27). Faith works for everyone, everywhere, in the same way, much like the law of gravity. God cannot—because He will not—violate His own laws. When God says something, that's the way it is. Some people—whom God loves with all of His heart—die, not because it's His will, but because they violate His laws of faith.

1. A. Read Acts 3:6-8, 5:15, 9:39-40; 2 Peter 1:1; and Romans 12:3. Do we earn this faith through good works? (No)
    B. When did we obtain this *"like precious faith"*? (When we were born again)
    C. In order to see the supernatural results Peter did, what do we need to learn? (How to exercise this faith)
2. A. Read Romans 10:17; Galatians 2:16, 20; and 2 Peter 1:2-4. What comes by hearing the Word of God? (Faith for salvation)
    B. Is faith already present when we study the Bible and hear God's Word preached as a Christian? (Yes)
    C. What does the Word teach us so that we can cooperate and receive the manifestation of our salvation benefits more completely? (How faith works)
3. A. Read Romans 3:27. How does faith work? (According to the laws God created to govern its use)
    B. Much like the law of gravity, how does faith work? (It works for everyone, everywhere, in the same way)
    C. Why do people—whom God loves with all of His heart—die? (Because they violate His laws of faith)

THE LAW OF FAITH
LESSON 20 – DISCIPLESHIP QUESTIONS

1. Did Peter ask God to heal the man in Acts 3:6-8?

2. Did Peter give, command, and minister the healing power of God that he already had?

3. According to Acts 5:15, why did people bring the sick forth in the streets?

4. Read Acts 9:39-40. After kneeling down and praying, Peter turned to the body and said what to Tabitha?

5. According to 2 Peter 1:1, like precious faith came _____ the righteousness of our God and Savior Jesus Christ.

6. According to Romans 12:3, God has _____ to each one the measure of faith.

7. Romans 10:17 reveals that faith comes how?

8. According to Galatians 2:16, how are we justified?

9. According to Galatians 2:20, how do we live the life we now live?

10. According to 2 Peter 1:2-4, what is multiplied unto us through the knowledge of God and of Jesus our Lord?

11. According as His divine power has given us what?

12. God has given us exceeding great and precious promises that by these we might what?

13. Ephesians 4:5 reveals one what?

    A. Lord
    B. Faith
    C. Baptism (into Christ)
    D. All of the above
    E. None of the above

14. According to Romans 3:27, is boasting excluded?

15. By the law of works?

THE LAW OF FAITH
LESSON 20 – ANSWER KEY

1. No

2. Yes

3. That at least the shadow of Peter passing by might overshadow some of them

4. Arise

5. Through

6. Dealt

7. By hearing the Word of God

8. By the faith of Jesus Christ

9. By the faith of the Son of God

10. Grace and peace

11. All things

12. Be partakers of the divine nature

13. D. All of the above

14. Yes

15. No, by the law of faith

THE LAW OF FAITH
LESSON 20 – SCRIPTURES

ACTS 3:6-8
Then Peter said, Silver and gold have I none; but such as I have give I thee: In the name of Jesus Christ of Nazareth rise up and walk. [7] And he took him by the right hand, and lifted him up: and immediately his feet and ankle bones received strength. [8] And he leaping up stood, and walked, and entered with them into the temple, walking, and leaping, and praising God.

ACTS 5:15
Insomuch that they brought forth the sick into the streets, and laid them on beds and couches, that at the least the shadow of Peter passing by might overshadow some of them.

ACTS 9:39-40
Then Peter arose and went with them. When he was come, they brought him into the upper chamber: and all the widows stood by him weeping, and showing the coats and garments which Dorcas made, while she was with them. [40] But Peter put them all forth, and kneeled down, and prayed; and turning him to the body said, Tabitha, arise. And she opened her eyes: and when she saw Peter, she sat up.

2 PETER 1:1-4
Simon Peter, a servant and an apostle of Jesus Christ, to them that have obtained like precious faith with us through the righteousness of God and our Saviour Jesus Christ: [2] Grace and peace be multiplied unto you through the knowledge of God, and of Jesus our Lord, [3] According as his divine power hath given unto us all things that pertain unto life and godliness, through the knowledge of him that hath called us to glory and virtue: [4] Whereby are given unto us exceeding great and precious promises: that by these ye might be partakers of the divine nature, having escaped the corruption that is in the world through lust.

ROMANS 12:3
For I say, through the grace given unto me, to every man that is among you, not to think of himself more highly than he ought to think; but to think soberly, according as God hath dealt to every man the measure of faith.

ROMANS 10:17
So then faith cometh by hearing, and hearing by the word of God.

GALATIANS 2:16

Knowing that a man is not justified by the works of the law, but by the faith of Jesus Christ, even we have believed in Jesus Christ, that we might be justified by the faith of Christ, and not by the works of the law: for by the works of the law shall no flesh be justified.

GALATIANS 2:20

I am crucified with Christ: nevertheless I live; yet not I, but Christ liveth in me: and the life which I now live in the flesh I live by the faith of the Son of God, who loved me, and gave himself for me.

EPHESIANS 4:5

One Lord, one faith, one baptism.

ROMANS 3:27

Where is boasting then? It is excluded. By what law? of works? Nay: but by the law of faith.

FAITH SPEAKS
LESSON 21

One of the laws of faith is this: You will have what you say.

A man's belly shall be satisfied with the fruit of his mouth; and with the increase of his lips shall he be filled. [21] Death and life are in the power of the tongue: and they that love it shall eat the fruit thereof.

PROVERBS 18:20-21

Death and life are in the power of your tongue. This is a law of faith.

God created the worlds by faith through speaking them into existence (Gen. 1). Everything natural—what we can see, taste, hear, smell, and feel—was created by words. God's faith-filled words are what framed this universe and are what continue to hold it together (Heb. 1:3 and 11:3). If He were to violate His own words—the laws He created—the whole universe would self-destruct. Why? Because creation is held together by the power of God's living Word!

God's creation is governed by laws. One of the laws of God is that we have what we say. There is power in words. We speak words.

The ability to speak reflects God's image in us. This is one very important characteristic that sets the human creation apart from plants and animals—we speak words. In a sense, it's God-like because words have the ability to create.

LEARN TO SPEAK LIFE

Jesus confirmed this law (Matt. 21:18-22; Mark 11:12-14, and 20-24). He spoke to a fig tree and commanded it to die. The next morning, His disciples discovered that overnight, the tree had done exactly that. In response to their amazement, Jesus declared,

Have faith in God. [23] For verily I say unto you, That whosoever shall say *unto this mountain, Be thou removed, and be thou cast into the sea; and shall not doubt in his heart,* but shall believe *those things which he saith shall come to pass;* he shall have whatsoever he saith.

MARK 11:22-23, EMPHASIS MINE

Faith is released by words. It is one of the laws that govern faith. Death *and* life—not just life only—are in the power of your tongue.

If you've been born again, you have the faith of the Son of God. Since most Christians don't know this, they don't use it. The few who do believe still may not see it work properly, because they don't understand and cooperate with the laws that govern faith.

If your doctor tells you you're going to die soon, your words will affect what you receive. If you know that God has already healed you and you are trying to believe, your words will determine what you experience. You will get life or death according to what you say. If someone asks you how you are, you release death by answering, "I'm going to die. The doctor said I've only got a week left." If you start planning your funeral and giving in to grief, you are empowering death. Even though you have the faith of the Son of God inside you, it won't be released. Instead, what Satan wants to do will be released through those words of death. Your words are that powerful!

HEART AND MOUTH TOGETHER

You may have heard an extreme version of this truth through the "faith" or "confession" movements. Some people have even termed this "name it and claim it" or "blab it and grab it."

This truth—you will have what you say—has been abused in many ways. If someone said "That tickles me to death!" the self-appointed "confession police" would immediately jump up and condemn that person. However, Romans 10:10 clarifies the issue:

For with the heart man believeth unto righteousness; and with the mouth confession is made unto salvation.

It's only when the heart and mouth work together in faith that the confession is brought to pass. The reason people don't drop dead when they use a slang expression like "It tickles me to death!" is because they didn't mean it in their hearts. I'm not saying it's good to continue using such an expression, but it didn't come to pass because the words weren't what the heart truly believed.

Regardless of how this truth has been misrepresented and abused, it's still a truth. Many Christians are missing out on what God has provided for them in the spirit, because they aren't using their words properly. You must learn to speak life instead of death.

SPEAK TO THE MOUNTAIN

Just speaking your faith isn't enough; you must also speak directly to the mountain.

Whosoever shall say unto this mountain, Be thou removed.

MARK 11:23

Most Christians are busy talking to God about their mountain instead of talking to their mountain about God. The mountain is your problem, or whatever you want to see changed. Speak to it!

Don't say, "O God, I'm sick. Please take this disease from me!" or "Father, please remove this debt." That's a violation of what this scripture is telling you to do. You're talking to God about your mountain. Speak to the sickness. Talk to your bills. Address your depression, or whatever else the problem may be. Tell it that God has already set you free. Then command it to leave you alone. That is why you must understand the authority God has given you and how it works.

I stayed with a couple while ministering in Charlotte, North Carolina. They watched the video *Niki Ochenski: The Story of a Miracle!* This testimony of how the revelation of grace and faith helped a teenage girl on the brink of death receive her healing deeply touched the wife. She had a friend who was suffering from the same thing (fibromyalgia and chemical sensitivities). So she immediately invited her over so I could pray with and minister to her.

Once the friend arrived, I shared God's Word and countered this woman's wrong thinking for about half an hour. When she was ready to pray, I commanded all pain to leave her body and—BOOM—it was instantly gone. She started praising God, but a few minutes later, she remarked, "I still have a burning across my waist in the back. Why didn't it leave with all the other pain?"

I shared with her Mark 11:23 and answered, "The Bible says you have to speak to the mountain. You told me you had pain throughout your body, so I spoke to pain. Now, watch this. I'm going to speak to burning." Then I commanded burning to go in Jesus' name. Immediately, it was gone, and she was praising God!

"BURNING, IN THE NAME OF JESUS..."

I taught her how to stand on the Word and what to do if a symptom returned. Then, as she was getting ready to leave twenty minutes later, she said, "That burning is back."

I told her, "Well, I've just instructed you in what to do. Now I want you to pray and rebuke this."

So she prayed, "Father, I thank You that it's Your will to heal me and that You've already healed me. By Your stripes, I was healed. I now claim my healing, I stand on it, and I thank You for it in Jesus' name." That's a pretty good prayer coming from a woman who less than an hour before had thought God sent her this sickness to glorify Himself.

However, I knew that burning hadn't left. So I asked, "How do you feel?"

She responded, "The burning is still there."

"Do you know why?"

"No."

"You talked to God about your mountain instead of talking to your mountain about God. You didn't speak to it."

"What do you mean?" she asked.

"You didn't speak to burning."

"You mean I'm supposed to actually call it by name and talk to it?"

"Yes, that's exactly what you're supposed to do. Talk to that burning." Many people think that's weird, but Jesus spoke to a fig tree. In fact, the Word says that He "answered" it (Mark 11:14). You can't answer something unless it has been talking to you first. That's why when your checkbook speaks to you and says, "God's Word doesn't work. You're going to fail. You're in the red again!" you need to answer it with, "God's Word does work. He's El Shaddai—more than enough! I command you, checkbook, in the name of Jesus to come into the black and stay there!" You must speak directly to your mountain.

This time, this woman said, "Burning, in the name of Jesus…" She stopped right there and shouted, "It's gone!" She didn't even get so far as to command it. Just by addressing it directly and using her faith in Jesus—BOOM—it left. What an awesome example of this principle in action!

ELECTRICITY

Words are important! You can't speak death, discouragement, defeat, and depression and then expect to receive blessings. It's not going to work. Why? One of the laws that govern faith states that you will have what you say. Not only must you believe God's Word in your heart and speak in agreement with it from your mouth; you must also speak directly to your problem and command it to get in line. Thank God for what He's already done, and then command your body to quit hurting, your finances to work, the devil to get off your case, etc. Take your authority and use it. These are some of the laws that govern faith.

You already have the faith of the Son of God; you just need to learn how to use it. Once you understand how it works and begin to cooperate, you'll start seeing results.

God created the natural laws that govern electricity. Even though man didn't discover them and how they operated until recently, they've been here on the earth since the very beginning. People 4,000 years ago could have used electricity, but they were ignorant of its laws. Now that we've learned the laws of electricity, we use it. In fact, we use it all the time, and it's dependable.

God didn't withhold electricity from people because they were bad. David was a very godly man, but he didn't know about it. Neither did Moses, Gideon, or Solomon. It was simply their ignorance of electricity and the laws that govern its use that prevented them from receiving its benefits. If they had known, they could have taken advantage of its benefits.

People hurt themselves and die today, not because they are bad people, but because they violate the law of faith. God isn't against them. It's just that He has established laws regarding how His power flows—and they are not cooperating.

Learn what those laws are, and put them into practice for your benefit. Until you do, God is not going to change all of creation *for* you. He won't suspend the law of gravity to save your life and kill millions of others just because you jumped off the Empire State Building. That's not how it works. Discover the laws that govern faith and cooperate.

RELEASE YOUR FAITH

I have only discussed a few laws thus far (mostly related to speaking), but there are many, many more. As you study God's Word, you will see them. You will learn that Jesus encouraged people to act on their faith. Since *"faith without works is dead,"* actions are another very important way to release your faith (James 2:26). There is also forgiving others (Mark 11:25-26), and so forth.

God's Word brings you the original faith when you're born again. Then, after you are saved, it teaches you how that faith works. If you can believe that you have already dwelling on the inside of you the same faith that raised Jesus Christ from the dead, then the rest is just learning how to cooperate with the laws governing how it works.

LESSON 21 – ADDITIONAL INFORMATION

You must understand the authority God has given you and how it works. My teachings "The Laws of Faith" and *The Believer's Authority* thoroughly address these issues.

Niki Ochenski: The Story of a Miracle! is a testimony DVD of how the revelation of grace and faith helped a teenage girl on the brink of death receive her healing. You will be greatly encouraged!

FAITH SPEAKS
LESSON 21 – OUTLINE

I.   One of the laws of faith is this: You will have what you say.

A man's belly shall be satisfied with the fruit of his mouth; and with the increase of his lips shall he be filled. [21] Death and life are in the power of the tongue: and they that love it shall eat the fruit thereof.

PROVERBS 18:20-21

    A.   Death and life are in the power of your tongue.

    B.   God's faith-filled words are what framed this universe and continue to hold it together (Heb. 1:3 and 11:3).

    C.   If He were to violate His own words—the laws He created—the whole universe would self-destruct because creation is held together by the power of God's living Word.

    D.   The ability to speak reflects God's image in us.

    E.   In a sense, it's God-like because words have the ability to create.

II. Jesus confirmed this law (Matt. 21:18-22; Mark 11:12-14, and 20-24).

Have faith in God. [23] For verily I say unto you, That whosoever shall say *unto this mountain, Be thou removed, and be thou cast into the sea; and shall not doubt in his heart,* but shall believe *those things which he saith shall come to pass;* he shall have whatsoever he saith.

MARK 11:22-23, EMPHASIS MINE

    A.   Faith is released by words.

    B.   This truth—you will have what you say—has been abused in many ways.

    C.   It's only when the heart and mouth work together in faith that the confession is brought to pass.

For with the heart man believeth unto righteousness; and with the mouth confession is made unto salvation.

ROMANS 10:10

D. Many Christians are missing out on what God has provided for them in the spirit, because they aren't using their words properly.

III. Just speaking your faith isn't enough—you must also speak directly to the mountain.

Whosoever shall say unto this mountain, Be thou removed.

MARK 11:23

A. The mountain is your problem, or whatever you want to see changed.

B. Speak to it!

C. Tell it that God has already set you free.

D. Then command it to leave you alone.

IV. Words are important!

A. You can't speak death, discouragement, defeat, and depression and then expect to receive blessings.

B. Not only must you believe God's Word in your heart and speak in agreement with it from your mouth; you must also speak directly to your problem and command it to get in line.

C. Thank God for what He's already done, and then command your body to quit hurting, your finances to work, the devil to get off your case, etc.

D. Take your authority and use it.

V. People hurt themselves and die today, not because they are bad people, but because they violate the law of faith.

A. God isn't against them; it's just that He has established laws regarding how His power flows—and they are not cooperating.

B. Learn what those laws are, and put them into practice for your benefit.

C. Discover the laws that govern faith and cooperate.

VI. God's Word brings you the original faith when you're born again.

A. Then, after you are saved, it teaches you how that faith works.

B. If you can believe that you have already dwelling on the inside of you the same faith that raised Jesus Christ from the dead, then the rest is just learning how to cooperate with the laws governing how it works.

LESSON 21 – ADDITIONAL INFORMATION

You must understand the authority God has given you and how it works. My teachings "The Laws of Faith" and *The Believer's Authority* thoroughly address these issues.

Niki Ochenski: The Story of a Miracle! is a testimony DVD of how the revelation of grace and faith helped a teenage girl on the brink of death receive her healing. You will be greatly encouraged!

FAITH SPEAKS
LESSON 21 – TEACHER'S GUIDE

1.   One of the laws of faith is this: We will have what we say (Prov. 18:20-21). Death and life are in the power of our tongue. God's faith-filled words are what framed this universe and continue to hold it together (Heb. 1:3 and 11:3). If He were to violate His own words—the laws He created—the whole universe would self-destruct because creation is held together by the power of God's living Word. The ability to speak reflects God's image in us. In a sense, it's God-like because words have the ability to create.

2.   Jesus confirmed this law (Matt. 21:18-22; Mark 11:12-14, and 20-24). Faith is released by words. This truth—we will have what we say—has been abused in many ways. It's only when the heart and mouth work together in faith that the confession is brought to pass (Rom. 10:10). Many Christians are missing out on what God has provided for them in the spirit, because they aren't using their words properly.

3.   Just speaking our faith isn't enough—we must also speak directly to the mountain (Mark 11:23). The mountain is our problem, or whatever we want to see changed. We must speak to it! We need to tell it that God has already set us free. Then we must command it to leave us alone.

1. A.   Read Proverbs 18:20-21; Hebrews 1:3, and 11:3. What are in the power of our tongue? (Death and life)
   B.   What framed this universe and continue to hold it together? (God's faith-filled words)
   C.   What does the ability to speak reflect in us? (God's image)
2. A.   Read Matthew 21:18-22; Mark 11:12-14, 20-24; and Romans 10:10. When is the confession brought to pass? (Only when the heart and mouth work together in faith)
   B.   Why are many Christians missing out on what God has provided for them in the spirit? (Because they aren't using their words properly)
3. A.   Read Mark 11:23. What must we speak directly to? (The mountain)
   B.   What is the mountain? (Our problem, or whatever we want to see changed)

4.   Words are important. We can't speak death, discouragement, defeat, and depression and then expect to receive blessings. Not only must we believe God's Word in our hearts and speak in agreement with it from our mouths; we must also speak directly to our problem and command it to get in line. Let's thank God for what He's already done and then command our bodies to quit hurting, our finances to work, the devil to get off our case, etc. Let's take our authority and use it.

5.   People hurt themselves and die today, not because they are bad people, but because they violate the law of faith. God isn't against them; it's just that He has established laws regarding how His power flows—and they are not cooperating. Let's learn what those laws are and put them into practice for our benefit. Let's discover the laws that govern faith and cooperate.

6.   God's Word brings us the original faith when we're born again. Then, after we are saved, it teaches us how that faith works. If we can believe that we have already dwelling on the inside of us the same faith that raised Jesus Christ from the dead, then the rest is just learning how to cooperate with the laws governing how it works.

4.   A.   If we expect to receive blessings, what must we not speak? (Death, discouragement, defeat, and depression)

     B.   What must we speak directly to and command to get in line with God's Word? (Our problem)

5.   A.   What has God established regarding how His power flows? (Laws)

     B.   We need to learn what those laws are and do what with them for our benefit? (Put them into practice—cooperate)

6.   A.   What does God's Word bring us when we're born again? (The original faith)

     B.   Then, after we are saved, what does God's Word teach us? (How that faith works)

     C.   What kind of faith do we already have dwelling on the inside of us? (The same faith that raised Jesus Christ from the dead)

FAITH SPEAKS
LESSON 21 – DISCIPLESHIP QUESTIONS

1. According to Proverbs 18:20-21, a man's belly shall be satisfied with the words of his mouth and be filled with _____.

2. Death and life are in _____ of the tongue.

3. According to Hebrews 1:3, what does God uphold by the word of His power?

4. According to Hebrews 11:3, what were the worlds framed by?

5. According to Mathew 21:18-22, when Jesus came to the fig tree and didn't see figs, what did He do?

6. When did the fig tree wither away?

7. All things we shall ask in prayer, believing, we shall what?

8. According to Mark 11:12-14, where were they coming from?

9. Why was there nothing but leaves?

10. Who heard Jesus answer the fig tree?

11. According to Mark 11:20-24, what did they see as they passed by?

12. *"Whosoever shall say unto this _____."*

13. *"And shall not doubt in his _____."*

14. *"But shall _____ that those things he says shall come to pass."*

15. What shall he have?

16. According to Romans 10:10, with what do we believe unto righteousness?

17. With the mouth, confession is made unto what?

18. According to James 2:26, just as the body is dead without the spirit, so faith without _____ is dead also.

19. According to Mark 11:25-26, when we stand praying, we should what?

20. Why?

FAITH SPEAKS
LESSON 21 – ANSWER KEY

1. The increase of his lips

2. The power

3. All things

4. The Word of God

5. He said to it, *"Let no fruit grow on thee henceforward for ever"*

6. Presently

7. Receive

8. Bethany

9. The time of figs was not yet

10. His disciples

11. The fig tree dried up from the roots

12. *"Mountain"*

13. *"Heart"*

14. *"Believe"*

15. *"Whatsoever he says"*

16. Our hearts

17. Salvation

18. Works

19. Forgive

20. That our Father in heaven may forgive us our trespasses

FAITH SPEAKS
LESSON 21 – SCRIPTURES

PROVERBS 18:20-21

A man's belly shall be satisfied with the fruit of his mouth; and with the increase of his lips shall he be filled. [21] Death and life are in the power of the tongue: and they that love it shall eat the fruit thereof.

HEBREWS 1:3

Who being the brightness of his glory, and the express image of his person, and upholding all things by the word of his power, when he had by himself purged our sins, sat down on the right hand of the Majesty on high.

HEBREWS 11:3

Through faith we understand that the worlds were framed by the word of God, so that things which are seen were not made of things which do appear.

MATTHEW 21:18-22

Now in the morning as he returned into the city, he hungered. [19] And when he saw a fig tree in the way, he came to it, and found nothing thereon, but leaves only, and said unto it, Let no fruit grow on thee henceforward for ever. And presently the fig tree withered away. [20] And when the disciples saw it, they marvelled, saying, How soon is the fig tree withered away! [21] Jesus answered and said unto them, Verily I say unto you, If ye have faith, and doubt not, ye shall not only do this which is done to the fig tree, but also if ye shall say unto this mountain, Be thou removed, and be thou cast into the sea; it shall be done. [22] And all things, whatsoever ye shall ask in prayer, believing, ye shall receive.

MARK 11:12-14

And on the morrow, when they were come from Bethany, he was hungry: [13] And seeing a fig tree afar off having leaves, he came, if haply he might find any thing thereon: and when he came to it, he found nothing but leaves; for the time of figs was not yet. [14] And Jesus answered and said unto it, No man eat fruit of thee hereafter for ever. And his disciples heard it.

MARK 11:20-26

And in the morning, as they passed by, they saw the fig tree dried up from the roots. [21] And Peter calling to remembrance saith unto him, Master, behold, the fig tree which thou cursedst is withered away. [22] And Jesus answering saith unto them, Have faith in God. [23] For verily I say unto you, That whosoever shall say unto this mountain, Be thou removed, and be thou cast into the sea; and shall not doubt in his heart, but shall believe that those things which he saith shall come to pass; he shall have whatsoever he saith. [24] Therefore I say unto you, What things soever ye desire, when ye pray, believe that ye receive them, and ye shall have them. [25] And when ye stand praying, forgive, if ye have aught against any: that your Father also which is in heaven may forgive you your trespasses. [26] But if ye do not forgive, neither will your Father which is in heaven forgive your trespasses.

ROMANS 10:10

For with the heart man believeth unto righteousness; and with the mouth confession is made unto salvation.

JAMES 2:26

For as the body without the spirit is dead, so faith without works is dead also.

AGGRESSIVE RECEIVING
LESSON 22

Mark's Gospel records an awesome example of the laws of faith in operation. A woman with an issue of blood came to Jesus seeking healing. She simply touched the hem of His garment and was instantly made whole. The Lord felt virtue flow out of Him and turned around, asking, *"Who touched my clothes?"* (Mark 5:30).

Jesus disciples were amazed. There was a multitude of people surrounding Him, and they were all pushing up against Him. But there was something very different about this woman's touch. She touched Him in faith—and instantly the power of God flowed!

Most people believe that, as God, Jesus knew all things. Therefore, when He inquired *"Who touched my clothes?"* He was simply asking a rhetorical question. Even though Jesus was totally God in His spirit, He lived in a physical body. Although it was a sinless physical body, Luke 2:52 reveals, *"And Jesus increased in wisdom and stature, and in favour with God and man."*

SHE SAID

Jesus didn't know all things in His human mind. I believe He meant just exactly what He said when He asked, "Who touched Me?"

This is a significant point. If Jesus didn't know who touched Him, then how did this healing virtue of God flow out of Him to effect this woman's cure? Think about that!

Most people think God sizes us up when we come to Him with a request. Depending on how much we've prayed, studied the Word, fasted, lived holy, or a multitude of other things, He either grants or rejects our request. But that's not what happened here. How did this woman receive her healing? She put the laws of faith into action, and the power of God automatically flowed.

For she said, If I may touch but his clothes, I shall be whole.

MARK 5:28, EMPHASIS MINE

It's a law of God that we have what we say (Mark 11:23). She said and she received.

EARNEST ACTION

It's also a law of God that *"faith without works is dead"* (James 2:20). This woman acted on her faith. She didn't just speak about being healed; she acted on that faith even at great personal risk.

In that day, anyone with an issue of blood was unclean, and everyone they touched became unclean also. Therefore, people with this uncleanness had to avoid crowds because they would defile everyone they touched. This woman could have been stoned to death by this multitude if they knew her secret. This is probably the reason she was hesitant to come forward with what she had done.

Notice also that this woman touched the hem of Jesus' garment. How do you touch the hem of a garment when there's a multitude thronging the one wearing it? The only logical explanation is that this woman was probably on her hands and knees, crawling through the mass of people.

Why is that important? It illustrates another law of faith—earnestness. You can't receive the things of God by just passively seeking them.

And ye shall seek me, and find me, when ye shall search for me with all your heart.

JEREMIAH 29:13

As long as you can live without your healing, you will. But when you get aggressive, like this woman, where you are willing to risk even your own life in order to receive, you will receive.

WHO'S CRAZY?

This woman had been suffering from this condition for twelve long years (Mark 5:25). She spent all the money she had trying all the different cures of that day, but just became worse (Mark 5:26). No one faulted her for going the natural route. I'm sure people gave her much sympathy and pity. But if her friends knew what she intended to do—to approach Jesus in the midst of a multitude—I'm sure someone would have told her that was crazy.

It's not crazy when we let doctors experiment on us. We allow them to treat us in ways that would kill a well person and cost us everything we have. But when we openly trust God for our healing, then we're "fanatics."

However, it takes this type of aggressive attitude to effectively receive from God.

This woman put a number of the laws of faith into operation, and the healing virtue of God flowed to her automatically.

IT'S NOT PERSONAL

Remember the laws of electricity? When someone flips the light switch on the wall, the electrical power just flows. They don't have to call the electric company and ask for the power to be sent; it's already available. We just have to take the authority granted us and command the power to flow.

Likewise, when someone touches a live electrical wire, if they are grounded, the current just flows. The electric company doesn't size them up and say, "I'll teach them a lesson. I'll give them the shock of their lives!" No. There are just laws that govern how electricity flows. It's not personal.

That's the way it is with God. The Lord isn't healing one and refusing another. There are laws that govern how His power works. We can violate those laws and miss out on the blessings He has already given us, or we can learn what the laws are, cooperate with them, and experience the abundant life He has provided. It's up to us.

IGNORANT OF GOD'S LAWS

People could have been using electricity thousands of years ago. It wasn't the Lord who just recently made electricity available. It was man's ignorance—lack of specific knowledge—that kept us in the dark.

My use of the word *ignorance* isn't intended as a derogatory statement. Leonardo da Vinci was a brilliant man. He invented a helicopter and many other things that were centuries ahead of his time. But he was ignorant of electricity.

In the same way, there are many wonderful Christians who are sincere and very godly people in many ways. But they are ignorant of God's laws of faith. Therefore, they aren't receiving the results they desire. They aren't bad people; they just don't know the laws that govern how God's kingdom works.

Receiving from God isn't about how He feels toward you. If that were the only issue, then we would all be perfect in every way. It's what He wants for each and every one of us! But there are laws that must be put into effect in order to receive the things He has for us. It's our misuse of these laws that is literally killing us.

AGGRESSIVE RECEIVING
LESSON 22 – OUTLINE

I.   Mark's Gospel records an awesome example of the laws of faith in operation (Mark 5:25-34).

   A.   The Lord felt virtue flow out of Him and turned around, asking, *"Who touched my clothes?"* (Mark 5:30).

And Jesus increased in wisdom and stature, and in favour with God and man.

LUKE 2:52

   B.   Most people think God sizes us up when we come to Him with a request.

   C.   But that's not what happened here.

   D.   She put the laws of faith into action, and the power of God automatically flowed.

For she said, If I may touch but his clothes, I shall be whole.

MARK 5:28, EMPHASIS MINE

II.   This woman acted on her faith.

Faith without works is dead.

JAMES 2:20

   A.   The only logical explanation for her touching the hem of Jesus' garment is that this woman was probably on her hands and knees, crawling through the mass of people.

   B.   This illustrates another law of faith—earnestness.

   C.   You can't receive the things of God by just passively seeking them.

And ye shall seek me, and find me, when ye shall search for me with all your heart.

JEREMIAH 29:13

   D.   When you get aggressive, like this woman, where you are willing to risk even your own life in order to receive, you will receive.

E. It takes this type of aggressive attitude to effectively receive from God.

III. This woman put a number of the laws of faith into operation, and the healing virtue of God flowed to her automatically.

    A. The Lord isn't healing one and refusing another.

    B. There are laws that govern how God's power works.

    C. We can violate those laws and miss out on the blessings God's has already given us, or we can learn what the laws are, cooperate with them, and experience the abundant life He has provided.

    D. It's up to us.

IV. Receiving from God isn't about how He feels toward you.

    A. If that were the only issue, then we would all be perfect in every way.

    B. It's what God wants for each and every one of us!

    C. But there are laws that must be put into effect in order to receive the things God has for us.

    D. It's our misuse of these laws that is literally killing us.

AGGRESSIVE RECEIVING
LESSON 22 – TEACHER'S GUIDE

1. Mark's Gospel records an awesome example of the laws of faith in operation (Mark 5:25-34). A woman with an issue of blood came to Jesus seeking healing. The Lord felt virtue flow out of Him and turned around, asking, *"Who touched my clothes?"* (Mark 5:30). Most people think God sizes us up when we come to Him with a request. But that's not what happened here. She put the laws of faith into action, and the power of God automatically flowed.

2. This woman acted on her faith (James 2:20) in touching the hem of Jesus' garment. The only logical explanation is that she was probably on her hands and knees, crawling through the mass of people. This illustrates another law of faith—earnestness. We can't receive the things of God by just passively seeking them (Jer. 29:13). When we get aggressive, like this woman, where we are willing to risk even our own lives in order to receive, we will receive. It takes this type of aggressive attitude to effectively receive from God.

3. This woman put a number of the laws of faith into operation, and the healing virtue of God flowed to her automatically. The Lord isn't healing one and refusing another. There are laws that govern how His power works. We can violate those laws and miss out on the blessings He has already given us, or we can learn what the laws are, cooperate with them, and experience the abundant life He has provided. It's up to us.

4. Receiving from God isn't about how He feels toward us. If that were the only issue, then we would all be perfect in every way. It's what He wants for each and every one of us! But there are laws that must be put into effect in order to receive the things He has for us. It's our misuse of these laws that is literally killing us.

1. A. Read Mark 5:25-34. What do most people think God does when we come to Him with a request? (We think He sizes us up)

   B. What happened when this woman put the laws of faith into action? (The power of God automatically flowed)

2. A. Read James 2:20 and Jeremiah 29:13. Can we receive the things of God by just passively seeking them? (No)

   B. What type of attitude does it take to effectively receive from God? (An aggressive attitude—where we are willing to risk even our own lives in order to receive)

3. A. Is the Lord healing one and refusing another? (No)

   B. How do we experience the abundant life He has provided? (We must learn what the laws of faith are and cooperate with them)

   C. Is it up to God or us? (Us)

4. A. If receiving from God was only about how He feels toward us, then we would all be what in every way? (Perfect)

   B. What is it that is literally killing us? (Our misuse of these laws)

AGGRESSIVE RECEIVING
LESSON 22 – DISCIPLESHIP QUESTIONS

1.   According to Mark 5:30, what did Jesus immediately know in Himself?

2.   What did He then do?

3.   What did He say?

4.   Luke 2:52 reveals that Jesus increased in what?

   A.   Wisdom
   B.   Stature
   C.   Favor with God
   D.   Favor with man
   E.   All of the above
   F.   None of the above

5.   According to Mark 5:28, what did the woman do?

6.   *"If I may touch but His _____."*

7.   *"I shall be _____."*

8.   Mark 11:23 instructs us to do what unto this mountain?

9.   We should believe that what things shall come to pass?

10.   We shall have whatsoever we what?

11.   According James 2:20, what is dead?

12.   Jeremiah 29:13 reveals that we'll find God when?

13.   According to Mark 5:25-26, what did a certain woman have?

14.   How long?

15.   What had she suffered?

16.   Of whom?

17.   What had she spent?

18.   Was she bettered?

AGGRESSIVE RECEIVING
LESSON 22 – ANSWER KEY

1. That virtue had gone out of Him

2. He turned about in the press

3. *"Who touched my clothes?"*

4. E. All of the above

5. She said

6. *"Clothes"*

7. *"Whole"*

8. Say

9. Those things which we say

10. Say

11. Faith without works

12. When we search for Him with all of our heart

13. An issue of blood

14. Twelve years

15. Many things

16. Many physicians

17. All that she had

18. No, she grew worse

AGGRESSIVE RECEIVING
LESSON 22 – SCRIPTURES

MARK 5:30

And Jesus, immediately knowing in himself that virtue had gone out of him, turned him about in the press, and said, Who touched my clothes?

LUKE 2:52

And Jesus increased in wisdom and stature, and in favour with God and man.

MARK 5:28

For she said, If I may touch but his clothes, I shall be whole.

MARK 11:23

For verily I say unto you, That whosoever shall say unto this mountain, Be thou removed, and be thou cast into the sea; and shall not doubt in his heart, but shall believe that those things which he saith shall come to pass; he shall have whatsoever he saith.

JAMES 2:20

But wilt thou know, O vain man, that faith without works is dead?

JEREMIAH 29:13

And ye shall seek me, and find me, when ye shall search for me with all your heart.

MARK 5:25-26

And a certain woman, which had an issue of blood twelve years, [26] And had suffered many things of many physicians, and had spent all that she had, and was nothing bettered, but rather grew worse.

UNBELIEF COUNTERACTS FAITH
LESSON 23

Just because you understand that you already have the faith of God doesn't mean it will automatically produce victory in your life. Your unbelief will counterbalance and short-circuit that faith until you get rid of it. Your problem isn't a lack of faith but rather too much unbelief! Jesus and three of His disciples went up on the Mount of Transfiguration. He was glorified, and they saw Moses and Elijah speak with Him. Immediately after this, they came down from the mountain to a multitude. A man came forward to Jesus,

Kneeling down to him, and saying, [15] Lord, have mercy on my son: for he is lunatick, and sore vexed: for ofttimes he falleth into the fire, and oft into the water. [16] And I brought him to thy disciples, and they could not cure him. [17] Then Jesus answered and said, O faithless and perverse generation, how long shall I be with you? how long shall I suffer you? bring him hither to me.

MATTHEW 17:14-17

This man brought his "lunatic" son to Jesus. Mark 9:17-22 reveals that this "dumb spirit" produced violent seizures, much like what we would call "epilepsy" today. The father had brought his boy to the disciples first, but they weren't able to cast the demon out. Jesus was not pleased! Notice His reaction:

O faithless and perverse generation, how long shall I be with you? how long shall I suffer you? bring him hither to me.

MARK 17:17

This is important because there aren't very many people operating in the supernatural power of God in the body of Christ today. We aren't seeing very many demons cast out or people healed. As a whole, the church seems powerless to expel devils and cure sicknesses.

EXCUSES, EXCUSES

Basically, much of the body of Christ excuses this by saying "Well, we're just people. We pray and ask God to do it, but if we don't see anything happen, that's just because God is sovereign and it must not be His will" or "Those things passed away with the apostles." We've come up with all these different doctrines to justify our powerlessness and ineffectiveness.

Jesus didn't respond that way. If He were like a modern-day touchy-feely, feel-good type of minister, He would have said, "Guys, I'm sorry! I shouldn't have been up on the mountain being transfigured and talking to My Father for so long. I left you alone to handle problems that are beyond your ability. After all, you're only human. Forgive me. I'm sorry. I'm here now. Bring the boy to Me." Jesus didn't do that. Instead, He became angry and thundered, "O faithless and perverse generation! This isn't the way it's supposed to be. How long am I going to be with you? How long must I be here to do these things?"

Jesus had been training His disciples. He had already given them authority to cast out devils and heal the sick. They should have been able to handle this. So Jesus, in effect, was saying, "Guys, this isn't acceptable. You are faithless and perverse. This is not the way it's supposed to be!"

Although I say this in love, I pray that it registers and makes the impact it should: *Our Christianity today is faithless and perverse!* The church is supposed to have the answers for the world, but we are not using what we've got. God has already given us everything, but we aren't releasing it. We are powerless and ineffective. Most believers have simply lowered the standard by saying, "Miracles and supernatural power passed away with the first-century church," and those who do look for miracles approach it as "O God, we ask You to do it," instead of receiving what He's already done, taking their authority, commanding, and making it come to pass. It's twisted from what the Lord meant it to be!

Jesus' response to the disciples is the same for us today: "This is wrong! It's not the way I intended it to be." People ought to be able to come to us for healing, deliverance, and blessing (emotional and financial). But when the sick come to a typical minister today, that minister will send them to a doctor. The poor are sent to the government or some other social agency. When the mentally or emotionally disturbed ask for help, they are sent to a "shrink." This should not be! God's answers are in the Word and the church. We shouldn't have to send people anywhere else! The body of Christ has really failed in this area.

This is a big reason that more people aren't coming to Christ. The church has failed to portray the Lord as the one with the answers to all the problems of life. The typical church deals only with issues of eternity, and it leaves all the present issues to man's ability. People just don't see the relevance of the church to everyday life. This should not be! Jesus isn't any more pleased with this today than He was in this situation with the child suffering from seizures.

DESPITE PRIOR SUCCESS

And Jesus rebuked the devil; and he departed out of him: and the child was cured from that very hour. [19] Then came the disciples to Jesus apart, and said, Why could not we cast him out?

MATTHEW 17:18-19

That's a valid question because Jesus had already given them power over the devil.

And when he [Jesus] had called unto him his twelve disciples, he gave them power against unclean spirits, to cast them out, *and* to heal all manner of sickness and all manner of disease.

MATTHEW 10:1, BRACKETS AND EMPHASIS MINE

Not only did they already have all the power they needed to see that demonized boy set free; they had prior success in using it!

And they [the disciples previously] *cast out many devils, and anointed with oil many that were sick and healed them.*

MARK 6:13, BRACKETS MINE

These were not people who had never flowed in God's power and the miraculous; these were followers of Jesus who apparently had a 100 percent success rate before this, which makes their question even more significant.

These were believers who had seen God's power flow through them before to heal the sick and cast out devils. They knew it was God's will and that He had already given them the power. Yet they had exercised their faith, acted on it, and spoke to the mountain but still didn't see the desired results. Sound familiar?

You've probably had a situation in your life when you released your faith, acted on it, spoke to the mountain but still didn't receive your desired results. You believed God for healing, prosperity, deliverance, or whatever, but it didn't come to pass. I'm not talking about those who pray "God, if it be Your will" and aren't surprised when nothing happens. These disciples were shocked, hurt, and surprised. They asked this question because they *did* believe, and they had seen it work in the past.

Why do you think certain demons don't come out? Why are specific individuals not healed? Why don't financial breakthroughs come sometimes? Why do you think people pray, really believing, but what they ask for doesn't come to pass? Although there are multiple reasons for this, the dominant answer to this question is, "It must not have been God's will." Hogwash!

GOD'S WILL?

God wants you to prosper in every area of your life! It's not God's will for you to be sick, to not have your needs met, to be oppressed. It's not God's will for you to be discouraged and defeated. He is not punishing you or trying to teach you something. That's simply not true!

A large segment of the body of Christ lumps every "unanswered" prayer into "Well, God is sovereign." God is Almighty and He can do anything He wants to, but He has already done what He wants and has given us the authority and power to bring His will to pass.

Many things happen today, not because it's God's will, but because we are reaping what we have sown. Take, for instance, the terrorist attacks that happened on September 11, 2001. Many people viewed them as "God's judgment on America." Well, America is worthy of being judged, but the Lord isn't releasing His judgment. Neither did He "sovereignly" allow it. God has set up laws that we reap what we sow.

America has been systematically trying to become a secular nation. We have kicked God out of our schools and public life. We've been busy doing our own thing and ignoring Him. By denying God the right to move freely in our society, we let our defenses down.

Satan attacks whether you're godly or not. You don't have to be doing something wrong in order to draw his attack. You could actually be doing something right and be attacked. David had people attack him when he was seeking and serving God. Although he won, he was still attacked and had to fight. It's just that there's often more damage when your defense is down.

"BECAUSE OF YOUR UNBELIEF"

When we ask the question "Why don't things work?" two main perspectives—both wrong—come forth. First, many people think, *Que sera, sera. Whatever will be, will be. God is sovereign and He controls everything.* Second, a popular charismatic—"faith"—answer would be, "They don't have enough faith." That's presented as being the *only* reason people don't see their answer to prayer. But it's too simplistic and condemns people because it puts all the responsibility on them without any grace. This drives them away from faith-oriented teaching. It is *a* reason, but not an *all-encompassing* one!

In ministering to other people, their faith does affect the process. You can't make them receive based on your faith alone. Jesus quickened people's faith when He ministered to them. He told them *"Sin no more, lest a worse thing come unto thee"* (John 5:14), implying that they had a part to play in their healing. We know that Jesus operated in faith perfectly.

Yet He couldn't do many miracles in His own hometown. This wasn't because of any problem with His faith, but because the people were full of unbelief. There needs to be some degree of faith present on the part of the person receiving. However, if the healing doesn't manifest, it could also be a problem with the minister's faith and ability to receive from God.

It's just not always as simple as, "Believe and receive or doubt and do without." Sometimes you can believe and still not receive. That is what happened to the disciples here (Matt. 17). They asked, "Jesus, why couldn't we cast the demon out? We believed and received, but we didn't get our desired results."

And Jesus said unto them, Because of your unbelief.

MATTHEW 17:20A

Many people mistakenly think that they can't have both unbelief and faith at the same time. They believe that faith and unbelief are mutually exclusive. That's not true.

When Jesus told them "It's because of your unbelief," He wasn't saying, "You didn't have faith." He didn't mention that. In fact, Christ's very next statement was,

I say unto you, If ye have faith as a grain of mustard seed, ye shall say unto this mountain, Remove hence to yonder place; and it shall remove; and nothing shall be impossible unto you.

MATTHEW 17:20B

It doesn't require a "great" faith or a "big" faith to do great things; you just need to minimize the unbelief working against your faith.

"ONLY BELIEVE!"

That's why Jesus answered the disciples' request, "Lord, increase our faith," with, "Guys, you don't need more faith; just use what you've already got. If your faith is the size of a mustard seed, it is enough to cause this tree to be uprooted and planted in the sea. Nothing is impossible to you" (Luke 17:5-6, paraphrase mine). Notice the same terminology in Mark 11:23:

For verily I say unto you, That whosoever shall say unto this mountain, Be thou removed, and be thou cast into the sea; and shall not doubt in his heart.

EMPHASIS MINE

It's possible to be in faith and have doubt in your heart at the same time!

When Jesus was on His way to minister to Jairus' daughter, the woman with the issue of blood touched Jesus' garment and received healing. During this delay, news came from Jairus' house: "Don't trouble the Master any longer—your daughter is dead."

As soon as Jesus heard the word that was spoken, he saith unto the ruler of the synagogue, Be not afraid, only believe.

MARK 5:36

Only believe! Why would Jesus tell him to only believe? Because you can believe and disbelieve at the same time!

Jesus told the father of the lunatic boy who needed deliverance, *"If thou canst believe, all things are possible to him that believeth"* (Mark 9:23).

Immediately, the man *"cried out, and said with tears, Lord, I believe; help thou mine unbelief"* (Mark 9:24).

Jesus didn't rebuke this man for saying he had both faith and unbelief; He just ministered to his son and saw him delivered. This lack of rebuke speaks volumes!

According to God's Word, you can have a true faith—that under normal circumstances would bring about the desired deliverance—but still not see it produce the right results. The problem isn't an absence of faith, but the presence of unbelief.

THE NET EFFECT

Faith and unbelief are opposing forces. Unbelief counteracts your faith. Instead of trying to get more and more faith, you need to deal with the unbelief that is counterbalancing it. That's how you get your faith to work!

If you hitched a horse up to a 1,000-pound weight and had it exert enough force, the weight would move. However, if you hooked up another horse to it on the other side and had it pull with equal power in the opposite direction, the weight wouldn't move. Even though tremendous power is being released, the net effect on the weight would be zero. That's the way it is with faith and unbelief.

Your faith is sufficient. Jesus Himself said that even a mustard seed of faith can uproot a tree or move a mighty mountain. Therefore, your faith is more than enough to see a healing, cast out a demon, or anything else. The problem is unbelief countering your faith and causing a net effect of zero.

I have seen people who obviously didn't believe it was God's will for them to be well.

They fought against it when I came to pray for them. Since they didn't believe, they died. That's relatively easy to deal with. But I've also seen other people who believed it was God's will for them to be well. They were praying and trying to trust God for their healing. Some had even seen others healed or been healed themselves before. However, they still died. Now, that is harder to deal with.

CONFUSED

Many people wonder *Why weren't they healed? I know there was faith present!* I've seen people who loved God with all their heart and were facing death with joy, yet had an expectancy and an anticipation that they would see physical healing manifest. But still they died. Even though faith is intangible, you can tell if it's present or not when you are seeking God. When you recognize that faith is present but you see different results than what the Word of God promises, it can cause a tremendous amount of confusion.

This is why the disciples were confused when they couldn't cast the demon out of the lunatic boy (Matt. 17:19). They had faith, power, and authority and had successfully used it, until then. They spoke to the mountain and commanded the demon to come out. They acted in agreement with their faith, but still the results remained contrary. Why?

Because of your unbelief.

MATTHEW 17:20A

Unbelief is subtle. Many people don't recognize it. They just look at a person and if they perceive faith, they think that faith will automatically work. Not necessarily! Jesus told His disciples, "It's not that you didn't have faith; it's because you had unbelief." Then, to reinforce His point, Jesus added, "If your faith is only the size of a mustard seed, it's enough to cast a mountain into the sea" (Matt. 17:20, paraphrase mine). As a born-again Christian, your God-given supernatural faith is more than enough to accomplish anything you need—as long as there isn't any unbelief counteracting it!

LESSON 23 – ADDITIONAL INFORMATION

The religious doctrine commonly referred to as "the sovereignty of God" is a real faith killer. It misrepresents the Lord and renders people passive. My message "The Sovereignty of God" soundly debunks it.

UNBELIEF COUNTERACTS FAITH
LESSON 23 – OUTLINE

I. Just because you understand that you already have the faith of God doesn't mean it will automatically produce victory in your life.

    A. Your unbelief will counterbalance and short-circuit that faith until you get rid of it.

    B. Your problem isn't a lack of faith but rather too much unbelief.

II. The father had brought his boy to the disciples first, but they weren't able to cast the demon out (Mark 9:17-22).

There came to him a certain man, kneeling down to him, and saying, [15] Lord, have mercy on my son: for he is lunatick, and sore vexed: for ofttimes he falleth into the fire, and oft into the water. [16] And I brought him to thy disciples, and they could not cure him. [17] Then Jesus answered and said, O faithless and perverse generation, how long shall I be with you? how long shall I suffer you? bring him hither to me.

MATTHEW 17:14-17

    A. Jesus was not pleased!

O faithless and perverse generation, how long shall I be with you? how long shall I suffer you? bring him hither to me.

MATTHEW 17:17

    B. This is important because there aren't very many people operating in the supernatural power of God in the body of Christ today.

    C. Jesus' response to the disciples is the same for us today.

    D. God's answers are in the Word and the church.

III. Not only did they already have all the power they needed to see that demonized boy set free; they had prior success in using it.

And Jesus rebuked the devil; and he departed out of him: and the child was cured from that very hour. [19] Then came the disciples to Jesus apart, and said, Why could not we cast him out?

MATTHEW 17:18-19

And when he [Jesus] had called unto him his twelve disciples, he gave them power against unclean spirits, to cast them out, *and* to heal all manner of sickness and all manner of disease.

MATTHEW 10:1, BRACKETS AND EMPHASIS MINE

And they [the disciples previously] cast out many devils, and anointed with oil many that were sick and healed them.

MARK 6:13, BRACKETS MINE

A. These were believers who had seen God's power flow through them before to heal the sick and cast out devils.

B. They knew it was God's will and that He had already given them the power.

C. Yet they exercised their faith, acted on it, and spoke to the mountain but still didn't see the desired results.

IV. Many people mistakenly think that they can't have both unbelief and faith at the same time.

And Jesus said unto them, Because of your unbelief...I say unto you, If ye have faith as a grain of mustard seed, ye shall say unto this mountain, Remove hence to yonder place; and it shall remove; and nothing shall be impossible unto you.

MATTHEW 17:20, EMPHASIS MINE

A. It's possible to be in faith and have doubt in your heart at the same time!

For verily I say unto you, That whosoever shall say unto this mountain, Be thou removed, and be thou cast into the sea; and shall not doubt in his heart.

MARK 11:23, EMPHASIS MINE

B. The reason Jesus told Jairus to only believe is because you can believe and disbelieve at the same time!

As soon as Jesus heard the word that was spoken, he saith unto the ruler of the synagogue, Be not afraid, only believe.

MARK 5:36

C. Jesus told the father of the lunatic boy who needed deliverance, *"If thou canst believe, all things are possible to him that believeth"* (Mark 9:23).

And straightway the father of the child cried out, and said with tears, Lord, I believe; help thou mine unbelief.

MARK 9:24

D. According to God's Word, you can have a true faith—that under normal circumstances would bring about the desired deliverance—but still not see it produce the right results.

E. The problem isn't an absence of faith, but the presence of unbelief.

V. Faith and unbelief are opposing forces.

A. Unbelief counteracts your faith.

B. Instead of trying to get more and more faith, you need to deal with the unbelief that is counterbalancing it.

C. That's how you get your faith to work!

VI. Your faith is sufficient.

A. The problem is unbelief countering your faith and causing a net effect of zero.

B. Unbelief is subtle—many people don't recognize it.

C. As a born-again Christian, your God-given supernatural faith is more than enough to accomplish anything you need—as long as there isn't any unbelief counteracting it.

LESSON 23 – ADDITIONAL INFORMATION

The religious doctrine commonly referred to as "the sovereignty of God" is a real faith killer. It misrepresents the Lord and renders people passive. My message "The Sovereignty of God" soundly debunks it.

UNBELIEF COUNTERACTS FAITH
LESSON 23 – TEACHER'S GUIDE

1.   Just because we understand that we already have the faith of God doesn't mean it will automatically produce victory in our lives. Our unbelief will counterbalance and short-circuit that faith until we get rid of it. Our problem isn't a lack of faith but rather too much unbelief.

2.   A father had brought his boy to the disciples first, but they weren't able to cast the demon out (Mark 9:17-22 and Matt. 17:14-17). Jesus was not pleased! This is important because there aren't very many people operating in the supernatural power of God in the body of Christ today. Jesus' response to the disciples is the same for us today. God's answers are in the Word and the church.

3.   Not only did they already have all the power they needed to see that demonized boy set free; they had prior success in using it (Matt. 17:18-19, 10:1; and Mark 6:13)! These were believers who had seen God's power flow through them before to heal the sick and cast out devils. They knew it was God's will and that He had already given them the power. Yet they exercised their faith, acted on it, and spoke to the mountain but still didn't see the desired results.

1. A. What will counterbalance and short-circuit our faith until we get rid of it? (Our unbelief)
    B. Is our problem a lack of faith or too much unbelief? (Too much unbelief)
2. A. Read Mark 9:17-22 and Matthew 17:14-17. Was Jesus pleased with these disciples? (No)
    B. Where are God's answers? (In the Word and the church)
3. A. Read Matthew 17:18-19, 10:1; and Mark 6:13. What had these believers seen before? (God's power flow through them to heal the sick and cast out devils)
    B. They exercised their faith, acted on it, and spoke to the mountain but still didn't see what? (The desired results)

4.   Many people mistakenly think that they can't have both unbelief and faith at the same time (Matt. 17:20). It's possible to be in faith and have doubt in our hearts at the same time (Mark 11:23). The reason Jesus told Jairus to only believe is because we can believe and disbelieve at the same time (Mark 5:36). Jesus told the father of the lunatic boy who needed deliverance, *"If thou canst believe, all things are possible to him that believeth"* (Mark 9:23-24). According to God's Word, we can have a true faith that under normal circumstances would bring about the desired deliverance, but we can still not see it produce the right results. The problem isn't an absence of faith, but the presence of unbelief.

5.   Faith and unbelief are opposing forces. Unbelief counteracts our faith. Instead of trying to get more and more faith, we need to deal with the unbelief that is counterbalancing it. That's how we get our faith to work!

6.   Our faith is sufficient. The problem is unbelief countering our faith and causing a net effect of zero. Unbelief is subtle—many people don't recognize it. As born-again Christians, our God-given supernatural faith is more than enough to accomplish anything we need—as long as there isn't any unbelief counteracting it!

4.   A.   Read Matthew 17:20; Mark 11:23, 5:36, and 9:23-24. Is it possible to be in faith and have doubt in our hearts at the same time? (Yes)

    B.   Why did Jesus tell Jairus to only believe? (Because we can believe and disbelieve at the same time)

5.   A.   What are opposing forces? (Faith and unbelief)

    B.   Instead of trying to get more and more faith, how do we get our faith to work? (By dealing with the unbelief that's counterbalancing it)

6.   A.   What does unbelief cause as it counters our faith? (A net effect of zero)

    B.   As long as there isn't any unbelief counteracting it, our God-given supernatural faith is more than enough to accomplish what? (Anything we need)

UNBELIEF COUNTERACTS FAITH
LESSON 23 – DISCIPLESHIP QUESTIONS

1. According to Matthew 17:14-17, who had the man brought his son to before?

2. Could the disciples cure him?

3. How did Jesus then describe that generation?

4. According to Mark 9:17-22, how did the man address Jesus?

5. What had that dumb spirit been doing to the boy?

   A. Takes him
   B. Tears him
   C. Causes him to foam at the mouth
   D. Causes him to gnash his teeth
   E. Causes him to pine away
   F. All of the above
   G. None of the above

6. What did the man ask the disciples to do?

7. What did the man ask Jesus?

8. According to Matthew 17:18-19, whom did Jesus rebuke?

9. What did the devil (demon) then do?

10. What happened to the child?

11. According to Matthew 10:1, what had Jesus already given the disciples?

    A. Power to cast out unclean spirits
    B. Fear and loathing
    C. Power to heal all manner of sickness and disease
    D. All of the above
    E. Both A. and C.

12. According to Mark 6:13, what did the disciples cast out?

13. According to John 5:14, what did Jesus tell the man who had been made whole?

14. According to Matthew 17:20, why could the disciples not cast the demon out?

15. According to Luke 17:5-6, what did the apostles ask Jesus to increase?

16. What could faith as a mustard seed command to be plucked up by the root and be planted in the sea?

17. Mark 11:23 reveals that we should not doubt in our what?

18. According to Mark 5:36, when did Jesus speak to the ruler of the synagogue?

19. According to Mark 9:23-24, all things are possible to whom?

20. The father said, *"Lord, I believe; help thou mine _____."*

UNBELIEF COUNTERACTS FAITH
LESSON 23 – ANSWER KEY

1. The disciples

2. No

3. Faithless and perverse

4. Master

5. F.   All of the above

6. Cast the dumb spirit out

7. To have compassion on them and help them

8. The devil (demon)

9. Departed out of the boy

10. He was cured

11. E.   Both A. and C.

12. Many devils

13. *"Sin no more, lest a worse thing come unto thee"*

14. Because of their unbelief

15. Their faith

16. A sycamine tree

17. Hearts

18. As soon as He heard the word that was spoken

19. Those who believe

20. *"Unbelief"*

UNBELIEF COUNTERACTS FAITH
LESSON 23 – SCRIPTURES

MATTHEW 17:14-20

And when they were come to the multitude, there came to him a certain man, kneeling down to him, and saying, [15] Lord, have mercy on my son: for he is lunatick, and sore vexed: for ofttimes he falleth into the fire, and oft into the water. [16] And I brought him to thy disciples, and they could not cure him. [17] Then Jesus answered and said, O faithless and perverse generation, how long shall I be with you? how long shall I suffer you? bring him hither to me. [18] And Jesus rebuked the devil; and he departed out of him: and the child was cured from that very hour. [19] Then came the disciples to Jesus apart, and said, Why could not we cast him out? [20] And Jesus said unto them, Because of your unbelief: for verily I say unto you, If ye have faith as a grain of mustard seed, ye shall say unto this mountain, Remove hence to yonder place; and it shall remove; and nothing shall be impossible unto you.

MARK 9:17-24

And one of the multitude answered and said, Master, I have brought unto thee my son, which hath a dumb spirit; [18] And wheresoever he taketh him, he teareth him: and he foameth, and gnasheth with his teeth, and pineth away: and I spake to thy disciples that they should cast him out; and they could not. [19] He answereth him, and saith, O faithless generation, how long shall I be with you? how long shall I suffer you? bring him unto me. [20] And they brought him unto him: and when he saw him, straightway the spirit tare him; and he fell on the ground, and wallowed foaming. [21] And he asked his father, How long is it ago since this came unto him? And he said, Of a child. [22] And ofttimes it hath cast him into the fire, and into the waters, to destroy him: but if thou canst do any thing, have compassion on us, and help us. [23] Jesus said unto him, If thou canst believe, all things are possible to him that believeth. [24] And straightway the father of the child cried out, and said with tears, Lord, I believe; help thou mine unbelief.

MATTHEW 10:1

And when he had called unto him his twelve disciples, he gave them power against unclean spirits, to cast them out, and to heal all manner of sickness and all manner of disease.

MARK 6:13

And they cast out many devils, and anointed with oil many that were sick, and healed them.

JOHN 5:14

Afterward Jesus findeth him in the temple, and said unto him, Behold, thou art made whole: sin no more, lest a worse thing come unto thee.

LUKE 17:5-6

And the apostles said unto the Lord, Increase our faith. [6] And the Lord said, If ye had faith as a grain of mustard seed, ye might say unto this sycamine tree, Be thou plucked up by the root, and be thou planted in the sea; and it should obey you.

MARK 11:23

For verily I say unto you, That whosoever shall say unto this mountain, Be thou removed, and be thou cast into the sea; and shall not doubt in his heart, but shall believe that those things which he saith shall come to pass; he shall have whatsoever he saith.

MARK 5:36

As soon as Jesus heard the word that was spoken, he saith unto the ruler of the synagogue, Be not afraid, only believe.

WIGGLESWORTH HAD LESS
LESSON 24

I went to Omaha, Nebraska, to minister not long after seeing someone raised from the dead. I knew my faith was working, and things were going good. A paralyzed man in a wheelchair had come to the service. In my excitement, I reasoned, *Since my faith has developed to the point of seeing someone raised from the dead, surely it can handle a man in a wheelchair!* So, I walked over, grabbed this fellow by the hand, and lifted him up out of his wheelchair. He immediately fell right over on his face!

When that happened, my faith evaporated. Everyone in the audience gasped, moaned, and groaned. I then wrestled this guy back up into his wheelchair and said the scriptural equivalent of:

Depart in peace, be ye warmed and filled.

JAMES 2:16

Although I tried to encourage this man to continue believing God, I couldn't help him.

I returned to my hotel room that night totally perplexed. "Lord, what happened? I know I had faith!" It takes faith to do something like that! Have you ever yanked someone up out of their wheelchair and immediately seen them nosedive into the carpet? Most people haven't. Why? They don't believe they would be healed. The reason I pulled him up out of the wheelchair was because I truly believed he would walk. Even though faith was present, I didn't see the desired result. This brought me much confusion.

I sought the Lord for an answer to this dilemma for two or three years. Then, finally, I recognized my problem while reading a book about Smith Wigglesworth.

MEET SMITH WIGGLESWORTH

Wigglesworth lived in England in the early 1900s and had a powerful miracle ministry. He traveled to several countries and saw many great things happen. In the book I read, Smith's son-in-law recounted numerous testimonies.

At the beginning of a meeting, Wigglesworth liked to boldly announce, "The first person up here will be healed!" Someone would come forward, he would pray for them, and they would be healed. Smith used this as his attention-getter before delivering the message. Then, after the Word, he would pray for the rest of the sick.

One time, an elderly woman with cancer in her stomach came to the meeting. The cancer was so large that she appeared to be nine months' pregnant. She was so frail and weak, her two lady friends had to each take an arm and hold her upright in her seat. They knew what Smith was going to say, so when he made his usual announcement at the beginning of the meeting, they popped right up and brought their friend to the front for prayer.

Wigglesworth looked at her, saw this huge tumor on her belly, and told the two women holding her, "Let her go!" They answered, "We can't let her go! She doesn't have strength!" He raised his voice and said it again, "Let her go!" So they did. This woman fell forward on that tumor and groaned in pain. The audience immediately gasped in unbelief.

It was the exact same response I'd received after that man in the wheelchair fell on his face. I started feeling pity, sympathy, and embarrassment for both this man and myself. In my situation, I responded in a manner of unbelief. However, Wigglesworth stood his ground and simply said, "Pick her up."

Those two ladies picked her up. Then he said, "Let her go!" They cried, "We can't let her go!" Smith boomed, "Let her go!" When they finally did, she fell face first on that tumor again. The crowd moaned and groaned. Wigglesworth said, "Pick her up." So they picked her up once more.

Then Smith said for the third time, "Let her go!" The two women argued, "We will not let her go!" Smith commanded, "You let her go!" Then a man in the audience stood up and yelled, "You beast! Leave that poor woman alone!" Wigglesworth shouted back, "You mind your business; I know my business." He turned to the two ladies again and barked, "Let! Her! Go!"

When they did, the tumor fell out of her dress onto the stage, and she walked off totally healed.

THE DIFFERENCE

So what was the difference? Smith and I both had *"the measure of faith"* (Rom. 12:3). I had enough faith to grab the man by the hand and lift him up out of the wheelchair, fully expecting him to walk. However, I also had unbelief.

I was too easily swayed by what other people thought, as well as by fear, embarrassment, and pity for this guy.

> *How can ye believe, which receive honour one of another, and seek not the honour that cometh from God only?*
>
> **JOHN 5:44**

When you're worried about looking good in the sight of people, it can hinder your faith. Wigglesworth didn't have more than I did; he had less—less unbelief.

Smith was often criticized as being "too hard." He would hit, punch, and even kick people at times. When asked why, he responded, "I'm just out to get the devil. I can't help it if their body gets in the way!" He once kicked a baby with a head injury off the stage and into the front row. But that baby was healed! Wigglesworth understood the difference between godly compassion and human pity. He recognized that pity stops the power of God from operating. So, he was hard, insensitive, and unfeeling toward unbelief.

DRAIN IT TO ZERO!

Like Jesus' disciples in Matthew 17, I had both faith and unbelief working at the same time when I was in Omaha. It's not that my, or their, faith wasn't strong enough; there was just too much unbelief counteracting it.

Picture two outdoor thermometers: one measures faith, the other measures unbelief. Most people ignore the unbelief and concentrate on their faith. If their faith is up an inch but what they have prayed for still hasn't come to pass, they think they need to push their faith up another inch or two. So they go on an all-out effort to increase their faith, saying, "O God, give me more faith. I need more faith!"

The Lord said, "It's your unbelief that's the problem. Without unbelief working against it, your faith doesn't need to be any bigger than a mustard seed to get the job done" (Matt. 17:20, paraphrase mine). Instead of trying to shoot your faith through the roof, pull the plug on your unbelief, drain it to zero, and you'll find that your faith is strong enough to accomplish anything you need.

Most Christians don't receive what God has already supplied, not because of a lack of faith, but because of unbelief. These are two opposite situations. If someone doesn't believe, of course they won't receive. Faith is the bridge that brings God's provision from the spiritual world over into the physical world. Faith must be present, but it's not that big of a deal. It's not hard. As Christians, we have the supernatural faith of God. It's just that most believers haven't yet realized or dealt with their unbelief.

What is unbelief? It could be fear, worry, or care. If the doctor tells you you're going to die and you start trying to believe God by confessing "Jesus, I believe that by Your stripes I've been healed," but in your mind you're still worried, that's being double-minded. Double-minded people won't receive anything from the Lord (James 1:7-8).

Mark 11:23 says, *"That whosoever shall say unto this mountain, Be thou removed, and be thou cast into the sea; and shall not doubt in his heart"* (emphasis mine).

You can't believe, be saying and doing some of the right things, and yet have a split heart. To get the results you're after, you must be single minded and focused!

"HE CONSIDERED NOT"

Abraham didn't allow himself to think on anything contrary to what God had told him. He was strong in faith because the promise was all he considered.

Who against hope believed in hope, that he [Abraham] might become the father of many nations, according to that which was spoken, So shall thy seed be. [19] And being not weak in faith, he considered not his own body now dead, when he was about an hundred years old, neither yet the deadness of Sarah's womb.

ROMANS 4:18-19, BRACKETS MINE

You can't be tempted with anything you don't think. Therefore, overcoming temptation, unbelief, and failure begins in your thoughts. If your thoughts are only on God, then all you will be tempted with is to believe and trust Him. But if your thoughts are on things other than God, then you could be tempted with those things.

Abraham didn't consider—study, ponder, deliberate, examine—his own body now dead nor the deadness of Sarah's womb. When God told him that Sarah would conceive and give birth to a child the next year, Abraham didn't dwell on his age or the fact that Sarah had long since passed the time of childbearing. The thought may have crossed his mind, but he didn't consider it.

Just because an occasional contrary thought crosses your mind doesn't mean you are in unbelief. You can't stop the devil from giving you a thought, but you don't have to keep it. As Kenneth E. Hagin often said, "You can't stop a bird from flying over your head, but you can prevent it from making a nest there." A fleeting thought doesn't mean you're in unbelief. But when you consider, entertain, study, deliberate, examine, and ponder it, you will be tempted.

BAPTIZED IN UNBELIEF

Most people in Abraham's shoes today would blow it. If the Lord came to them at ninety-nine years old and said "Your wife will have a child next year," they would feel bound to seek a doctor for medical confirmation. "Is this possible? Have you ever heard of anyone one hundred years old having a baby? Please, examine my wife. She's already quit having her menstrual cycles. How could she possibly have a child now?" The doctors would agree and speak forth their unbelief, saying, "No, it's never happened before. And it can't happen now either!" Then they'd go back to God in prayer and ask, "Lord, did You really say this?" He would answer, "Yes, I did!" Then they'd try to believe Him after accumulating and pondering on all of these contrary thoughts. And they would wonder, *Why is it so hard to receive from God?*

The reason Abraham was such a strong man of faith wasn't because he had more than we do. He had less—less unbelief! This man was so mentally disciplined at age ninety-nine that when he was told by God that he would have a child, he didn't even think about, focus on, or study his own body nor the deadness of his wife's womb. Abraham only looked at the promise of God!

Unbelief comes through your thought process.

It doesn't take a lot of faith to receive from God; it only takes just a pure, simple, childlike faith. However, most of us as Christians are baptized in unbelief. We're still so plugged in to the world's negativity that it's a miracle our faith has accomplished what it has. We take in all the junk on television, radio, and movies. After subjecting ourselves to all of this bad news, God tells us He's going to do something contrary to what the rest of the world is experiencing, and we have a hard time only believing. We know God wants to bless us. We're asking for it and heading in that direction, but we're loaded down with all of this unbelief.

A SEPARATED LIFE

As a young man, Lester Sumrall once visited Smith Wigglesworth. With a newspaper rolled up under his arm, he knocked on the door. After introducing himself, he asked, "May I come in and visit with you?" Smith answered, "You can come in, but that paper has to stay outside."

Now, reading the newspaper isn't a sin. I read it on occasion—once every month or two. I'll also watch a news program on television about the same. In the car, I'll listen to the two-minute news summary on the radio. But that's basically the news I get. I don't do more, because there's so much negativity and unbelief in there.

Smith probably missed a dozen or two good things in the newspaper over those thirty-five years or so. He could have used them in his messages to help make a point (like I do sometimes). But he also missed hundreds of thousands of negative thoughts and statements that could have produced unbelief in him. To Smith, it just wasn't worth the risk!

Since Wigglesworth lived such a separated life, he simply wasn't as susceptible to unbelief as I was when I tried to pull that man out of the wheelchair. Now that God has shown me this, I've started living a more separated life too. I don't watch or listen to things I used to. Because of this, some people say my faith is stronger. Actually, it's purer. It's not as diluted now. I don't have as many thoughts of unbelief as before, because I quit opening myself up to things that give me opportunity for it.

THE PROBLEM

Jesus told His disciples, "Your unbelief is the problem. If you had faith as small as a grain of mustard seed, it would be sufficient. You could have seen this boy delivered if you would have only believed" (Matt. 17:20, paraphrase mine).

Taking into account the parallel passage (Mark 9:14-29), we can see some of the reasons the disciples had unbelief in this instance. The boy had a seizure, fell down, and foamed at the mouth. I don't know if you've ever been around someone having an epileptic seizure, but I have. It'll make the hair stand up on the back of your neck!

When that happens, it'll foster unbelief, worry, and fear. It's going to look contrary to what you're praying for. And unless you've spent time specifically fighting against that type of unbelief, you'll succumb to it.

That's what happened to me when I pulled that man out of the wheelchair and didn't see the right results. I was worried about what the audience thought. I let other people's unbelief and the fear of their rejection influence me. It hindered my faith.

Faith was present, but so was unbelief. If I had stood the way Smith Wigglesworth did, then my faith would have worked the way his worked. The difference wasn't our faith, but it was our unbelief. I had more than Wigglesworth—more unbelief!

LESSON 24 – ADDITIONAL INFORMATION

My teaching *Hardness of Heart* will answer many of your questions about this Lesson. It's one of the greatest things the Lord has ever shown me!

WIGGLESWORTH HAD LESS
LESSON 24 – OUTLINE

I. I went to Omaha, Nebraska, to minister not long after seeing someone raised from the dead.

    A. I knew my faith was working, and things were going good.

    B. So, I walked over, grabbed this fellow by the hand, and lifted him up out of his wheelchair.

    C. Even though faith was present, I didn't see the desired result.

    D. This brought me much confusion.

    E. Then, finally, I recognized my problem while reading a book about Smith Wigglesworth.

II. Smith and I both had *"the measure of faith"* (Rom. 12:3).

    A. But I was too easily swayed by what other people thought, as well as by fear, embarrassment, and pity for this guy.

How can ye believe, which receive honour one of another, and seek not the honour that cometh from God only?

JOHN 5:44

    B. Wigglesworth didn't have more than I did; he had less—less unbelief.

    C. Wigglesworth understood the difference between godly compassion and human pity.

    D. So, he was hard, insensitive, and unfeeling toward unbelief.

III. Like Jesus' disciples in Matthew 17, I had both faith and unbelief working at the same time when I was in Omaha.

    A. The Lord said, "It's your unbelief that's the problem. Without unbelief working against it, your faith doesn't need to be any bigger than a mustard seed to get the job done" (Matt. 17:20, paraphrase mine).

    B. Instead of trying to shoot your faith through the roof, pull the plug on your unbelief, drain it to zero, and you'll find that your faith is strong enough to accomplish anything you need.

That whosoever shall say unto this mountain, Be thou removed, and be thou cast into the sea; and shall not doubt in his heart.

MARK 11:23, EMPHASIS MINE

IV. To get the results you're after, you must be single-minded and focused (James 1:7-8)!

    A. Abraham didn't allow himself to think on anything contrary to what God had told him.

Who against hope believed in hope, that he [Abraham] might become the father of many nations, according to that which was spoken, So shall thy seed be. [19] And being not weak in faith, he considered not his own body now dead, when he was about an hundred years old, neither yet the deadness of Sarah's womb.

ROMANS 4:18-19, BRACKETS MINE

    B. You can't be tempted with anything you don't think.

    C. If your thoughts are only on God, then all you will be tempted with is to believe and trust Him.

    D. But if your thoughts are on things other than God, then you could be tempted with those things.

    E. A fleeting thought doesn't mean you're in unbelief, but when you consider, entertain, study, deliberate, examine, and ponder it, you'll be tempted.

V. Unbelief comes through your thought process.

    A. It doesn't take a lot of faith to receive from God; it takes a pure, simple, childlike faith.

    B. However, most of us as Christians are baptized in unbelief.

    C. We're still so plugged in to the world's negativity that it's a miracle our faith has accomplished what it has.

    D. We know God wants to bless us.

    E. We're asking for it and heading in that direction, but we're loaded down with all of this unbelief.

VI. Now that God has shown me this, I've started living a more separated life.

    A. I don't watch or listen to things I used to.

    B. Because of this, my faith is purer—it's not as diluted now.

    C. I don't have as many thoughts of unbelief as before, because I quit opening myself up to things that give me opportunity for it.

LESSON 24 – ADDITIONAL INFORMATION

My teaching *Hardness of Heart* will answer many of your questions about this Lesson. It's one of the greatest things the Lord has ever shown me!

WIGGLESWORTH HAD LESS
LESSON 24 – TEACHER'S GUIDE

1.   Andrew went to Omaha, Nebraska, to minister not long after seeing someone raised from the dead. He knew his faith was working, and things were going good. So he walked over, grabbed this fellow by the hand, and lifted him up out of his wheelchair. Even though faith was present, Andrew didn't see the desired result. This brought him much confusion. Then, finally, he recognized his problem while reading a book about Smith Wigglesworth.

2.   Smith and Andrew both had *"the measure of faith"* (Rom. 12:3). But Andrew was too easily swayed by what other people thought, as well as by fear, embarrassment, and pity for this guy (John 5:44). Wigglesworth didn't have more than Andrew did; he had less—less unbelief. Wigglesworth understood the difference between godly compassion and human pity. So, he was hard, insensitive, and unfeeling toward unbelief.

3.   Like Jesus' disciples in Matthew 17, Andrew had both faith and unbelief working at the same time when he was in Omaha. The Lord said, "It's your unbelief that's the problem. Without unbelief working against it, your faith doesn't need to be any bigger than a mustard seed to get the job done" (Matt. 17:20, Andrew's paraphrase). Instead of trying to shoot our faith through the roof, let's pull the plug on our unbelief. If we drain it to zero, we'll find that our faith is strong enough to accomplish anything we need (Mark 11:23).

1. A.   Andrew went to Omaha, Nebraska, to minister not long after what? (Seeing someone raised from the dead)
    B.   He knew his faith was working, so he walked over, grabbed this fellow by the hand, and what? (Lifted him up out of his wheelchair)
    C.   Even though faith was present, what happened? (Andrew didn't see the desired result)
2. A.   Read Romans 12:3 and John 5:44. What was Andrew too easily swayed by? (What other people thought, as well as by fear, embarrassment, and pity for this guy)
    B.   How was Smith Wigglesworth toward unbelief? (Hard, insensitive, and unfeeling)
3. A.   Read Matthew 17:20 and Mark 11:23. Like Jesus' disciples in Matthew 17, Andrew had what working at the same time when he was in Omaha? (Both faith and unbelief)
    B.   How will we find that our faith is strong enough to accomplish anything we need? (By pulling the plug on our unbelief and draining it to zero)

4.   To get the results we're after, we must be single-minded and focused (James 1:7-8). Abraham didn't allow himself to think on anything contrary to what God had told him (Rom. 4:18-19). We can't be tempted with anything we don't think. If our thoughts are only on God, then all we will be tempted with is to believe and trust Him. But if our thoughts are on things other than God, then we could be tempted with those things. A fleeting thought doesn't mean we're in unbelief, but when we consider, entertain, study, deliberate, examine, and ponder it, we'll be tempted.

5.   Unbelief comes through our thought process. It doesn't take a lot of faith to receive from God; it just takes a pure, simple, childlike faith. However, most of us as Christians are baptized in unbelief. We're still so plugged in to the world's negativity that it's a miracle our faith has accomplished what it has. We know God wants to bless us. We're asking for it and heading in that direction, but we're loaded down with all of this unbelief.

6.   Now that God has shown us this, let's start living more separated lives. Let's not watch or listen to the things we used to. Because of this, our faith will be purer—it won't be as diluted. We won't have as many thoughts of unbelief as before, because we would have quit opening ourselves up to things that give us opportunity for it.

4. A. Read James 1:7-8 and Romans 4:18-19. What must we be in order to get the results we're after? (Single-minded and focused)
    B. Can we be tempted with anything we don't think? (No)
    C. When will we be tempted? (When we consider, entertain, study, deliberate, examine, and ponder a thought)
5. A. How does unbelief come? (Through our thought process)
    B. What kind of faith does it take to receive from God? (A pure, simple, childlike faith)
6. A. How do we start living a more separated life? (By not watching or listening to the things we used to)
    B. How will this affect our faith? (It'll be purer—less diluted)
    C. What will happen when we quit opening ourselves up to things that give us opportunity for unbelief? (We won't have as many thoughts of unbelief as before)

WIGGLESWORTH HAD LESS
LESSON 24 – DISCIPLESHIP QUESTIONS

1. According to James 2:16, does wishing someone well but not giving them what they need profit?

2. Paul said what he said in Romans 12:3 through what?

3. Who did he say it to?

4. Should we think more highly of ourselves than we ought?

5. According to John 5:44, does seeking one another's honor hinder our believing?

6. From whom should we seek honor only?

7. According to Matthew 17:20, the disciples couldn't cast the demon out of the boy because of what?

8. According to James 1:7-8, who is unstable in all their ways?

9. Will they receive anything from the Lord?

10. Double-mindedness hinders our ability to what from the Lord?

11. According to Mark 11:23, what are we to speak to?

12. According to Romans 4:18-19, who believed in hope?

13. God had spoken that Abraham would become the father of what?

14. Was he weak in faith?

15. What did Abraham consider not?

    A. His own body now dead
    B. He was about a hundred years old
    C. The deadness of Sarah's womb
    D. All of the above
    E. None of the above

16. According to Mark 9:14-18, what did this boy have?

17. According to Mark 9:19-24, all things are possible to whom?

18. According to Mark 9:25-29, whom did Jesus rebuke?

19. What did the boy appear like once the deaf and dumb spirit came out of him?

20. What happened when Jesus took the boy by the hand and lifted him up?

WIGGLESWORTH HAD LESS
LESSON 24 – ANSWER KEY

1. No

2. The grace given unto him

3. Everyone that is among you

4. No

5. Yes

6. God

7. Their unbelief

8. A double-minded person

9. No

10. Receive

11. This mountain

12. Abraham

13. Many nations

14. No

15. D. All of the above

16. A dumb spirit

17. Those who believe

18. The foul spirit

19. Dead

20. He arose

WIGGLESWORTH HAD LESS
LESSON 24 – SCRIPTURES

JAMES 2:16
And one of you say unto them, Depart in peace, be ye warmed and filled; notwithstanding ye give them not those things which are needful to the body; what doth it profit?

ROMANS 12:3
For I say, through the grace given unto me, to every man that is among you, not to think of himself more highly than he ought to think; but to think soberly, according as God hath dealt to every man the measure of faith.

JOHN 5:44
How can ye believe, which receive honour one of another, and seek not the honour that cometh from God only?

MATTHEW 17:20
And Jesus said unto them, Because of your unbelief: for verily I say unto you, If ye have faith as a grain of mustard seed, ye shall say unto this mountain, Remove hence to yonder place; and it shall remove; and nothing shall be impossible unto you.

JAMES 1:7-8
For let not that man think that he shall receive any thing of the Lord. [8] A double minded man is unstable in all his ways.

MARK 11:23
For verily I say unto you, That whosoever shall say unto this mountain, Be thou removed, and be thou cast into the sea; and shall not doubt in his heart, but shall believe that those things which he saith shall come to pass; he shall have whatsoever he saith.

ROMANS 4:18-19
Who against hope believed in hope, that he might become the father of many nations, according to that which was spoken, So shall thy seed be. [19] And being not weak in faith, he considered not his own body now dead, when he was about an hundred years old, neither yet the deadness of Sarah's womb.

MARK 9:14-29

And when he came to his disciples, he saw a great multitude about them, and the scribes questioning with them. [15] And straightway all the people, when they beheld him, were greatly amazed, and running to him saluted him. [16] And he asked the scribes, What question ye with them? [17] And one of the multitude answered and said, Master, I have brought unto thee my son, which hath a dumb spirit; [18] And wheresoever he taketh him, he teareth him: and he foameth, and gnasheth with his teeth, and pineth away: and I spake to thy disciples that they should cast him out; and they could not. [19] He answereth him, and saith, O faithless generation, how long shall I be with you? how long shall I suffer you? bring him unto me. [20] And they brought him unto him: and when he saw him, straightway the spirit tare him; and he fell on the ground, and wallowed foaming. [21] And he asked his father, How long is it ago since this came unto him? And he said, Of a child. [22] And ofttimes it hath cast him into the fire, and into the waters, to destroy him: but if thou canst do any thing, have compassion on us, and help us. [23] Jesus said unto him, If thou canst believe, all things are possible to him that believeth. [24] And straightway the father of the child cried out, and said with tears, Lord, I believe; help thou mine unbelief. [25] When Jesus saw that the people came running together, he rebuked the foul spirit, saying unto him, Thou dumb and deaf spirit, I charge thee, come out of him, and enter no more into him. [26] And the spirit cried, and rent him sore, and came out of him: and he was as one dead; insomuch that many said, He is dead. [27] But Jesus took him by the hand, and lifted him up; and he arose. [28] And when he was come into the house, his disciples asked him privately, Why could not we cast him out? [29] And he said unto them, This kind can come forth by nothing, but by prayer and fasting.

DEAL WITH YOUR UNBELIEF
LESSON 25

Unbelief comes in three different types: ignorance, disbelief, and natural.

Ignorance is when someone just doesn't know the truth. They might not have grown up in church, or they might have been raised in a traditional denomination. Therefore, their idea of Christianity is skewed. They think Christians are just waiting on heaven and that there's no real victory to be experienced in this life. Due to their lack of knowledge, they have unbelief.

This type of unbelief is relatively easy to deal with: Just tell them the truth! If their heart is open to the Lord, they will receive it. Then, ignorance leaves and they are able to believe God.

Disbelief comes from being taught wrong. Someone told them, "God doesn't heal or do miracles anymore. All of that supernatural stuff passed away with the apostles." That's beyond "Well, I've never heard of a person being healed today" (ignorance); it's, "If tongues, healing, or miracles happen today, it's of the devil." That's wrong teaching!

Disbelief is more difficult to overcome than ignorance. A person who's been taught wrong has prejudices against the truth. It's a lot harder for them to renew their mind and receive.

I had to struggle to renew my mind to the truth. I'd been taught many excuses for why God doesn't do miracles today, how tongues were of the devil, and why the supernatural things in the book of Acts don't happen now. Although it is a little harder to overcome, the antidote for this second type of unbelief is the same as the first. I had to receive the truth of God's Word above man's traditions in order to overcome this unbelief that came through wrong teaching.

NATURAL UNBELIEF

The third kind of unbelief is what I call "natural" unbelief. It's not ignorance or wrong teaching but simply natural input that's contrary to the truth. The demonized boy had a seizure and foamed at the mouth (Mark 9:14-29, parallel to Matt. 17:14-21). When something like that happens, your mind, emotions, eyes, and ears are all going to tell you, "The demon didn't come out. Look, it didn't work!" That's not necessarily evil, just natural.

You go through life receiving input from your eyes, ears, and feelings and making your decisions based on that. It's not wrong, or evil; it's just natural. If you were driving me somewhere in your car, I'd want you to have some of this "natural" input. I certainly wouldn't want you driving "by faith" with your eyes closed! However, there are things you can't perceive with just your five physical senses, and there are times when the Lord will ask you to take a step of faith. That's when you must be able to get beyond this kind of unbelief that comes from natural things.

If you pray for someone to be healed and they fall over dead, some natural unbelief will come at you. You prayed for them to be well, but now they're dead. What's going to happen? Unless you are really strong, you're naturally going to listen to fear and unbelief say, "Well, it didn't work. Why? Because you can't see it!"

Most people are dominated by their physical senses. It was this kind of unbelief—natural unbelief—that hindered the disciples in Matthew 17. They believed they could cast out devils. They had done it before. The very fact that they asked, *Why could not we cast him out?* (Matt. 17:19) showed they had faith. They had ministered to the boy, believing, but when he began going into convulsions, they were moved more by what they saw than by what they believed.

"THIS KIND"

How do you overcome this kind of unbelief? By knowing the truth and renewing your mind to it, you can get over ignorance and disbelief. But how do you get beyond what you see and feel? How do you get to where you're believing only and not letting that pain you feel in your body convince you that "No, it didn't work"? Jesus gave the answer in Matthew 17:21, which says,

Howbeit this kind [of unbelief] *goeth not out but by prayer and fasting.*

BRACKETS MINE

Many people have misinterpreted this verse. They think Jesus was talking about "this kind of demon." So they've invented different doctrines saying that certain demons are stronger than others and can only be cast out through prayer and fasting. That's not what Jesus was talking about.

You will never encounter a demon—or even the devil himself—that won't cower and flee at the name of Jesus and faith in His name. Your fasting and prayer doesn't add anything to it. If the name of Jesus and faith in His name won't defeat the devil, neither will your prayer and fasting!

Unbelief is the consistent subject of both verses (Matt. 17:20-21). *"This kind"* in verse 21 refers to *"unbelief"* in verse 20, not to the demon in verse 19. Therefore, Jesus was saying that this type of unbelief—natural unbelief—can only come out by much prayer and fasting.

"COME BACK INTO THAT BODY"

Your faith is enough. I know. I've seen three people raised from the dead—including my own son. I didn't have "big" faith; I just had simple faith.

God set me up the first time. I'd been praying for months for this man who was paralyzed from the waist down. He had been unable to move before, but I'd helped him to where he could move his legs, get around, and do things. I just went by his house every day to pray for and minister to him.

Then one evening, while I was preparing to start a service, this man's son came in and waved me down. When I walked over, he threw me—and my guitar—into his car and drove us straight to his parents' house. It didn't take but a second to get there (Pritchett, Colorado, only had 144 people at the time). I just thought we were going to pray for his father, that maybe he'd had a heart attack and was in some pain.

As I walked in, the sheriff was there trying to get his oxygen mask out. The man's wife was crying and praying, "O God, please bring Everett back from the dead!" That's the first time I realized he was dead. Since I already had so much time and effort invested in this man and his healing, the first thought that came to me was, *No way!* So I walked over and said, "Everett, in the name of Jesus, come back into that body." BOOM—he just sat up healed! (Later that day, the doctor checked him out and confirmed it.)

Just a tiny bit of faith is sufficient if there isn't anything to counterbalance it. If you would've told me two days before that somebody was going to die and I'd have to raise them from the dead, my mind would have had time to start thinking. Thoughts of natural unbelief would have come at me, and it's very possible that I wouldn't have seen him raised from the dead. But the way it happened was a divine setup. God brought me over there in my ignorance. I prayed and didn't have time to disbelieve God. That's why it worked!

PRAYER & FASTING

However, natural unbelief normally kicks in through your senses whenever you pray and something contrary happens. This is because you've been trained to go by your five natural senses—what you can see, taste, hear, smell, and feel. Jesus said that the only way you can overcome this kind of unbelief is through prayer and fasting (Matt. 17:21).

Unbelief that comes from your physical senses isn't necessarily evil; it's just natural. Living in this physical world, you must take into account what your senses are telling you.

A man once tried to fly an airplane "by faith," and I was stupid enough to go with him. It didn't take long before he realized he didn't have the skill it took to fly. So he curled up into a fetal position on the floor and cried, "My God, we're going to die—we're going to die!" While he freaked out, I had to fly this tiny little plane. I'd never flown an airplane before. I didn't know what was going on. Besides all that, we were in a terrible storm. I actually had to fly that thing for an hour until this guy pulled himself together and landed us!

I don't recommend trying to fly an airplane by faith. You should have some aviation knowledge and be able to follow the instruments. You need to be able to respond to what you see and hear. There's nothing wrong with that.

However, there are times in your life when responding to what you can see, taste, hear, smell, and feel will not get the job done. You must be able to move beyond your natural senses and into the spirit realm. How do you do that? Through prayer and fasting.

DEAL WITH YOUR UNBELIEF
LESSON 25 – OUTLINE

I.   Unbelief comes in three different types: ignorance, disbelief, and natural.

    A.   Ignorance is when someone just doesn't know the truth.

        i.   Due to their lack of knowledge, they have unbelief.

        ii.   This type of unbelief is relatively easy to deal with.

        iii.   Just tell them the truth!

    B.   Disbelief comes from being taught wrong.

        i.   Disbelief is more difficult to overcome than ignorance.

        ii.   Although it is a little harder to overcome, the antidote for this second type of unbelief is the same as the first.

        iii.   I had to receive the truth of God's Word above man's traditions in order to overcome this unbelief that came through wrong teaching.

II.   Natural unbelief isn't ignorance or wrong teaching but simply natural input that's contrary to the truth (Mark 9:14-29, parallel to Matt. 17:14-21).

    A.   You go through life receiving input from your eyes, ears, and feelings and making your decisions based on that. It's not wrong, or evil; it's just natural.

    B.   However, there are things you can't perceive with just your five physical senses, and there are times when the Lord will ask you to take a step of faith.

    C.   That's when you must be able to get beyond the kind of unbelief that comes from natural things.

    D.   Most people are dominated by their physical senses.

    E.   It was this kind of unbelief—natural unbelief—that hindered the disciples in Matthew 17.

    F.   They had ministered to the boy, believing, but when he began going into convulsions, they were moved more by what they saw than by what they believed.

III.   How do you overcome this kind of unbelief?

Howbeit this kind [of unbelief] *goeth not out but by prayer and fasting.*

MATTHEW 17:21, BRACKETS MINE

A. Many people have misinterpreted this verse.

B. Unbelief is the consistent subject of both verses (Matt. 17:20-21)—*"this kind"* in verse 21 refers to *"unbelief"* in verse 20, not to the demon in verse 19.

C. Therefore, Jesus was saying that this type of unbelief—natural unbelief—can only come out by much prayer and fasting.

IV. Just a tiny bit of faith is sufficient if there isn't anything to counterbalance it.

A. However, natural unbelief normally kicks in through your senses whenever you pray and something contrary happens.

B. This is because you've been trained to go by your five natural senses—what you can see, taste, hear, smell, and feel.

C. Jesus said that the only way you can overcome this kind of unbelief is through prayer and fasting (Matt. 17:21).

D. There are times in your life when responding to what you can see, taste, hear, smell, and feel will not get the job done.

E. You must be able to move beyond your natural senses and into the spirit realm. How? Through prayer and fasting.

DEAL WITH YOUR UNBELIEF
LESSON 25 – TEACHER'S GUIDE

1.   Unbelief comes in three different types: ignorance, disbelief, and natural. Ignorance is when someone just doesn't know the truth. Due to their lack of knowledge, they have unbelief. This type of unbelief is relatively easy to deal with: Just tell them the truth! Disbelief comes from being taught wrong and is more difficult to overcome than ignorance. Although it is a little harder to overcome, the antidote for this second type of unbelief is the same as the first. We have to receive the truth of God's Word above man's traditions in order to overcome the unbelief that comes through wrong teaching.

2.   Natural unbelief isn't ignorance or wrong teaching but simply natural input that's contrary to the truth (Mark 9:14-29, parallel to Matt. 17:14-21). We go through life receiving input from our eyes, ears, and feelings and making our decisions based on that. It's not wrong, or evil; it's just natural. However, there are things we can't perceive with just our five physical senses, and there are times when the Lord will ask us to take a step of faith. That's when we must be able to get beyond the kind of unbelief that comes from natural things. Most people are dominated by their physical senses. It was this kind of unbelief—natural unbelief—that hindered the disciples in Matthew 17. They had ministered to the boy, believing, but when he began going into convulsions, they were moved more by what they saw than by what they believed.

1.   A.   What are the three different types of unbelief? (Ignorance, disbelief, and natural)
     B.   What is the antidote for lack of knowledge and wrong teaching? (We have to receive the truth of God's Word)
2.   A.   Read Mark 9:14-29 and Matthew 17:14-21. What does natural unbelief come from? (Natural input that's contrary to the truth)
     B.   Are there things we can't perceive with just our five physical senses? (Yes)
     C.   When must we be able to get beyond this kind of unbelief that comes from natural things? (When the Lord asks us to take a step of faith)

3.   How do we overcome this kind of unbelief? By prayer and fasting. Many people have misinterpreted Matthew 17:20-21. Unbelief is the consistent subject of both verses. *"This kind"* in verse 21 refers to *"unbelief"* in verse 20, not to the demon in verse 19. Therefore, Jesus was saying that this type of unbelief—natural unbelief—can only come out by much prayer and fasting.

4.   Just a tiny bit of faith is sufficient if there isn't anything to counterbalance it. However, natural unbelief normally kicks in through our senses whenever we pray and something contrary happens. This is because we've been trained to go by our five natural senses—what we can see, taste, hear, smell, and feel. Jesus said that the only way we can overcome this kind of unbelief is through prayer and fasting (Matt. 17:21). There are times in our lives when responding to what we can see, taste, hear, smell, and feel will not get the job done. We must be able to move beyond our natural senses and into the spirit realm. How do we do that? Through prayer and fasting!

3. A. Read Matthew 17:19-21. How do we overcome natural unbelief? (By prayer and fasting)
    B. Unbelief is the consistent subject of what two verses? (Verses 20 and 21)
4. A. When does natural unbelief normally kick in through our senses? (Whenever we pray and something contrary happens)
    B. Why? (Because we've been trained to go by our five natural senses—what we can see, taste, hear, smell, and feel)
    C. What did Jesus say is the only way we can overcome this kind of unbelief and move beyond our natural senses and into the spirit realm? (Through prayer and fasting)

DEAL WITH YOUR UNBELIEF
LESSON 25 – DISCIPLESHIP QUESTIONS

1. According to Mark 9:14-18, who couldn't cast the demon out?

2. According to Mark 9:19-24, what would this evil spirit do to the boy attempting to destroy him?

3. What did the father cry out with tears?

4. According to Mark 9:25-29, what did Jesus charge the dumb and deaf spirit to do?

5. Did the spirit obey?

6. Where was Jesus when the disciples asked Him about this privately?

7. According to Matthew 17:14-18, who brought the boy to the disciples?

8. What two questions did Jesus ask when He found out that the disciples had failed to cast the demon out?

9. Jesus told them to bring the boy to whom?

10. According to Matthew 17:19-21, unbelief hindered the disciples' faith when they tried to do what?

11. If our faith is pure—without any unbelief counteracting it—what shall be impossible for us?

12. How do we get rid of this kind of natural unbelief?

DEAL WITH YOUR UNBELIEF
LESSON 25 – ANSWER KEY

1. The disciples

2. Often cast him into fire and water

3. *"Lord, I believe; help thou mine unbelief"*

4. *"Come out of him, and enter no more into him"*

5. Yes

6. *"When he was come into the house"*

7. His father

8. *"How long shall I be with you?"* and *"How long shall I suffer you?"*

9. Him

10. Cast the demon out

11. Nothing

12. By prayer and fasting

DEAL WITH YOUR UNBELIEF
LESSON 25 – SCRIPTURES

MARK 9:14-18

And when he came to his disciples, he saw a great multitude about them, and the scribes questioning with them. [15] And straightway all the people, when they beheld him, were greatly amazed, and running to him saluted him. [16] And he asked the scribes, What question ye with them? [17] And one of the multitude answered and said, Master, I have brought unto thee my son, which hath a dumb spirit; [18] And wheresoever he taketh him, he teareth him: and he foameth, and gnasheth with his teeth, and pineth away: and I spake to thy disciples that they should cast him out; and they could not. [19] He answereth him, and saith, O faithless generation, how long shall I be with you? how long shall I suffer you? bring him unto me. [20] And they brought him unto him: and when he saw him, straightway the spirit tare him; and he fell on the ground, and wallowed foaming. [21] And he asked his father, How long is it ago since this came unto him? And he said, Of a child. [22] And ofttimes it hath cast him into the fire, and into the waters, to destroy him: but if thou canst do any thing, have compassion on us, and help us. [23] Jesus said unto him, If thou canst believe, all things are possible to him that believeth. [24] And straightway the father of the child cried out, and said with tears, Lord, I believe; help thou mine unbelief. [25] When Jesus saw that the people came running together, he rebuked the foul spirit, saying unto him, Thou dumb and deaf spirit, I charge thee, come out of him, and enter no more into him. [26] And the spirit cried, and rent him sore, and came out of him: and he was as one dead; insomuch that many said, He is dead. [27] But Jesus took him by the hand, and lifted him up; and he arose. [28] And when he was come into the house, his disciples asked him privately, Why could not we cast him out? [29] And he said unto them, This kind can come forth by nothing, but by prayer and fasting.

MATTHEW 17:14-21

And when they were come to the multitude, there came to him a certain man, kneeling down to him, and saying, [15] Lord, have mercy on my son: for he is lunatick, and sore vexed: for ofttimes he falleth into the fire, and oft into the water. [16] And I brought him to thy disciples, and they could not cure him. [17] Then Jesus answered and said, O faithless and perverse generation, how long shall I be with you? how long shall I suffer you? bring him hither to me. [18] And Jesus rebuked the devil; and he departed out of him: and the child was cured from that very hour. [19] Then came the disciples to Jesus apart, and said, Why could not we cast him out? [20] And Jesus said unto them, Because of your unbelief: for verily I say unto you, If ye have faith as a grain of mustard seed, ye shall say unto this mountain, Remove hence to yonder place; and it shall remove; and nothing shall be impossible unto you. [21] Howbeit this kind goeth not out but by prayer and fasting.

RESPONSIVE TO GOD
LESSON 26

What do you do when your body hurts, you've already prayed, believed, received, and acted on your faith for healing—but you're still in pain? Under normal circumstances, you've been trained to respond to your body. Since it still hurts, which is contrary to what you prayed, your natural senses have conditioned you to conclude, "It didn't work." How do you overcome that and receive the manifestation of God's provision? By fasting.

Fasting retrains your body to respond to God's Word and your born-again spirit. When you fast, you're telling your body what to do. You're breaking the natural domination and control your body has been exerting over you. Your body isn't bad; it's just been trained wrong. You've been responding primarily to what you can see, taste, hear, smell, and feel.

That's okay most of the time, but you need to learn—experientially—that man does not live by bread alone but by every word that proceeds from the mouth of God (Matt. 4:4). By fasting, you say to your body, "Body, you need to understand that the spirit is more important than the physical. There are realities you can't perceive with this little peanut brain. In order to help you learn this, we're going on a fast. By not eating or drinking like we normally do, we are going to recognize that God is our Source. Instead of going by my appetite and letting food supply my needs, the Lord and His Word will give me strength!"

If you haven't trained it, your body will rebel at that, and your appetite will go wild. Many people have told me that they felt like they were going to die by noon the first day of their fast. They felt weak all over, had a headache, and so forth.

Did you know that it's a proven medical fact that fasting one day a week is good for you? It will purge your body of toxins. In fact, you don't physically begin to die until about forty days into a fast. Prior to that, it's mostly just your appetite talking, not physical necessity. Many of us could live off the fat of the land for quite some time!

WHO RULES WHOM?

When you fast, your body will try to maintain its control. It'll cause you to feel like "I'll never make it through the day" and attempt to coerce you to go against what you believe God has told you to do. Your body will exert itself, and your sense knowledge—what you can see, taste, hear, smell, and feel—will try to dominate you. That's when you'll have a choice: Either let your physical realm rule, or rule your physical realm.

By choosing to continue your fast, you're telling your body, "Get in line! You need to learn that you won't starve by noon the first day. You're being retrained so you can do the things God tells you to do and get your needs met through His Word." Your body will rebel and answer, "No, I'll die!" That's when you say, "Okay, we'll make it a two-day fast." And your body will respond, "Two days! I'll die for sure!" You reply, "All right, three days!"

Pretty soon your body will conclude, "If I'm going to survive this, I'd better shut up. Every time I complain, another day gets added to the fast!" Over time, your body will yield.

After you get through the initial hunger pain, you can actually reach a place where you aren't hungry at all. It just doesn't bother you. If you go on a prolonged fast (the longest I've done was ten or eleven days) without food or liquids—other than water—you can actually get to a place where it seems like you don't ever have to eat again. You can bring your body into subjection to where God is literally ministering to you in a supernatural way.

Once that happens and you get off the fast, your body has learned something. Your mind now knows that when you say "By His stripes, I was healed" and it still feels pain that there are realities beyond its ability to detect. You declare, "I'm healed whether or not I can see, taste, hear, smell, or feel it yet!" Your body will answer "Okay" and submit.

However, if you haven't ever fasted and disciplined your body, you'll pray "By His stripes, I was healed," and your body will say, "You're still hurting. You aren't healed." You'll counter "No, body, I am healed," and it'll respond, "Wait a minute here! Who are you to tell me anything? I tell you when to eat, what to eat, and how much to eat. You haven't given me an instruction in years. You're completely dominated by your senses. Don't tell me what to do!" Your body will rebel, and you'll submit to the natural unbelief that comes through your senses.

Fasting breaks the dominance of your natural realm over your spirit. Prayer does too!

TRAIN YOUR BODY

When you pray, you're speaking and listening to Someone you can't physically see or feel. Your natural mind and sense knowledge just go bonkers, saying, "This is stupid! What am I doing?" But if you continue in prayer and make it a practice, you'll start seeing miracles and other things happen. There will be so much evidence that your prayer time is valid and God is real that it will help retrain your physical senses. Your body will begin to recognize that there's more than what it can see, taste, hear, smell, and feel. Then when you want your body to act like it is well when it doesn't feel well, your body will go ahead and respond because it knows that there's more to it than what the natural senses can perceive.

This won't work for a person who doesn't spend time in prayer and fasting. When they start trying to command their body to go against what they perceive with their natural senses, it'll rebel because they've never disciplined it.

Your body isn't evil; it's just natural and has to be trained. However, no one else can do this for you. You must train yourself and exercise your senses (Heb. 5:14).

You may not realize it, but you had to train yourself to submit to your physical senses. As a soldier in Vietnam, many nights I had bunker guard. Both my hearing and my smell became much more acute in that life-or-death situation. I usually smelled the enemy before I could see them. You can actually train yourself in these things!

SIXTH SENSE

Just as your natural senses can be trained in the physical realm, they can also be educated in spiritual things. They don't have to remain carnal. They can be trained to discern spiritual truth. This is what fasting and prayer does!

I believe the Lord originally created mankind with six senses. That sixth sense was faith. Adam and Eve used faith just as much as they used their other five senses. When mankind fell, our sense of faith began to atrophy to the point that today many people are total strangers to it. But this ability to walk by faith does exist within us all. It just has to be nurtured and trained.

But strong meat belongeth to them that are of full age, even those who by reason of use have their senses exercised to discern both good and evil.

HEBREWS 5:14

Our senses must be exercised in order to operate in faith. That's what fasting and prayer do. They don't make God respond to you better; fasting and prayer make you respond to Him better.

STICK WITH IT!

When you spend so much time in God's presence, His Word becomes like a sixth sense. You might not see, taste, hear, smell, or feel what He said, but you have faith based on His Word. Your natural mind will just accept that and say, "It's not discernible by these other senses, but that's faith. I recognize it and that's the way it is." You can train yourself that way!

That's what Smith Wigglesworth did. He spent so much time in prayer, fasting, and the Word that he hardened himself toward unbelief and what other people thought. He was sensitive to God and hard toward other things. When he prayed for someone and didn't see the manifestation right away, he just kept at it until he did.

Since the Lord has shown me these things, I stick with it now until I see the manifestation. If I pray and don't see a physical manifestation, I just make it happen. I know in my heart that God has already done His part. I understand that He's already released His power. Therefore, I'm not just asking and pleading with Him to do something; I'm aggressively receiving what's already been done, and I'm standing against Satan who's hindering the manifestation. I'm taking my authority, speaking to the mountain, and commanding things to happen!

When ministering to other people, there are things you can do that will quicken their faith. Sometimes I discern unbelief while praying for someone. It may not be evil or disbelief, but maybe this person is just dominated by natural things. If they are having a hard time receiving healing from God, I'll just push over into a gift of the Spirit. Then, using a word of wisdom or a word of knowledge, I'll talk to them about something emotional—perhaps about how they've been hurt. Maybe depression, grief, or tragedy had struck. So I'll use this gift of the Spirit to speak to them on something totally unrelated to their physical healing. Then they start receiving, saying in their heart, *There's no way he could have known this. God is speaking to me through this man.* All at once, they open up and faith starts flowing. Once their faith is quickened, their heart says, *Yes, this is God. Father, I receive.*

Then I'll come back and speak to that physical healing that didn't manifest before. All of a sudden, they will be healed. I've at least doubled or tripled the amount of people I've seen healed by doing this. That's what I mean by "making" it happen.

POSITIONED TO RECEIVE

God has already done everything to heal everyone. It's not a matter of asking the Lord to heal, but rather our receiving the healing He has already given. That's the basic principle, but there are laws that govern how it works. You have to speak. So I talk to the specific parts of people's bodies and command them to respond. I take authority over the devil. Sometimes I do things to quicken their faith. I don't do all of these things to manipulate God, but to help people move into a position to receive.

Since understanding and applying these powerful truths, I'm seeing much better results than ever before—and you will too!

RESPONSIVE TO GOD
LESSON 26 – OUTLINE

I. Fasting retrains your body to respond to God's Word and your born-again spirit.

    A. When you fast, you're telling your body what to do.

    B. You're breaking the natural domination and control your body has been exerting over you.

    C. You've been responding primarily to what you can see, taste, hear, smell, and feel.

    D. That's okay most of the time, but you need to learn—experientially—that man does not live by bread alone but by every word that proceeds from the mouth of God (Matt. 4:4).

II. When you fast, your body will try to maintain its control.

    A. Your body will exert itself, and your sense knowledge—what you can see, taste, hear, smell, and feel—will try to dominate you.

    B. That's when you'll have a choice: Either let your physical realm rule, or rule your physical realm.

    C. You can bring your body into subjection to where God is literally ministering to you in a supernatural way.

    D. Once that happens and you get off the fast, your body has learned something.

    E. Fasting breaks the dominance of your natural realm over your spirit.

III. Prayer does too!

    A. When you pray, you're speaking and listening to Someone you can't physically see or feel.

    B. Your natural mind and sense knowledge just go bonkers.

    C. But if you continue in prayer and make it a practice, you'll start seeing miracles and other things happen.

    D. There will be so much evidence that your prayer time is valid and that God, whom you cannot see, is real that it will help retrain your physical senses.

    E. Your body will begin to recognize that there's more than what it can see, taste, hear, smell, and feel.

IV. Your body isn't evil; it's just natural and has to be trained.

A. Just as your natural senses can be trained in the physical realm, they can also be educated in spiritual things.

B. This is what fasting and prayer does!

But strong meat belongeth to them that are of full age, even those who by reason of use have their senses exercised to discern both good and evil.

HEBREWS 5:14

C. Our senses must be exercised in order to operate in faith.

D. Fasting and prayer don't make God respond to you better—they make you respond to Him better.

E. You can train yourself that way!

V. God has already done everything to heal everyone.

A. It's not a matter of asking the Lord to heal, but rather our receiving the healing He has already given.

B. That's the basic principle, but there are laws that govern how it works.

C. We don't do all of these things to manipulate God, but to help people move into a position to receive.

D. As we understand and apply these powerful truths, we will see much better results than ever before.

RESPONSIVE TO GOD
LESSON 26 – TEACHER'S GUIDE

1.   Fasting retrains our bodies to respond to God's Word and our born-again spirits. When we fast, we're telling our bodies what to do. We're breaking the natural domination and control our bodies have been exerting over us. We've been responding primarily to what we can see, taste, hear, smell, and feel. That's okay most of the time, but we need to learn—experientially—that man does not live by bread alone but by every word that proceeds from the mouth of God (Matt. 4:4).

2.   When we fast, our bodies will try to maintain control. Our bodies will exert themselves, and our sense knowledge—what we can see, taste, hear, smell, and feel—will try to dominate us. That's when we'll have a choice: Either let our physical realm rule, or rule our physical realm. We can bring our bodies into subjection to where God is literally ministering to us in a supernatural way. Once that happens and we get off the fast, our bodies have learned something. Fasting breaks the dominance of our natural realm over our spirits.

3.   Prayer does too! When we pray, we're speaking and listening to Someone we can't physically see or feel. Our natural minds and sense knowledge just go bonkers. But if we continue in prayer and make it a practice, we'll start seeing miracles and other things happen. There will be so much evidence that our prayer time is valid and that God, whom we cannot see, is real that it will help retrain our physical senses. Our bodies will begin to recognize that there's more than what they can see, taste, hear, smell, and feel.

1.   A.   Read Matthew 4:4. What retrains our bodies to respond to God's Word and our born-again spirits? (Fasting)
      B.   What do we need to learn experientially? (That man does not live by bread alone but by every word that proceeds from the mouth of God)
2.   A.   When we fast, what choice will we have to make when our bodies exert themselves and our sense knowledge tries to dominate us? (Either let our physical realm rule, or rule our physical realm)
      B.   What does fasting break? (The dominance of our natural realm over our spirits)
3.   A.   When we pray, to whom are we speaking and listening? (Someone we can't physically see or feel)
      B.   What will happen if we continue in prayer and make it a practice? (We'll start seeing miracles and other things happen—there will be so much evidence that our prayer time is valid and that God, whom we cannot see, is real that it will help retrain our physical senses)
      C.   What will begin to recognize that there's more than what they can see, taste, hear, smell, and feel? (Our bodies)

4.   Our bodies aren't evil; they're just natural and have to be trained. Just as our natural senses can be trained in the physical realm, they can also be educated in spiritual things (Heb. 5:14). This is what fasting and prayer does! Our senses must be exercised in order to operate in faith. Fasting and prayer don't make God respond to us better—they make us respond to Him better. We can train ourselves that way!

5.   God has already done everything to heal everyone. It's not a matter of asking the Lord to heal, but rather our receiving the healing He has already given. That's the basic principle, but there are laws that govern how it works. We don't do all of these things to manipulate God, but to help people (including ourselves) move into a position to receive. As we understand and apply these powerful truths, we will see much better results than ever before—glory to God!

4. A. Read Hebrews 5:14. Are our bodies evil? (No, they're just natural and have to be trained)
    B. Do fasting and prayer make God respond to us better? (No, they make us respond to Him better)
5. A. It's not a matter of asking the Lord to heal but rather what? (Our receiving the healing He has already given)
    B. Why do we do all of these things—cooperating with the laws that govern faith? (To help people—including ourselves—move into a position to receive)
    C. When will we see much better results than before? (As we understand and apply these powerful truths)

RESPONSIVE TO GOD
LESSON 26 – DISCIPLESHIP QUESTIONS

1. Who was speaking in Matthew 4:4?

2. Who was being spoken to?

3. Shall man live by bread alone?

4. What does man live by?

5. What three words indicate to us that Jesus was quoting Scripture?

6. According to Hebrews 5:14, who does strong meat belong to?

7. How do we exercise our senses?

8. What do we learn to discern between?

RESPONSIVE TO GOD
LESSON 26 – ANSWER KEY

1. Jesus

2. Satan

3. No

4. Every word that proceeds from the mouth of God

5. *"It is written"*

6. *"Them that are of full age"*

7. *"By reason of use"*

8. *"Both good and evil"*

RESPONSIVE TO GOD
LESSON 26 – SCRIPTURES

MATTHEW 4:4

But he answered and said, It is written, Man shall not live by bread alone, but by every word that proceedeth out of the mouth of God.

HEBREWS 5:14

But strong meat belongeth to them that are of full age, even those who by reason of use have their senses exercised to discern both good and evil.

CONCLUSION

God has already done His part. His transmitter works perfectly twenty-four hours a day. He's constantly giving us everything we need.

Our receivers are the problem, not God's transmitter. We must learn to understand the spiritual realm and cooperate in faith to bring His provision into physical manifestation.

We must stop giving the devil extra power and glory. He has been completely stripped and defeated. Remember the parade!

We already have the supernatural faith of God. Therefore, our problem isn't lack of faith but unbelief. Our simple, childlike, mustard seed of faith is more than enough to see anything done if there's no unbelief to counteract it.

If we truly believe God's Word and are acting in faith upon it but still aren't seeing the right results—nine times out of ten it's natural unbelief. Through prayer and fasting, we can break the domination of our physical senses and begin to exercise our natural realm to respond to the Lord and His Word.

This foundational revelation has totally transformed my life! I trust that this same revolution has now also begun in you. Therefore, I pray...

That the God of our Lord Jesus Christ, the Father of glory, may give unto you the spirit of wisdom and revelation in the knowledge of him: [18] The eyes of your understanding being enlightened; that ye may know what is the hope of his calling, and what the riches of the glory of his inheritance in the saints, [19] And what is the exceeding greatness of his power to us-ward who believe.

EPHESIANS 1:17-19

Amen!

RECEIVE JESUS AS YOUR SAVIOR

Choosing to receive Jesus Christ as your Lord and Savior is the most important decision you'll ever make!

God's Word promises *"that if thou shalt confess with thy mouth the Lord Jesus, and shalt believe in thine heart that God hath raised him from the dead, thou shalt be saved. [10] For with the heart man believeth unto righteousness; and with the mouth confession is made unto salvation"* (Rom. 10:9-10). *"For whosoever shall call upon the name of the Lord shall be saved"* (Rom. 10:13).

By His grace, God has already done everything to provide salvation. Your part is simply to believe and receive.

Pray out loud, "Jesus, I confess that You are my Lord and Savior. I believe in my heart that God raised You from the dead. By faith in Your Word, I receive salvation now. Thank You for saving me!"

The very moment you commit your life to Jesus Christ, the truth of His Word instantly comes to pass in your spirit. Now that you're born again, there's a brand-new you!

RECEIVE THE HOLY SPIRIT

As His child, your loving heavenly Father wants to give you the supernatural power you need to live this new life.

For every one that asketh receiveth; and he that seeketh findeth; and to him that knocketh it shall be opened...how much more shall your heavenly Father give the Holy Spirit to them that ask him?

LUKE 11:10 & 13

All you have to do is ask, believe, and receive!

Pray, "Father, I recognize my need for Your power to live this new life. Please fill me with Your Holy Spirit. By faith, I receive it right now! Thank You for baptizing me! Holy Spirit, You are welcome in my life!"

Congratulations—now you are filled with God's supernatural power!

Some syllables from a language you don't recognize will rise up from your heart to your mouth (1 Cor. 14:14). As you speak them out loud by faith, you're releasing God's power from within and building yourself up in the spirit (1 Cor. 14:4). You can do this whenever and wherever you like.

It doesn't really matter whether you felt anything or not when you prayed to receive the Lord and His Spirit. If you believed in your heart that you received, then God's Word promises you did. *"Therefore I say unto you, What things soever ye desire, when ye pray, believe that ye receive them, and ye shall have them"* (Mark 11:24). God always honors His Word—believe it!

Please contact me and let me know that you've prayed to receive Jesus as your Savior or to be filled with the Holy Spirit. I would like to rejoice with you and help you understand more fully what has taken place in your life. I'll send you a free gift that will help you understand and grow in your new relationship with the Lord. *Welcome to your new life!*

RECOMMENDED MATERIALS

SPIRIT, SOUL & BODY

Understanding the relationship of your spirit, soul, and body is foundational to your Christian life. You will never truly know how much God loves you or believe what His Word says about you until you do. In this series, learn how they're related and how that knowledge will release the life of your spirit into your body and soul. It may even explain why many things are not working the way you had hoped.

Item Code: 1027-C   4-CD Series

Item Code: 1027-D   As-Seen-on-TV DVD Series

Item Code: 318   Paperback Book

Item Code: 418   Study Guide

Item Code: 701   Spanish Book

THE TRUE NATURE OF GOD

Are you confused about the nature of God? Is He the God of judgment found in the Old Testament or the God of mercy and grace found in the New Testament? Andrew's revelation on this subject will set you free and give you a confidence in your relationship with God like never before. This truly is nearly-too-good-to-be-true news.

Item Code: 1002-C   5-CD Series

Item Code: 308   Paperback Book

LIVING IN THE BALANCE OF GRACE AND FAITH

This book explains one of the biggest controversies in the church today. Is it grace or faith that releases the power of God? Does God save people in His sovereignty, or does your faith move Him? You may be surprised by the answers as Andrew reveals what the Bible has to say concerning these important questions and more. This will help you receive from God in a greater way and will change the way you relate to Him.

Item Code: 1064-C   5-CD Series

Item Code: 1064-D   As-Seen-on-TV DVD Series

Item Code: 3208-D   Recorded Live DVD Series

Item Code: 328   Paperback Book

Item Code: 428   Study Guide

Item Code: 737   Spanish Book

THE BELIEVER'S AUTHORITY

Like it or not, every one of us is in a spiritual war. We can't be discharged from service, and ignorance of the battlefield only aids the enemy. In war, God is always for us, and the devil is against us; whichever one we cooperate with will win. And there's only one way the enemy can get our cooperation—and that's through deception! In this teaching, Andrew exposes this war and the Enemy for what he is.

Item Code: 1045-C	6-CD Series
Item Code: 1045-D	As-Seen-on-TV DVD Series
Item Code: 3205-D	Recorded Live DVD Series
Item Code: 327	Paperback Book
Item Code: 427	Study Guide
Item Code: 735	Spanish Book

THE EFFECTS OF PRAISE

Every Christian wants a stronger walk with the Lord. But how do you get there? Many don't know the true power of praise. It's essential. Listen as Andrew teaches biblical truths that will not only spark understanding but will help promote spiritual growth so you will experience victory.

| Item Code: 1004-C | 3-CD Series |
| Item Code: 309 | Paperback Book |

GOD WANTS YOU WELL

Health is something everyone wants. Billions of dollars are spent each year trying to retain or restore health. So, why does religion say that God uses sickness to teach you something? It even tries to make you believe that sickness is a blessing. That's just not true. God wants you well.

Item Code: 1036-C	4-CD Series
Item Code: 1036-D	As-Seen-on-TV DVD Series
Item Code: 330	Paperback Book
Item Code: 430	Study Guide
Item Code: 740	Spanish Book